know your islam

W9-CDP-604

This is a joint venture with

A. AZA KHANA-E-ZAHRA
1365 EXETER STREET
BALDWIN, NEW YORK 11510

TAHRIKE TARSILE QUR'AN INC.
Publishers and Distributors of Holy Qur'an
P.O. BOX 1115
CORONA-ELMHURST STA.
ELMHURST, NEW YORK 11373-1115

Published by
Tahrike Tarsile Qur'an, Inc.
Publishers and Distributors of Holy Qur'an
P.O. Box 1115
Corona Elmhurst Sta.
Elmhurst, New York 11373-1115

Second U.S. Edition 1986

Library of Congress Catalog Number; 81-51707

British Library Cataloguing in Publication Data

ISBN: 0-940368-74

Distributors for Canada

Syed Mohammed Zaki Baqri
The Council of Islamic Guidance
72 Pilkey Crescent
Scarborough, Ont. M1B 2A9
Canada

Distributors for United Kingdom

MIHRAB PUBLISHERS & BOOK DISTRIBUTORS
20 Potters Lane, Kiln Farm
Milton Keynes, MK11 3HF

هٰذَا مِنْ فَضْلِ رَبِّیّ

This is by the Grace of God

Compiled by :

YOUSUF N. LALLJEE

"If any religion has a chance of ruling over England, nay Europe, within the next hundred years, it can only be Islam. I have always held the religion of Muhammad in high estimation, because of its wonderful vitality. It is the only religion, which appears to me, to possess the assimilating capability to the changing phase of existence, which can make its appeal to every age. I believe, that if a man like Muhammad were to assume the dictatorship of the modern world, he would succeed in solving its problem, in a way that would bring it much needed peace and happiness."

George Bernard Shaw.

Compiled and published by YOUSUF N. LALLJEE,
Bakhtawar Annexe, 22, Narayan Dabholkar Road, Bombay 400 006.

BISM-ILLAH-IR-RAHMAN-IR-RAHEEM

(In the name of God, the most Compassionate, the Merciful)

AL-HAMDU L'ILLAH

(All praise be to God)

"*Be quick in the race of forgiveness from your Lord, and for a Garden whose width is that (of the whole) of the heavens and of the earth, prepared for the righteous.*"   3:133

"Be virtuous when there is still time for you to realise and adopt virtues, when repentance can do you good, when prayers are heard, when you are enjoying peace and comfort and when the angels are still writing your good and bad actions (when you still have power and opportunities to do good or to be wicked). Do good before old age or disability stops you from doing anything, before protracted illness sends you down exhausted and unfit for any work and before death takes you away from this sphere of activities (life). Because death, sooner or later, will put an end to all your pleasures and all your enjoyments, it will send you far away from your cherished surroundings.

SERMONS OF HAZRAT ALI from Nahj-ul-Balagha

This book is not based on the Fatwa (religious decisions) of any one Mujtahed. In case of any difficulty in understanding any particular subject, one should consult the Mujtahed under whose Taqleed (guidance) one is.

Dedicated to the loving memory of our beloved
AYATULLAH SHAIKH MOHAMED HASAN NAJAFI
(Shaikh Sahab) this is how we used to call him.
Died on 7th June 1967, (28th Safar 1387) at Tehran and
buried in Masjid-e-Tabatabaee adjoining the Roza of
Janabe Masooma (sister of Imam Reza) at Qum,
(About 60 miles from Teheran).

Contents

1

On obeying the Holy Prophet: And those who annoy the Prophet: On the Prophets Ahl-ul-Bait: The Hour of Death: On Prayers: The Righteous: On Weights and Measures: On the most trustworthy handle: On the Mercy of God: On Parents: On Patience: On Food: On those who are slain in the way of God: On whom is the curse of God: On entering the houses of others: On scandal mongers: On scandal and suspicion: On gambling and intoxicants: Blessings on the Prophet: On Charity: The parable of a goodly word and an evil word: The parable of a city enjoying security: The parable of those who reject their Lord: The parable of Light: The parable of Truth and Vanity: On your possessions and your progeny: On respite: On greeting: On Fasting: On the Day of Reckoning: The life of this world compared to the hereafter: For whom is the final attainment: On death: On Friday prayers: Who are the true believers: Those who reject our signs: What will happen to the rejectors of God: When will our condition change: To escape from Satan: Whom to adore: God's favour on us: Whom will God not guide: Jesus testifies the coming of the Holy Prophet: On the birth of Jesus: Jesus was not crucified: On leaders who misguide people: Devouring Inheritance: On justice: Who will be foremost in the hereafter: Whom will God forgive: Partners in a good cause and an evil one: On those who are niggardly: The hypocrites: The signs of God: When trouble touches man: The certainty of Resurrection: On vain discourse: Those who take their religion to be mere play:

Hazrat Ali says that as a caliph and a ruler, he promises safety and security of life, property, honour, social status and religious freedom to non-muslims and they should not be maltreated and looked down upon. So long as they do not try to betray and injure the cause of the state of Islam they should not be molested and should be allowed to practice their religion and trades freely and openly. Islam teaches us to carry a message of peace with us and improve the status of society wherever we go and the best way to achieve this is to create amity, friendliness and concord amongst human beings. Therefore, Muslims should try to develop friendship of these people and should never resort to wrong use of power, force or arrogance. They should not be over-taxed, humiliated, and should not be forced out of their homes, lands and trades. Their priests should be treated with due respect. Their monasteries should be protected, they should be allowed to carry on their lectures, teachings and preachings as usual, and their religious ceremonies should not be prohibited. If they want to build their places of worship then fallow ownerless lands should be allotted to them. One who disobeys this order is going against the orders of God and the Holy Prophet (A.S.) and will deserve His Wrath.

Sermons of Hazrat Ali from Nahj-ul-Balagha

Preface

"O Lord! Increase me in knowledge"—The Holy Quran
20 : 114

*This book is a compilation of the essential fundamental princi-
ples governing the religion of Islam. The object of compiling
this work is to interest people in Islam and to correct the misleading propaganda that Islam has been established by the
sword and to prove the point that Islam is essentially a religion
of peace. The very name Islam means peace. The reader will
get acquainted with the great personalities in Islam who have
striven and sacrificed even their lives to show that aggression
finds no place in the practice of Islam. The life of the Holy Prophet Muhammad (S.A.) shows that neither he nor his progeny
ever started an aggressive war for the propagation of Islam. The
only wars they ever took part in were for the defence of Islam.
An attempt has thus been made to present a simple but complete outline of the subject. It is desinged for those who know
little or nothing about Islam and are puzzled by the multiplicity of interpretations and material offered to them on every
side. Hence three aims were in mind when compiling this book.
First, to cover as far as possible all the fundamentals of Islam;
second, to make them available as a check list for those who
know their Islam, and lastly as a guide book for those who are
keenly interested to know their Islam.*

*Twenty headings are chosen in this compilation each one deal-
ing with an important phase in the religion of Islam.*

*And now, once you go through the list of headings and say to
yourself what do I want to know? Surely you would like to*

7

know the lives of the fourteen Masooms who sacrificed their lives for the cause of Islam! You would like to know who the Ahl-ul-Bait of the prophet are and what instructions the Prophet left behind! You would like to know what the Holy Quran says on various subjects and understand for yourself in simple language! You would like to read Dua-e-Kumail and the daily prayers of Imam Zain-ul-Abedin to understand the charm of supplication!

Each chapter is a gem of information in itself. It is a beacon of light shining in the darkness which encompasses the world.

This book is meant for the seekers of knowledge, for once you go through the pages you will realise that it contains practically all the essentials whereby you will have grasped this knowledge.

The Ayat of the Holy Quran says:

And those who receive guidance, He increases the light of guidance, and bestows on them their piety and restraint from evil. 47 : 17.

And God doth advance in guidance those who seek guidance. 19 : 76.

The
Fundamentals
of
Islam

It is the privilege of the men of God to see the sublimest mysteries of the spiritual world and instruct men in righteousness; they warn and shield men against evil. But nothing can lessen each soul's personal responsibility for its own deeds. It carries its fate round its own neck. God's gifts are for all, but not all receive the same gifts, nor are all gifts of equal dignity or excellence.

9

Islam is a perfect code of life. In presenting this code of life, Islam provides both for the formation of basic ideas and also for the moulding of actions

KALEMA

LA ILAHA ILLALLAH
MUHAMMADUN RASOOLULLAH
ALIYUN WALI-ULLAH
WASI—O—RASOOLILLAH

LA ILAHA ILLALLAH: There is no God but Allah.

MUHAMMADUN RASOOLULLAH: (Our Prophet) Muhammad Mustafa (Peace of Allah be upon him and his Progeny!) is the Messenger of Allah.

ALIYUN WALI-ULLAH: Hazrat Ali (Peace of Allah be on him) is the guardian (Imam) appointed by Allah.

WASI—O—RASOOLILLAH: He (Hazrat Ali) is the rightful executor of the Will of the Prophet.

Note:

Whenever we utter or hear the name of our Prophet, we should recite Salawat. Similarly we should stand up, or lower our heads as a mark of reverence, whenever we utter or hear the name of our Imam of the Age (Twelfth Imam).

IMPORTANT ASPECTS

A. i) God is one.

  ii) Panjetan are five.

  iii) Imams are twelve

  iv) Masooms are fourteen.

  v) Prophets sent by Allah total one lakh twentyfour thousand.

B. NAMES OF PANJETAN:

  i) Muhammad (Peace of Allah be on him and his Progeny).

  ii) Ali (Peace of Allah be on him).

  iii) Fatema (Peace of Allah be on her).

iv) Hasan (Peace of Allah be on him).

v) Husain (Peace of Allah be on him).

C. NAMES OF IMAMS:

i) First Imam — Hazrat Ali (Alaihis-salam).

ii) Second Imam — Hazrat Hasan (Alaihis-salam).

iii) Third Imam — Hazrat Husain (Alaihis-salam).

iv) Fourth Imam — Hazrat Ali "Zain-ul-Abedeen" (Alaihis-salam).

v) Fifth Imam — Hazrat Muhammad "Baqir" (Alaihis-salam).

vi) Sixth Imam — Hazrat Jafar-e-"Sadiq" (Alaihis-salam).

vii) Seventh Imam — Hazrat Moosa-e-"Kazim" (Alaihis-salam).

viii) Eighth Imam — Hazrat Ali Ibn Moosa "Reza" (Alaihis-salam).

ix) Ninth Imam — Hazrat Muhammad "Taqee" (Alaihis-salam).

x) Tenth Imam — Hazrat Ali-yun-"Naqi" (Alaihis-salam).

xi) Eleventh Imam — Hazrat Hasan "Askari" (Alaihis-salam).

xii) Twelfth Imam — Hazrat Mehdi "Sahebuz-Zaman" (Alaihis-Salam).

D. FOURTEEN MASOOMS:

Our Holy Prophet Muhammad Mustafa (Peace of Allah be on him and his Progeny), his daughter Fatematuzzehra (Peace be on her) and the twelve Imams (Peace be on them) form the group of Fourteen Masooms. Masoom means sinless.

E. RECITATION OF SALAWAT:

Allahumma Salle Ala Muhammadin Wa-Ale Muhammad. (O Allah! bless Muhammad and the Progeny of Muhammad.)

F. NAMES OF ISLAMIC MONTHS:

1. Moharram
2. Safar
3. Rabi-ul-awwal
4. Rabi-ul-akhar
5. Jamadi-ul-Awwal

11

6. Jamadi-ul-Akhar
7. Rajab
8. Shaban
9. Ramazan
10. Shawwal
11. Zilkad
12. Zilhajj

Just as the tree has two parts, i.e. roots and shoots (branches), the teachings of Islam fall under two categories:

A. USOOL-E-DEEN means roots of religion.

B. FUROO-E-DEEN means branches of religion.

A. USOOL-E-DEEN :

Means the fundamental principles of religion. Usool-e-Deen which are five, are as mentioned below:

1. TAWHEED (ONENESS OF GOD).
2. ADL (JUSTICE).
3. NUBUWAT (PROPHETHOOD).
4. IMAMAT (VICEGERENCY OF THE PROPHET).
5. QIYAMAT (DAY OF JUDGMENT).

1. TAWHEED (Oneness of God)

Tawheed means God is one. He has neither a colleague nor a partner. He begets not, nor is He begotten, there is none like Him.

2. ADL (Justice)

It means that God is just. He will reward or punish any person according to his deeds.

3. NUBUWAT (Prophethood)

A Nabi (Prophet) excels all other persons for whom he is sent by Allah. He is Masoom (sinless). PROPHET MUHAMMAD MUSTAFA (blessings of Allah be on him and his Progeny) is the last of the Prophets sent by Him. The Prophets sent by Allah, including our Prophet, total one lakh twentyfour thousand.

4. IMAMAT (Guidance)

Nubuwat ended with Prophet Muhammad (blessings of Allah be on Him and his Progeny). Then Allah deputed Imams to guide us. They were Masooms (sinless). The Imam has his knowledge from God, and his verdict is the verdict of God.

Imams are twelve and they are the only rightful Imams. There is no successor to the Twelfth Imam. He is alive but invisible in accordance with the Will of Allah and will reappear when He commands, which will signify the coming end of the World.

5.   QIYAMAT (Resurrection)

It means the Day of Judgment.

B.   FUROO—E—DEEN:

Furoo-e-Deen, which are Ten, are as follows.

1. Namaz	6. Jehad
2. Roza	7. Amra-Bil-Ma'aroof
3. Hajj	8. Nahi-Anil-Munkar
4. Zakat	9. Tawalla
5. Khums	10. Tabarra

1.   NAMAZ OR SALAT (Prayer):

Salat, Namaz or Prayer is Wajib (Obligatory) for a Muslim five times a day. The prayers are obligatory on those who have become "Baligh". For the purpose of fulfilment religious obligation a boy becomes "baligh" on completion of his fifteenth year, and a girl on completion of her ninth year.

The following are the WAJIB PRAYERS (obligatory):

1.   The five daily Prayers: Namaz-e-Fajr, Namaz-e-Zohar, Namaz-e-Asr, Namaz-e-Maghrib, and Namaz-e-Isha.

2. Namaz-e-Ayaat.
3. Namaz-e-Tawaf.
4. Namaz-e-Qaza.
5. Namaz-e-Ahad.
6. Namaz-e-Istejara.
7. Namaz-e-Nazar.
8. Namaz-e-Mayyat.
9. Namaz-e-Qasam.
10. Namaz-e-Juma.
11. Namaz-e-Ehtiyat.

13

WAJIB (Compulsory): The offering of these prayers entitles one to Heavenly reward, while due to neglect the person will get retribution in the Hereafter.

(For further details refer section on PRAYERS.)

The Holy Prophet has said: "If Allah accepts one's Salat (Prayers), other good deeds of his will also be acceptable to Him. But if one's Salat is rejected by Allah, his other good actions will be surely rejected."

The Holy Prophet has further said:—

"Everything has something to embellish. And the thing that adorns Islam is the obligatory Salat, five times a day. Every· thing has a prop, and the prop for a Momin (Faithful) is this very Salat. Everything needs some sort of light, and for the heart of a Momin this Salat serves as a light. Everything carries some price, and the price of Paradise is this Salat. Salat is a way of penitence for a penitent and a source of prosperity. It is through this very Salat that the devotee can hope for Munificence of Allah, the acceptance of his supplications and the expiration of his sins."

Imam Jafar-e-Sadiq has said: "One who makes light of Salat and has no regard for it, does not belong to us, and will surely be deprived of the benefit of our intercession (on the Day of Judgment)."

"Praying," says the Prophet of Islam, "is the salvation of the true believer, the pillar of faith, and the light of heaven on earth."

"The best devotion," says Hazrat Ali, "is to abstain from what is prohibited; and the most agreeable of earthly acts co God, is to pray to Him, for prayer turneth away a decree even though ordained; it is the key of mercy, the means whereby needs are satisfied and every calamity warded off."

"Whosoever prays," says Imam Muhammad Baqir, "shall never want". And he once said to Mir (one of his followers), "O Mir, pray and do not say whatever is ordained shall come to pass. Verily there is a rank of nearness to God which cannot be obtained save by prayers and entreaty".

14

To the question, what was the best devotional act? He replied, that there was nothing more agreeable to God than praying and entreaty, for God loved those who pray to Him, and that there was nothing more hateful to Him, than those who are proud and abstain from devotion and prayer.

Hazrat Ali has said:

"Offer your prayers regularly, be careful when you are offering them, pray as often as you possibly can and through prayers seek the proximity of His Realm. Prayers are made compulsory for faithful Muslims. Have you not read in the Holy Quran the reply of those who would be thrown into Hell? When they will be asked: What has brought you to Hell, they will say, We were not amongst those who prayed."

2. ROZA: Observance of fasts becomes obligatory from the day following the appearance of the new moon of the month of Ramazan till the night when the new moon of the succeeding month appears,

"O ye who believe, fasting is prescribed to you as it was prescribed to those before you that ye may exercise self-restraint." 2 : 183

"So everyone of you who witnesseth this month should fast in it." 2 : 185

* * *

3. HAJJ: Going to Mecca for pilgrimage is called Hajj. The pilgrimage becomes obligatory on one who has funds enough for his return journey as well as maintenance of his family during his absence. The Hajj is performed on the 9th of the last month of the Islamic Calendar, namely, Zilhajj.

"Proclaim among people for the Hajj so that they come to you on foot or on camels of any kind from deep and distant places." 22 : 27

"The Hajj of the House of Allah (Kaaba) is obligatory on every one who has means for the journey to it." 3 : 97

* * *

4. ZAKAT (or poor rate):

This is payable at the rate of one out of every forty, on the value of one's capital possessions such as gold and silver coins, wheat, barley, dates, raisins, camels, cattle and sheep, after satisfying certain conditions.

* * *

> "And offer prayers
> And pay Zakat
> And bow down with those
> Who bow down (in worship)" 2 : 43

5. KHUMS:

Paying one-fifth of the amount of a year's saving (after deducting all legitimate expenses from the earnings of that year) is called Khums.

Sadaats (descendents of the Holy Prophet) have a right over half of this amount which should be paid to those amongst them who are poor and needy. The other half belongs to the Imam and should be paid to his Naaebs (Mujtaheds).

* * *

> "And know that out of all wealth you may acquire, one fifth of it is for Allah, and for the messenger and for his Kinsmen, and the Orphans, the poor and the wayfarer." 8 : 41

6. JEHAD:

Means to strive or fight in the way of God. Jehad literally means "strive" and as striving can be of various kinds and in different ways, it includes also fighting when it becomes the only alternative to defend the faith and the faithful.

* * *

> "And fight in the cause of Allah against those who fight against you, but do not transgress because Allah does not love transgressors." 2 : 190

7. AMRA-BIL-MA'AROOF: Means to enjoin what is right.

> "Let there arise out of you, a band of people inviting to all that is good, enjoining what is right and forbidding what is wrong. They are the ones to attain felicity." 3 : 104

* * *

8. NAHI-ANIL-MUNKAR: Means to forbid what is wrong.

> "Let there arise out of you, a band of people inviting to all

that is good, enjoining what is right and forbidding what is wrong. They are the ones to attain felicity."   3 : 104

9. TAWALLA: Means to love and respect the Ahl-ul-bait and to be friendly with their friends.

10. TABARRA: Means to disassociate or keep aloof from the enemies of the Ahl-ul-bait.

TAQLEED

Taqleed is to approach a living Mujtahed for the interpretation of problems concerning religion with the intention of acting in accordance with verdicts whenever the need arises.

Taqleed of a dead Mujtahed is permitted (Jaez) with the permission of a living one to the extent of his interpretations on which one has acted upon during the life of that Mujtahed. If an interpretation of a dead Mujtahed is not acted upon in his lifetime, the living Mujtahed should be approached for a verdict on the problem.

Performance of religious rites without adopting Taqleed of a Mujtahed will be considered void (batil).

SIFAT (Attributes of Allah):

The positive attributes are known as Sifate Subutiyah

The negative attributes are known as Sifate Salbiya.

SIFATE SUBUTIYAH:

Those attributes which are befitting ALLAH, are termed as Sifate Subutiyah. These are eight in number and are explained below:—

1.	QADEEM:	It means GOD is eternal. He has neither a beginning nor an end.
2.	QAADIR:	It means GOD is Omnipotent, i.e. He has power over every affair.
3.	ALIM:	It means GOD is Omniscient. He knows everything. Nothing remains secret from Him.
4.	HAI:	It means GOD is alive and will be so forever.
5.	MUREED:	It means that GOD does all things according to His will and intentions.

17

6.	MUDRIK:	It means GOD is aware of all affairs. He is All-Hearing and All-Seeing.
7.	MUTAKALLIM:	It means GOD can infuse speech in any-thing, e.g. trees, stones, etc.
8.	SADIQ:	It means GOD is truth personified.

SIFATE SALBIYA:

The negative attributes are seven in number. They are explained below:

1.	MURAKKAB:	Allah is not made or composed of any material.
2.	JISM:	Allah does not possess a body.
3.	MAKAN:	Allah does not have a place of abode. He exists everywhere.
4.	MOHTAJ:	Allah is not dependent on anyone or anything.
5.	MARA-EE:	Allah is never seen and will never be seen.
6.	MAHAL:	Allah is not subject to changes. No change of state takes place in Him.
7.	SHAREEK:	Allah has neither a colleague nor a part-ner.

What Others
Have to Say
About

Islam
The Holy Prophet
The Quran
Imam Husain

"History makes it clear, however, that the legend of fanatical Muslims sweeping through the world and forcing Islam at the point of the sword upon conquered races is one of the most fantastically absurd myths that historians have ever repeated."   (De Lacy O'Leary)

"Let there be no compulsion in religion: Truth stands out clear from error: Whoever rejects evil and believes in God hath grasped the most-trustworthy hand-hold, that never breaks. And God heareth and knoweth all things." (The Holy Quran)

2 : 256

What others have to say about:
Islam – The Holy Prophet – The Quran
and Imam Husain

ISLAM:

"Islam is the religion of the Universe, Islam is the destiny of mankind. That destiny must come to fulfilment sooner or later. Muslims carry a great responsibility on their shoulders in that respect, and the earlier they awaken to it the better." (Prof. Dr. C. Antonoff).

"Africa is a fair field for all religions; but the religion which the African will accept, is a religion which best suits his needs. And that religion, everyone who has the right to speak on the subject, says, is ISLAM." (H. G. Wells).

"Europe has continued to keep out of sight our scientific obligations to the Mussalmans. Surely they cannot be much longer hidden." (Rev. G. Margoliouth).

"As a reminder, of the blood-stained field of Kerbala, where the grandson of the Apostle of Allah fell at length, tortured by thirst and surrounded by the bodies of his murdered kinsmen, has been at any time since then sufficient to evoke, even in the most lukewarm and heedless, the deepest emotion, the most frantic grief and the exaltation of spirit before which pain, danger, and death shrink to unconsidered trifles. Verily on the tenth of Muharram, the tragedy is rehearsed in Persia, in Turkey, in Egypt, wherever a Shia community or colony exists. As I write it all comes back; the wailing chant, the sobbing multitudes, the white raiment red with blood from self-inflicted wounds, the intoxication of grief and sympathy." (Browne, "A Literary History of Persia".)

"Islam introduced a vigorous puritanism into Asia and Europe, deprecating even dancing and cardplaying." (Sadhu T. L. Vaswani).

"No religion in History spread so rapidly as Islam." (James A. Michener).

"If any religion has a chance of ruling over England, nay Europe, within the next hundred years, it can only be Islam.

I have always held the religion of Muhammad in high estimation because of its wonderful vitality. It is the only religion which appears to me to possess the assimilating capability to the changing phase of existence; which can make its appeal to every age. I believe that if a man like Muhammad were to assume the dictatorship of the modern world he would succeed in solving its problems in a way that would bring it much needed peace and happiness." (George Bernard Shaw).

THE HOLY PROPHET:

"Philosopher, orator, apostle, legislator, conqueror of ideas, restorer of rational dogmas, of a cult without images; the founder of twenty terrestrial empires and of one spiritual empire, that is Muhammad. As regards all standards by which human greatness may be measured, we may well ask, is there any man greater than He?" (Lamartine).

"His (Muhammad's) ability as a statesman faced with problems of extraordinary complexity is truly amazing." (Alfred Guillame).

"Muhammad was the soul of kindness, and his influence was felt and never forgotten by those around him." (Diwan Chand Sharma).

"Muhammad's immense contribution to civilization remains an outstanding and astounding fact of history, however we may judge it." (Lalla H. Dayal, M.A., Ph.D.).

"Of all men, Muhammad has exercised the greatest influence upon the human race." (Draper).

"It may be truly affirmed that of all known legislators and conquerors not one can be named, the history of whose life has been written with greater authenticity and full detail than that of Muhammad." (John Davenport).

"One of the finest things in the teaching of Muhammad is his injunction for every man to set apart a certain percentage of his annual income as the property of the poor." (H. & D. L. Thomas).

THE HOLY QURAN:

"Sincerity, in all senses, seems to me the merit of the Quran." (Thomas Carlyle).

21

"It (Quran) is the most esteemed and most powerful religious Book in the World." (J. C. Wilson).

"The Quran is powerful enough to conquer the hearts." (Rev. O. Leary, D.D.).

"It (Quran) is a literal revelation of God, dictated to Muhammad by Gabriel, perfect in every letter." (Harry Gaylord Dorman).

"It is this combination of dedication to one God, plus practical instruction, that makes the Quran unique." (James A. Michener).

IMAM HUSAIN:

"Husain marched with his little company not to glory, not to power or wealth, but to a supreme sacrifice and every member of that gallant band, male and female, knew that the foes around were implacable, were not only ready to fight, but to kill. Denied even water for the children, they remained parched under a burning sun, amid scorching sands, yet not one faltered for a moment but bravely faced the greatest odds without flinching." (Dr. K. Sheldrake).

"The best lesson which we get from the tragedy of Kerbala is that Husain and his followers were the rigid believers of God. They illustrated that numerical superiority does not count when it comes to Truth and Falsehood. The victory of Husain, despite his minority marvels me." (Thomas Carlyle).

"In a distant age and climate the tragic scene of the death of Husain will awaken the sympathy of the coldest reader." (Gibbon).

"Who falls for the love of God shall rise a STAR." (Ben Johnson).

Asma - ul - Husna

"God teaches us good, but how can we see if we make ourselves blind? At the end of all shall we know how small is our state, but for God's Grace : Let us bow to his Will and accept His true guidance: Let us praise Him and trust Him now and forever."

(THE BEAUTIFUL NAMES OF GOD)

The most beautiful names belong to God, so call on Him thereby. 7 : 180

Those who believe, and whose hearts find satisfaction in the remembrance of GOD, for without doubt in the remembrance of God do hearts find satisfaction. 13 : 28

1.	Ya Allah	.. ..	O God
2.	Ya Aadil	.. ..	O Equitable
3.	Ya Aakhir	.. ..	O Last
4.	Ya Alim	.. ..	O Knower
5.	Ya Ahad	.. ..	O The One and Only
6.	Ya Awwal	.. ..	O First
7.	Ya Azali	.. ..	O Eternal (in the past)
8.	Ya Aziz	.. ..	O Strong
9.	Ya Azeem	.. ..	O The Most High
10.	Ya Ba'ith	.. ..	O Raiser From Death
11.	Ya Baqi	.. ..	O Eternal (in the future)
12.	Ya Bari	.. ..	O Skilled Worker
13.	Ya Barr	.. ..	O Good
14.	Ya Basir	.. ..	O Seeing
15.	Ya Basit	.. ..	O Uncloser
16.	Ya Batin	.. ..	O Hidden
17.	Ya Fatih	.. ..	O Opener
18.	Ya Ghaffar	.. ..	O Pardoner
19.	Ya Ghafoor	.. ..	O Forgiver
20.	Ya Ghani	.. ..	O Sufficient
21.	Ya Hadi	.. ..	O Guide
22.	Ya Hafiz	.. ..	O Preserver
23.	Ya Haiy	.. ..	O Everlasting
24.	Ya Hakim	.. ..	O Wise
25.	Ya Hakim-al-Mutlak	..	O Judge of Judges
26.	Ya 'Ali	.. ..	O Exalted
27.	Ya Halim	.. ..	O Clement
28.	Ya Hamid	.. ..	O Praiseworthy

29.	Ya Haqq	.. ..	O Truth
30.	Ya Hasib	.. ..	O Reckoner
31.	Ya Hatim	.. ..	O Mighty
32.	Ya Jabbar	.. ..	O Compelling
33.	Ya Jaleel	.. ..	O Glorious
34.	Ya Jaame	.. ..	O Gatherer
35.	Ya Jamil	.. ..	O Beneficient
36.	Ya Kabir	.. ..	O Very Great
37.	Ya Karim	.. ..	O Generous
38.	Ya Khabir	.. ..	O He Who Knows
39.	Ya Khafiz	.. ..	O Abaser
40.	Ya Khaliq	.. ..	O Creator
41.	Ya Latif	.. ..	O Gracious
42.	Ya Majid	.. ..	O Glorious
43.	Ya Malik	.. ..	O King of Kings
44.	Ya Malik-ul-Mulk	.. ..	O King of the Kingdom
45.	Ya Mani'	.. ..	O Withholder
46.	Ya Momin	.. ..	O Faithful
47.	Ya Mateen	.. ..	O Firm
48.	Ya Mohyi	.. ..	O Quickener
49.	Ya Muakhkhir	.. ..	O Fulfiller
50.	Ya Mubdi	.. ..	O Beginner
51.	Ya Mughni	.. ..	O Sufficer
52.	Ya Muhaimin	.. ..	O Helper in Peril
53.	Ya Mu'id	.. ..	O Restorer
54.	Ya Mu'ti	.. ..	O Provider
55.	Ya Muizz	.. ..	O Honourer
56.	Ya Mujib	.. ..	O Hearer of Prayer
57.	Ya Mukhbir	.. ..	O One Who Informs
58.	Ya Mukit	.. ..	O Maintainer
59.	Ya Muqaddim	.. .	O Forewarner
60.	Ya Muqsit	.. ..	O Equitable
61.	Ya Muqtadir	.. ..	O Powerful
62.	Ya Mumit	.. ..	O Slayer
63.	Ya Muntaqim	.. ..	O Avenger
64.	Ya Musawwir	.. ..	O Sculptor
65.	Ya Mutaali	.. ..	O One above Reproach

66.	Ya Mutakabbir	O Majestic
67.	Ya Nafi	O Favourably inclined
68.	Ya Noor	O Light
69.	Ya Qadir	O Providence
70.	Ya Qahhar	O Dominant
71.	Ya Qawi	O Mighty
72.	Ya Qayyum	O Self Subsisting
73.	Ya Quddus	O Holy One
74.	Ya Rab	O Lord
75.	Ya Rafi	O Exalter
76.	Ya Raheem	O Beneficient
77.	Ya Rahman	O Merciful
78.	Ya Raqib	O Watchful
79.	Ya Rashid	O Unerring
80.	Ya Raoof	O Indulgent
81.	Ya Razzaq	O Provider
82.	Ya Saboor	O Patient
83.	Ya Salaam	O Peace
84.	Ya Samad	O Eternal
85.	Ya Sami	O One Who Hears
86.	Ya Shahid	O Witness
87.	Ya Shakir	O Thankful
88.	Ya Shakoor	O Appreciator
89.	Ya Vakil	O Guardian
90.	Ya Tawwab	O Relenting
91.	Ya Vali	O Nearest Friend
92.	Ya Wahhab	O Bestower
93.	Ya Wahid	O One
94.	Ya Wajid	O Perceiving
95.	Ya Wadood	O Loving
96.	Ya Wali	O Governor
97.	Ya Wasi	O Abundant
98.	Ya Warith	O Inheritor
99.	Ya Wali al Ahsan	O Friend of the believers
100.	Ya Zal-Jalal-Wal-Ikram	O Lord of Power & Majesty.

The
Holy
Quran

We have revealed for you (O Men) a Book in which is a Message for you : Will ye not then understand?
The Holy Quran 21 :10

The Holy Quran

Of all the heavenly books revealed to different Prophets for the guidance of mankind, the Holy Quran occupies a unique position in the sense that it is meant for all times and climes till the end of the world, because it is the last word of Allah after which no revealed Book is to come.

Islam is a perfect religion, so it touches every aspect of human activity: therefore the Quran, the Book of God, contains a complete code of life which may be required by man at any time in any place. J. Davenport says in his book, "Muhammad and the Quran":

"The Quran is the general code of the Muslim World; a social, civil, commercial, military, judicial, criminal, penal and yet a religious code, by it everything is regulated—from the ceremonies of religion to those of daily life, from the salvation of the soul to health of the body, from the rights of the general communities to those of each individual, from the interest of man to those of society, from morality to crime, from punishment here to that of the life to come."

The Quran is not a book containing theories but it is the Book which always exhorts mankind to practice and action. It always extends an invitation to think, to ponder and to contemplate over the mysteries of the Universe. It is the Book not only to recite but to understand and apply the instructions in one's own life. The Quran contains revolutionary ideas so that a man lying in the deep dark ditch of degradation, can come up and soar high to reach the zenith of greatness and glory; to come out of decline and rise up.

Hazrat Ali, the greatest expounder of the Holy Quran, the unmatched scholar of Islam and an orator of the highest calibre, speaks of the Quran in the following words:

"At such a time He made the Holy Prophet (S. A.) the means of revealing His Command bringing Muslims out of the world of chaos, carrying the message of peace and prosperity to mankind!"

Allah also revealed to the Holy Prophet (S.A.) His message through the Holy Book (Quran). This book contains such knowledge and enlightenment that it shall never be ineffective, futile, or fruitless. It carries in its words, wisdom so deep, that an ordinary man cannot actually reach those depths. It is a highway which will not mislead anybody. It is a light that will never die out. It creates such distinction between truth and falsehood that its decisions will never be challenged or refuted. Its exhortations cannot be proved wrong. It is the cure for perversity of minds. It is a power which cannot be overthrown. It is truth personified. Its supporters will never feel sorry for the support given to it. It is a mine of faith, a spring of knowledge and a fountain-head of equity and justice. The wisdom that this book contains and the learning which it imparts cannot be exhausted. It is such a destination that those who aim to reach it will never go astray. It is such a landmark that those who follow the path of truth will never miss it. It is such a sublime source of information that nothing can surpass it. God has made it a blessing for the learned, wise and pious persons, and an unfailing remedy for the wicked and a source of illumination for those in the depths of darkness. It is a powerful binding force to keep men within the bonds of truth, faith and love. It is the safest refuge from sin and vice. It is the harbinger of peace for humanity. It honours those who accept it, guides those who follow it, profits those who act according to its dictates, and it acts as a sound argument for those who speak through it. It brings success to those who embrace it. It is the quickest and the shortest way to salvation for those who formulate their lives according to its tenets. It is the easiest and the best form of explanation for those who want to understand the principles of truth and piety. So far as the history of mankind is concerned, it is the best source of information and so far as justice and equity is concerned, it is the best code of law.

It is an undeniable fact that the book by itself cannot teach and guide its readers because there is every possibility of misunderstandings and misinterpretations and so, it is but necessary that the teachings of the Quran be directly taken from the Prophet or his Ahl-ul-Bait (Progeny) who were always near him. Keeping this in view the Holy Prophet himself declared:

"I leave among you two weighty things, the Book of Allah (The Quran) and my Itrat (Progeny); if you hold fast to them you will never go astray, and these two shall never separate from each other till they meet me at the heavenly fountain of Kausar."

God's Command to obey the Holy Quran can be seen from a few Ayats amongst many, as noted below:

"This is the Book. In it is guidance sure without doubt, to those who fear God, who believe in the Unseen, are steadfast in Prayer, and spend out of what we have provided for them."   (2 : 2-3)

"These are verses of the wise Book. A guide and a mercy to the doers of Good, those who establish regular prayers, and give regular charity, and have in their hearts the assurance of the Hereafter." (31 : 2-3-4)

"That this is indeed a Quran most honourable, in a Book well-guarded, which none shall touch but those who are clean, a revelation from the Lord of the Worlds."   (56 : 77-80)

"We sent down the Quran in truth, and in truth has it descended:
And we sent thee but to give glad tidings and to warn (sinners)."   (17 : 105)

"When the Quran is read, listen to it with attention, and hold your peace: That ye may receive mercy."
                                                    (8 : 204)

AYAT-UL-KURSI: (The Throne verse of the Quran)

"O ye who believe! spend out of (the bounties) We have provided for you, before the day comes when no bargaining (will avail), nor friendship nor intercession. Those who reject Faith they are the wrong-doers.

GOD! There is no God but He,—the Living, the Self-Subsisting, Eternal. No slumber can seize Him. His are all things in the heavens and on earth. Who is there that can intercede in His presence except as He permitteth? He knoweth what (appeareth to His creatures as) before or after or behind them. Nor shall they compass aught of his Knowledge except as He willeth. His throne doth extend over the heavens and the earth, and he feeleth no fatigue in guarding and preserving them for He is the Most High, The Supreme (*in glory*). Let there be no compulsion in religion: Truth stands out clear from error: Whoever rejects evil and believes in God hath grasped the most trustworthy Hand-hold, that never breaks. And God heareth and knoweth all things. God is the protector of those who have faith: From the depths of darkness He will lead them forth into light. Of those who reject faith the patrons are the evil ones. From light they will lead them forth into the depths of darkness. They will be companions of the fire, to dwell therein (forever)."　　　　　(2 : 254, 255, 256, 557) The Holy Quran

Quranic Commandments
Prayers from the Holy Quran
Verses from the Holy Quran

When the Quran is read, listen to it with attention,
and hold your peace : That ye may receive mercy.
                    7 : 204 The Holy Quran

IN THE NAME OF GOD, MOST GRACIOUS, MOST MERCIFUL

ON OBEYING THE HOLY PROPHET:

O ye who believe! Obey God, and obey the Apostle, and those charged with authority among you. If ye differ in anything among yourselves refer it to God and His Apostle, if ye do believe in God and the last day. This is the best, and most suitable for final determination. 4 : 59

Obey God, and obey the Apostle: but if ye turn away, he is only responsible for the duty placed on him and ye for that placed on you. If ye obey him ye shall be on right guidance. The Apostle's duty is only to preach the clear (message). 24 : 54

O ye who believe! Obey God, and obey the Apostle, and make not vain your deeds. 18 : 33

AND THOSE WHO ANNOY THE PROPHET:

Those who annoy God and His Apostle — God has cursed them in this world and in the Hereafter, and has prepared for them a humiliating punishment. 33 : 57

ON THE PROPHET'S AHL-UL-BAIT:

Verily, verily, Allah intendeth but to keep off from you (every kind of) uncleanliness.

O ye People of the House, and purify you (with) a thorough purification. 33 : 33

O ye who believe! Fear God, and be with those who are true (in words and deeds). 9 : 119

THE HOUR OF DEATH:

Verily, the knowledge of the Hour is with God (alone). It is He who sends down rain, and He who knows what is in the wombs. Nor does any one know what it is that he will earn on the morrow.

Nor does any one know in what land he is to die. Verily, with God is full knowledge and He is acquainted (with all things). 31:34

The Hour will certainly come: Therein is no doubt: Yet most men believe not.   11:59

And serve thy Lord until there come unto thee The Hour that is certain.   15:99

ON PRAYERS:

Recite what is sent of the Book by inspiration to thee, and establish regular prayer. For prayer restrains from shameful and unjust deeds; and remembrance of God is the greatest (thing in life) without doubt. And God knows the (deeds) that ye do.   29:45

Then do ye remember Me: I will remember you.
Be grateful to Me, and Reject not faith.   2:152

If you are grateful, I will add more (favours unto you). But if ye show ingratitude, truly My punishment is indeed terrible.   14:7

Call on Me: I will answer your (prayer).
But those who are too arrogant to serve Me, will surely find themselves in Hell, in humiliation.   40:60

THE RIGHTEOUS:

It is righteousness to believe in God, and the Last Day, and the Angels, and the Book, and the Messengers; to spend of your substance, out of love for Him, for your kin, for orphans, for the needy, for the wayfarer, for those who ask, and for the ransom of slaves. To be steadfast in prayer, and practice regular charity, to fulfil the contracts which ye have made; and to be firm and patient, in pain (or suffering) and adversity, and throughout all periods of panic. Such are the people of truth, the God-fearing.   2:177

As to the righteous they will be in the midst of gardens and springs. Taking joy in the things which their Lord gives them because, before then, they lived a good life. They were in the habit of sleeping but little by night and in the early hours of dawn, they (were found) praying for forgiveness; and in their wealth and possessions (was remembered) the right of (the needy) him who asked, and him who (for some reason) was prevented (from asking).   51:15, 16, 17, 18, and 19

ON WEIGHTS AND MEASURES:

Give full measure when ye measure, and weigh with a balance that is straight. That is the most fitting and the most advantageous in the final determination.　　　17:35

Give just measure, and cause no loss (to others by fraud), and weigh with scales true and upright, and withhold not things justly due to men, nor do evil in the land, working mischief.　　　26:181, 182, 183

ON THE MOST TRUSTWORTHY HAND-HOLD:

Whoever submits his whole self to God and is a doer of good, has grasped indeed the most trustworthy hand-hold. And with God rests the end and Decision of (all) affairs.　　31:22

ON THE MERCY OF GOD:

Say: "O my servants who have transgressed against their souls! Despair not of the Mercy of God. For God forgives all sins. For He is Oft-forgiving Most Merciful. Turn ye to your Lord (in repentance) and bow to His (Will), before the penalty comes on you. After that ye shall not be helped."　　39:53-54

ON PARENTS:

Thy Lord hath decreed that ye worship none but Him, and that ye be kind to parents. Whether one or both of them attain old age in thy life.

Say not to them a word of contempt, nor repel them, but address them in terms of honour.

And, out of kindness, lower to them the wing of Humility, and say: "My Lord! bestow on them Thy Mercy even as they cherished me in childhood."　　17:23-24

"We have enjoined on man, kindness to parents; but if they (either of them) strive (to force) thee to join with Me (in worship) anything of which thou hast no knowledge, obey them not. Ye have (all to return to Me), and I will tell you (the truth) of all that ye did.　　29:8

ON PATIENCE:

"And Obey God and His Apostle and fall into no disputes, lest ye lose heart; and your power depart; and be patient and persevering:"

"For God is with those who patiently persevere."　　8:46

ON FOOD:

O ye people! Eat of what is on earth, lawful and good; and do not follow the footsteps of the evil one, for he is to you an avowed enemy. 2:168

O ye who believe! eat of the good things that we have provided for you; and be grateful to God, if it is Him ye worship.

He hath only forbidden you dead meat, and blood, and the flesh of swine, and that on which any other name hath been invoked besides that of God.

But if one is forced by necessity without wilful disobedience nor transgressing due limits—then he is guiltless. For God is Oft-Forgiving, Most Merciful. 2:172, 173

ON THOSE WHO ARE SLAIN IN THE WAY OF ALLAH:

"And say not of those who are slain in the way of God: "They are dead."

"Nay, they are living, though ye perceive (it) not." 2:155

"Think not of those slain in God's way as dead. Nay, they live, finding their sustenance in the Presence of their Lord." 3:169

THOSE ON WHOM IS THE CURSE OF ALLAH:

"Those who conceal the clear (signs) We have sent down, and the guidance after We have made it clear for the People in the Book, on them shall be God's curse, and the curse of those entitled to curse. Except those who repent and make amends and openly declare (the truth):

To them I turn; for I am Oft--returning, Most Merciful.

Those who reject Faith, and die rejecting, on them is God's curse and the curse of angels and of all mankind." 2:159, 160, 161

ON ENTERING THE HOUSES OF OTHERS:

"O ye who believe! Enter not houses other than your own, until ye have asked permission and saluted those in them; that is best for you, in order that ye may heed (what is seemly!) If ye find no one in the house, enter not until permission is given to you. If you are asked to go back, go back: that makes for greater purity for yourselves: and God knows well all that ye do."   24:27-28

ON SCANDAL MONGERS:

"Those who love (to see) scandal broadcast among the believers, will have a grievous penalty in this life and the Hereafter: God knows and ye know not."   24:19

ON SCANDAL AND SUSPICION:

"O ye who believe! if a wicked person comes to you with any news ascertain the truth, lest ye harm people unwittingly, and afterwards become full of repentance for what you have done."   49:6

"Nor defame nor be sarcastic to each other, nor call each other by (offensive) nicknmes: Ill-seeming is a name connoting wickedness."   49:11

"O ye who believe! Avoid suspicion as much (as possible). For suspicion in some cases is a sin. And spy not on each other, nor speak ill of each other behind their backs."   49:12

ON GAMBLING AND INTOXICANTS:

O ye who believe! Intoxicants and gambling, (Dedication) of stones, (Divination by) arrows, are an abomination of Satan's handiwork. Eschew such (abomination) that you may prosper.

Satan's plan is (but) to excite enmity and hatred between you with intoxicants and gambling and hinder you from the remembrance of God and from prayer: Will ye not then abstain?"   5:93-94

BLESSINGS ON THE PROPHET:

"God and His Angels send blessings on the Prophet: O ye that believe! send ye blessings on him, and salute him with all respect.   33.56

ON CHARITY:

"The Parable of those who spend their substance in the way of God is that of a grain of corn: it groweth seven ears, and each ear hath a hundred grains. God giveth manifold increase to whom He pleaseth: And God careth for all and He knoweth all things.

Those who spend their substance in the cause of God, and follow not up their gifts with reminders of their generosity or with injury, for them their reward is with their Lord.

On them shall be no fear nor shall they grieve.

Kind words and the covering of faults are better than charity followed by injury. God is free of all wants, and He is most forbearing."   2:261-262-263

If ye disclose (acts of) charity, even so it is well, but if ye conceal them, and make them reach those (really) in need, that is best for you. It will remove from you some of your (stains of) evil.

And God is well acquainted with what ye do.

Whatever of good ye give benefits your own souls and ye shall only do so seeking the "Face of God". Whatever good ye give, shall be rendered back to you, and ye shall not be dealt unjustly.

And they feed, for the love of God, the indigent, the orphan, and the captive, (saying), "We feed you for the sake of God alone. No reward do we desire from you, nor thanks."   126:8-9

THE PARABLE OF A GOODLY WORD AND AN EVIL WORD:

A goodly word is like a goodly tree, whose root is firmly fixed, and its branches (reach) to the Heavens. It brings forth its fruit at all times, by the leave of its Lord. So God set forth parables for men, in order that they receive admonition. And the parable of an evil word is that of an evil tree. It is torn up by the root from the surface of the earth. It has no stability.

"God will establish in strength those who believe, with the Word that stands firm in this world and in the Hereafter; But God will leave, to stray, those who do wrong. God doeth what He willeth."   12:24, 25, 26, 27

THE PARABLE OF A CITY ENJOYING SECURITY:

God sets forth a parable: A city enjoying security and quiet, is abundantly supplied with sustenance from every place.

Yet was it ungrateful for the favours of God. So God made it taste hunger and terror (in extremes), (closing in on it) like a garment (from every side), because of the (evil) which (its people) wrought. 16:112

THE PARABLE OF THOSE WHO REJECT THEIR LORD:

"The parable of those who reject their Lord is that their works are ashes, on which the wind blows furiously on a tempestuous day. No power have they over aught that they have earned. That is straying far, far (from the goal)." 14:18

THE PARABLE OF LIGHT:

"God is the light of the heavens and the earth. The parable of His Light is as if there were a Niche and within it a Lamp. The Lamp enclosed in glass. The glass as it were a brilliant star, lit from a blessed tree, an olive, neither of the east nor of the west, whose oil is well nigh luminous, though fire scarce touched it. Light upon Light! God doth guide whom He will to His Light. God doth set forth Parables for men and God doth know all things, (Lit is such a Light) in houses, which God hath permitted to be raised to honour, for the celebration in them of His name. In them is He glorified in the mornings and in the evenings (again and again), by men whom neither traffic nor merchandise can divert from the Remembrance of God, nor from regular prayers, nor from the practice of regular charity. Their (only) fear is for the Day when hearts and eyes will be transformed (in a world wholly new)."

"That God may reward them according to the best of their deeds, and add even more for them out of His Grace. For God doth provide for whom He will without measure."
24:35, 36, 37, & 38

THE PARABLE OF TRUTH AND VANITY:

"He sends down water from the skies, and the channels flow, each according to its measure; but the torrent bears away the foam that mounts up to the surface. Even so, from that (ore) which they heat in the fire to make ornaments or utensils therewith, there is a scum likewise. Thus doth God (by parables) show forth Truth and Vanity. For the scum disappears like froth cast out. While that which is for the good of Mankind remains on the earth. Thus doth God set forth parables."
13:17

"For those who respond to their Lord, are (all) good things. But those who respond not to Him even if they had all that is in the heavens and on the earth and as much more, (in vain) would they offer it for ransom. For them will the reckoning be terrible. Their abode will be Hell,—what a bed of Misery!"

ON POSSESSIONS AND PROGENY:

"And know ye that your possessions and your progeny are but a trial; and that it is God with whom lies your highest reward." 8:28

"O ye who believe! Let not riches or your children divert you from the remembrance of God. If any act thus, the loss is his own." 63:9

ON RESPITE:

And spend something (in charity) out of the substance which we have bestowed on you, before Death should come to any of you and ye should say, "O my Lord! Why didst thou not give me respite for a little while? I should then have given (largely) in charity, and I should have been one of the doers of good." But to no soul will God grant respite when the time appointed (for it) has come; and God is well acquainted with (all) that ye do. 6:10

ON GREETING:

"When a (courteous) greeting is offered to you, meet it with a greeting still more courteous, or (at least) of equal courtesy. God takes careful account of all things." 4:86

ON FASTING:

"O ye who believe! Fasting is prescribed to you, as it was prescribed to those before you, that you may learn self-restraint.

Ramazan is the (month) in which was sent down the Quran, as a guide to mankind, with clear (signs) for guidance and judgment (between right and wrong). So every one of you who is present (at home) during that month should spend it in Fasting. But if any one is ill, or on a journey, the prescribed period (should be made up) by days later. God intends every facility for you; He does not want to put you to difficulties (He wants you) to complete the prescribed period and to glorify Him. In

that He has guided you; and perchance ye shall be grateful."
2:183, 185

ON THE DAY OF RECKONING:

"The Trumpet will (just) be sounded, when all that is in the heavens and on the earth will swoon, except such as it will please God (to exempt). Then will a second one be sounded, when, behold, they will be standing and looking on!

And the Earth will shine with the glory of its Lord. The Record (of deeds) will be placed open. The Prophets and the witnesses will be brought forward; and a just decision pronounced between them; and they will not be wronged (in the least)."

"And to every soul will be paid in full (the fruit) of its deeds; and (God) knoweth best all that they do. The unbelievers will be led to Hell in crowds. Until when they arrive there, its gates will be opened. And its keepers will say, "Did not apostles come to you from among yourselves, rehearsing to you the signs of your Lord, and warning you of the Meeting of this day of yours?" The answer will be: "True: but the decree of punishment has been proved true against the unbelievers!"

(To them) will be said: "Enter ye the gates of Hell, to dwell therein. And evil is (this) abode of the arrogant!"

"And those who feared their Lord will be led to the garden in crowds. Until behold, they arrive there; its gates will be opened; and its Keepers will say: "Peace be upon you! Well have ye done! Enter ye here to dwell therein"

They will say: "Praise be to God, who has truly fulfilled His promise to us, and has given us (this) land in heritage. We can dwell in the Garden as we will. How excellent a reward for those who work (righteousness).

And thou will see the angels surrounding the Throne (Divine) on all sides, singing Glory and Praise to their Lord. The decision between them (at Judgment) will be in (perfect) justice and the cry (on all sides) will be "Praise be to God, the Lord of the worlds!" 39:68, 69, 70, 71, 72, 73, 74, 75

THE LIFE OF THIS WORLD COMPARED TO THE HEREAFTER:

"Know ye (all), that the life of this world is but play and amusement, pomp and mutual boasting and multiplying, (in rivalry) amongst yourselves, riches and children."

"In the Hereafter is a penalty severe (for the devotees of wrong). And forgiveness from God and (His) good pleasure (for the devotees of right). And what is the life of this world, but goods and chattels of deception." 57:20

And on the day that the unbelievers will be placed before the fire, (it will be said to them): "Ye received your good things in the life of the world, and ye took your pleasure out of them: but today shall ye be recompensed with a penalty and humiliation. For that ye were arrogant on earth without just cause, and that ye (ever) transgressed." 46:20

There are men who say: "Our Lord! Give us (Thy bounties) in this world!" But they will have no portion in the Hereafter.

And there are men who say: "Our Lord! Give us good in this world and good in the Hereafter, and defend us from the torment of the fire."

To these will be allotted what they have earned; and God is quick in account. 2:200,201

ON THE RE-UNION OF FAMILIES IN THE HEREAFTER:

"And those who believe and whose families follow them in faith, to them shall we join their families; nor shall we deprive them (of the fruit) of aught of their works: (yet) is each individual in pledge for his deeds."

"O ye who believe! Save yourselves and families from a fire whose fuel is men and stones, over which are (appointed) angels stern (and) severe, who flinch not (from executing) the Commands they receive from God, and do (precisely) what they are commanded."

FOR WHOM IS THE FINAL ATTAINMENT:

Those who patiently persevere seeking the Countenance of their Lord:

Establish regular prayers; spend out of (the gifts) We have bestowed for their sustenance, secretly and openly: and turn off evil with good: for such there is the final Attainment of the (eternal) Home.   13:22

Gardens of perpetual bliss; they shall enter there, as well as the righteous among their fathers, their spouses, and their offspring. And angels shall enter unto them from every gate (with the salutation):

Peace unto you that ye persevered in patience! Now how excellent is the Final Home!   13:23, 24

ON DEATH:

The Death from which ye flee will truly overtake you: then will ye be sent back to the knower of things secret and open: and He will tell you (the truth) of the things ye did. 62:8

ON FRIDAY PRAYERS:

O ye who believe! when the call is proclaimed to prayer on Friday (the day of assembly) hasten earnestly to the remembrance of God, and leave off business (and traffic). That is best for you if ye but knew! And when prayer is finished then may ye disperse through the land, and seek of the bounty of God: and celebrate the praises of God often (and without stint); that ye may prosper.   62:9, 10

THE TRUE BELIEVERS:

The Believers, men and women, are protectors one of another: They enjoin what is just, and forbid what is evil: They observe regular prayers, practice regular charity, and obey God and His Apostle. On them will God pour His mercy: For God is exalted in power, wise.   9:71

ON THOSE WHO REJECT DIVINE SIGNS:

Those who reject our signs, We shall gradually visit with punishment in ways they perceive not. Respite will I grant unto them: for My scheme is strong (And infallible). 7:182

They have hearts wherewith they understand not, eyes wherewith they see not, and ears wherewith they hear not. They are like cattle,—nay more misguided: for they are heedless (of warning).   7:179

Are the blind equal to those who see? or the depths of darkness equal to light?   13:16

To such as God rejects from His guidance, there can be no guide. He will leave them in their trespasses wandering in distraction.   7:186

WHAT WILL HAPPEN TO THE REJECTERS OF ALLAH:

At length, when comes the defening noise, that day shall man flee from his own brother, and from his father and mother, and from his wife and children. To make him indifferent to the others. Some faces that day will be beaming, laughing and rejoicing; and other faces that day will be dust-stained: blackness will cover them. Such will be rejecters of God, the doers of iniquity.   80:42

So leave them to babble and play (with vanities) until they meet that day of theirs, which they have been promised.   43:82

WHEN OUR CONDITION WILL CHANGE:

Verily never will God change the condition of a people until they change what is in themselves.   13:11

TO ESCAPE FROM SATAN:

If a suggestion from Satan assail thy (mind), seek refuge with God. For He heareth and knoweth (all things). Those who fear God, when a thought of evil from Satan assaults them, bring God to remembrance, when Lo! they see (aright).

WHOM TO ADORE: 7:200, 201

Adore not the sun and the moon, but adore God, Who created them, if it is Him ye wish to serve.   41:37

ALLAH'S FAVOUR ON US:

All that is on earth will perish; But will abide (for ever)
The Face of thy Lord, full of Majesty
Bounty and Honour.
Then which of the favours of your Lord will ye deny?
                                              56; 26, 27, 28

WHOM WILL ALLAH NOT GUIDE:

Those who believe not in the signs of God, God will not guide them, and theirs will be a grievous penalty.   16.104

This because they love the life of this world better than the hereafter: 16:107
And God will not guide those who reject Him.   26:107

If any men go astray, (God) Most gracious extends (the rope) to them, until, when they see the warnings of God (being fulfilled), either in punishment or in (the approach of) the Hour, they will at length realise who is worst in position, and (who) weakest in forces. 19:75

WHOM WILL ALLAH GUIDE:

Those who believe, and work in righteousness, the Lord will guide them because of their faith. 10:9

And to those who receive guidance, He increases the Light of Guidance, and bestows on them their piety and restraint from evil. 47:17

JESUS TESTIFIES TO THE COMING OF THE HOLY PROPHET:

And remember, Jesus the son of Mary said: "O Children of Israel! I am the Apostle of God (sent) to you confirming the law (which came) before me, and giving the glad tidings of an Apostle to come after me. Whose name shall be Ahmad. (Muhammad)" 61:6

ON THE BIRTH OF JESUS:

Related in the Book (the story of) Mary, when she withdrew from her family to a place in the East. She placed a screen (to screen herself) from them; then we sent to her Our angel, and he appeared before her as a man in all respects. She said: "I seek refuge from thee with (God) Most Gracious: (come not near) if thou dost fear God."

He said: "Nay, I am only a messenger from thy Lord, (to announce) to thee the gift of a Holy son."

She said: "How shall I have a son, seeing that no man has touched me, and I am not unchaste?"

He said: "So (it will be)." Thy Lord saith, "That is easy for Me: and (We wish) to appoint him as a sign unto men and Mercy from us. It is a matter (so) decreed."

So she conceived him, and she retired with him to a remote place. And the pains of childbirth drove her to the trunk of a palm-tree: She cried (in her anguish): "Ah. would that I had died before this! Would that I had been a thing forgotten and out of sight."

But (a voice) cried to her from beneath the (palm-tree). "Grieve not! for thy Lord hath provided a rivulet beneath thee. And shake towards thyself the trunk of the palm-tree: It will let fall fresh ripe dates upon thee. So eat and drink and cool (thine) eye. And if thou dost see any man, say, I have vowed a fast to (God) Most Gracious, and this day will I enter into no talk with any human being."

At length she brought the (babe) to her people, carrying him (in her arms). They said: "O Mary! truly an amazing thing hast thou brought! O Sister of Aaron! Thy father was not a man of evil nor thy mother a woman unchaste!" But she pointed to the babe. They said: "How can we talk to one who is a child in the cradle?" He (Jesus) said: "I am indeed a servant of God. He hath enjoined on me prayer and charity as long as I live. He hath made me kind to my mother, and not overbearing or miserable; so peace is on me the day I was born, the day that I die, and the day that I shall be raised up to life (again)." Such (was) Jesus the son of Mary: (it is) a statement of truth, about which they (vainly) dispute. It is not befitting to (the Majesty of God) that He should beget a son. Glory be to Him! When he determines a matter He only says to it, "Be" and it is.

19:16-35

JESUS WAS NOT CRUCIFIED:

That they said (in boast): "We killed Christ Jesus, the son of Mary, the Apostle of God," but they killed him not, nor crucified him, but it was made to appear to them, and those who differ therein are full of doubts, with no (certain) knowledge, but conjecture to follow, for a surety they killed him not. Nay, God raised him up unto Himself: And God is exalted in power and wise.

4:157,158

ON LEADERS WHO MISGUIDE PEOPLE:

He will go before his people on the day of Judgment and lead them into the fire (as cattle are led to water):

And woeful indeed will be this leading (and) the place led to! And they are followed by a curse in this (life) and on the day of judgment. And woeful is the gift which will be given (unto them).

11:98, 99

They have hearts wherewith they understand not, eyes wherewith they see not, ears wherewith they hear not. They are like cattle—nay more misguided: for they are heedless (of warning). 7:179

ON TRUST:

O ye that believe! Betray not the trust of God and the Apostle, nor misappropriate knowingly things entrusted to you. And know ye that your possessions and your progeny are but a trial and that it is God with whom lies the highest reward.
8:27, 28

And if one of you deposits a thing on trust with another, let the trustee (faithfuly) discharge his trust and let him fear God. Conceal not evidence: For whoever conceals it, his heart is tainted with sin. And God knoweth all that ye do. 2:283

ON DEVOURING INHERITANCE:

Those who unjustly eat up the property of orphans, eat up a fire into their own bodies; they will soon be enduring a blazing fire. 4:11

ON JUSTICE:

O ye who believe, stand out firmly for justice as witnesses to God even against yourselves or your parents or your kin and whether it be against rich or poor. For God can best protect both.

Follow not the lusts (of your heart) lest ye swerve, and if ye distort (justice) or decline to do justice, verily God is well acquainted with all that ye do. 4:135

WHO WILL BE FOREMOST IN THE HEREAFTER:

And those foremost (in faith) will be foremost (in the hereafter). These will be nearest to God. 56:10, 11

WHOM GOD WILL FORGIVE:

Be quick in the race of forgiveness from your Lord, and for a Garden whose width is that (of the whole) of the heavens and of the earth, prepared for the righteous, those who spend (freely) whether in prosperity or in adversity; who restrain anger, and pardon (all) men; for God loves those who do good: and those who, having done something to be ashamed of, or wronged their souls, earnestly bring God to mind, and ask for

47

forgiveness for their sins, and who can forgive sins except God? And are never obstinate in persising knowingly in (the wrong) they have done. For such the reward is forgiveness from their God.   3:133, 134, 135, 136

PARTNERS IN GOOD AND EVIL CAUSES

Whoever recommends and helps a good cause becomes a partner therein. And whoever recommends and helps an evil cause, shares in its burdens: and God hath power over all things.
                                                              4:85

ON THOSE WHO ARE MISERLY :

Behold, ye are those invited to spend (of your substance) in the way of God. But among you are some that are miserly. Any who are miserly are so at the expense of their own souls, God is free of all wants, and it is ye who are needy. If ye turn back (from the path), He will substitute in your stead another people; then they would not be like you.   47:38

THE HYPOCRITES:

There are amongst men some who serve God, as it were, on the verge. If good befalls them, they are, therewith, well content. But if a trial comes to them, they turn their faces. They lose both this world and the Hereafter. That is loss for all to see!   22:11

It is the wish of a section of the people of the Book to lead you astray.

But they shall lead astray (not you), but themselves, and they do not perceive!

Ye people of the Book! Why reject ye the signs of God, of which ye are (yourselves) witnesses?

Ye people of the Book! Why do ye clothe truth with falsehood, and conceal the truth, while ye have knowledge?
                                                       3:69, 70, 71

THE SIGNS OF GOD:

It is He who made the sun to be a shining glory and the moon to be a light (of beauty), and measured out stages for her; that ye might know the number of years and the count (of time).

God did create this in truth and righteousness. (Thus) doth He explain His signs in detail for those who understand. Verily, in the alternation of the night and the day and in all that God hath created in the heavens and the earth, are signs for those who fear. 10:5, 6

WHEN TROUBLE TOUCHES MAN:

When trouble toucheth a man, he crieth unto Us (in all postures) lying down on his side or sitting or standing. But when we have solved his trouble, he passeth on his way as if he had never cried to Us for a trouble that toucheth him! Thus do the deeds of the transgressors seem fair in their eyes! 10:12

THE CERTAINTY OF RESURRECTION:

O mankind! if ye have a doubt about Resurrection, (consider) that We created you out of dust, then out of sperm, then out of a leech like clot, then out of a morsel of flesh partly formed and partly unformed, in order that We may manifest (Our Power) to you; and We cause whom We will to rest in the wombs for an appointed term, then do We bring you out as babes, then (foster you) that ye may reach your age of full strength; and some of you are called to die and some are sent back to the feeblest old age so that they know nothing after having known (much). And (further), thou seest the earth barren and lifeless but when We pour down rain on it, it is stirred (to life), it swells and it puts forth every kind of beautiful growth (in pairs).

This is so, because God is the Reality. It is He who gives life to the dead, and it is He, who has power over all things. 22:5, 6

ON VAIN DISCOURSE:

When thou seest men in vain discourse about Our signs, turn away from them unless they turn to a different theme. If satan ever makes thee forget, then after recollection, sit not thou in the company of the ungodly. On their account no responsibility falls on the righteous, but (their duty) is to remind them that they may (learn to) fear God. 6: 68, 69

THOSE WHO TAKE THEIR RELIGION TO BE MERE PLAY:

Leave alone those who take their religion to be mere play and amusement, and are deceived by the life of this world.

But proclaim (to them) this (truth): That every soul delivers itself to ruin by its own acts. It will find for itself no protector or intercessor except God. If it offered every ransom, (or reparation), none will be accepted. Such is (the end of) those who deliver themselves to ruin by their own acts. They will have for drink (only) boiling water. 6:70

THE RIGHTEOUS COMPARED TO THE SINNERS:

The day We shall gather the righteous to (God) Most Gracious, like a band presented before the king for honours, and We shall drive the sinners to Hell, like thirsty cattle driven to water. 19:85-86

THE MOSQUE:

The Mosques of God shall be visited and maintained by such as believe in God and the last day, establish regular prayers and practise regular charity, and fear none (at all) except God. It is they who are expected to be on true guidance. 9:18

THE QURAN:

And that those on whom knowledge has been bestowed, may learn that the Quran is the truth from thy Lord and that they may believe therein, and their hearts may be made humble (open to it) For verily God is the guide of those who believe in the straight way. 22:54

Our Lord! give us good in this world and good in the Hereafter and defend us from the torment of the fire.　2:201

Our Lord! Pour out constancy on us and make our steps firm: Help us against those who reject faith.　2:250

Our Lord! Condemn us not if we forget or fall into error;

Our Lord! Lay not on us a burden like that which thou didst lay on those before us;

Our Lord! Lay not on us a burden greater than we have strength to bear. Blot out our sins and grant us forgiveness, have mercy on us. Thou are our Protector; help us against those who stand against Faith.　2:286

Our Lord! Let not our hearts deviate now after Thou hast guided us, but grant us mercy from Thine Own Presence; for Thou art the Grantor of bounties without measure.　3:8

Our Lord! We have indeed believed: forgive us then our sins, and save us from the agony of the fire.　3:16

Our Lord! Pour out on us Patience and Constancy, and take our souls unto Thee as Muslims (who bow to Thy will).　7:126

Our Lord! Truly Thou dost know what we conceal and what we reveal. For nothing whatever is hidden from God, whether on earth or heaven.　14:38

Our Lord! Cover us with thy forgiveness—me, my parents, and all believers, on the Day that the Reckoning will be established.　14:41

Our Lord! Bestow on us mercy from Thyself, and dispose of our affair for us in the right way.　18:10

Our Lord! We believe; then do Thou forgive us, and have mercy upon us. For thou art the Best of those who show mercy.　23:109

Our Lord! Avert from us the Wrath of Hell, for its Wrath is indeed an affliction grievous.　25:65

Our Lord! In Thee do we trust and to Thee do we turn in repentance. To Thee is our final Goal.　60:4

Our Lord! Perfect our Light for us, and grant us forgiveness. For Thou hast power over all things. 66:8

Our Lord! Forgive us our sins, blot out from us our iniquities, and take to Thyself our souls in the company of the righteous. 3:193

O Thou Creator of the heavens and the earth! Thou art my protector in this world and in the hereafter. Take Thou my soul (at death) as one submitting to Thy will (as a Muslim) and unite me with the righteous. 12:101

O my Lord! Advance me in knowledge. 20:114

All the above prayers can be recited in Arabic for Qunoot (Ardent supplication) in Namaz (Prayers).

INNA LILLAHAY WA INNA ILAIHAY RAAJAY-OON:
> To God we belong, and to Him we return.   2:156

WA KAFA BILLAHAY WALEEYA. WA KAFA BILLAHAY NASEERA:
> God is enough for a Protector and God is enough
for a Helper.   4:45

INNAL-LAHA SHAKAYROON ALEEM:
> Surely God is He who recogniseth and knoweth.   2:158

INNAL-LAHA YOU-HIBBOOL MOOTTAQEEN:
> God loves those who put their trust (in Him).   3:159

WALLAHO MA-AS-SAABAYREEN:
> God is with those who steadfastly persevere.   2:249

ALLAH HO KHAIROON HAAFAYZA: WA HOWA AR-HAMOOR RAAHAYMEEN:
> God is the best to take care, and He is the Most
Merciful of those who show mercy.   12:64

> *This Dua is recited in both the ears when a person
goes on a journey.

NASROOM MINALLAHAY WA FATH-HOON QAREEB:
> When help comes from God it results in a speedy
victory.   61:13

INNAL-LAHA YOU-HIBBOOL MOOQSAY-TEEN:
> God loveth those who are just.   60:8

INNAL-LAHA GHAFOOROOR RAHIM:
> God is oft-forgiving, Most Merciful.   60:12

INNAL-LAHA ALA KOOLLAY SHAI-IN QADEER:
> God hath power over all things.   2:259

ALLAH-HO RA-OOFOOM BIL AYBAAD:
> God is full of kindness to those who serve Him.   3:30

INNAL-LAHA LAA YOU-HIBBOOL KAAFAYREEN:
> God loveth not those who reject faith.   3:32

ALLAHO WALEE-YAL MOMENEEN:
> God is the Protector of those who have faith.   3:68

TAWAKKAL ALAL-LAH: ...
> Put thy trust in God.   33:3

ASTAGHFIROOLLAHA INNAL-LAHA KAANA GHAFOORAR RAHEEMA:

Seek the forgiveness of God; for God is Oft-forgiving, Most Merciful. 4:106

HAAZA MIN FAZLAY RABBEE:

This is by the Grace of God. 27:40

AM-MAI YOUJEEBOOL MUZTARRA IZA DA-AA-HO WA YAKSHEE FOOSSOO:

(God is He) Who listens to the (soul) distressed when it calls on Him and Who relieves its suffering. 27:62

MASHAA ALLAHO LA QOOWATA ILLA BILLAH:

(It is) as God willeth! there is no power but with God. 8:39

The Kaaba

"O ye servants of the Lord: fulfil the duties that are imposed on you, for in their neglect there is abasement. Your good work alone will render easy the road to death and to Heaven. Remember each sin increases the debt and makes the chain heavier. The message of mercy has come, the path of truth (Haq) is clear; obey the command that has been laid on you; live in purity and work with nobility of purpose and ask God to help you in your endeavours and to forgive your past transgressions. Cultivate humility and for-bearance, comfort yourself with sincere truth."

Hazrat Ali in Nahjul Balagha.

The Kaaba

(THE HOUSE OF GOD)

"Verily the first House of God made for mankind is the one at Mecca, a blessing and a guidance for the world. In it are clear signs, the standing place of Abraham, and whoever entereth it is secure; and (purely) for God is incumbent upon mankind, the pilgrimage to the House, for those who can afford to journey thither; and whoever denieth then verily God is self-sufficient and Independent of the Worlds."   3:96-97

The sanctity of Kabbat-ullah or Bait-ullah (House of God) has been established since times immemorial. The antiquity of Kaaba has been admitted by Sir Willam Muir with reference to the universal reverence and regard paid to it from the earliest time beyond any human memory.

From authentic traditions of the Prophets S.A. and quotations of Aale Muhammad A.S., it is evident that there is the Baitful Mamoor which is a place for worship in Heaven. Hazrat Ali says: "The heavenly place of worship (Baitul Mamoor) is visited by angels every day in multitude."

God through His infinite Mercy ordained the angels to build a similar place for his creatures on earth. The Angels descended with a tent and fixed it on earth. This was the first phase of Kaaba. When Adam and Hawa (Eve) descended on this earth they met at a place in Mecca called Arafat. They paid their homage in this tent. Thereafter, Adam and all the other Prophets held this place in high esteem and had great regard for it as a sacred place.

The first House of God was rebuilt and renovated at the Command of Allah, by the Prophet Abraham assisted by his worthy successor his son Ismail, under the guidance and supervision of angel Gabriel. Says the Quran:

"And remember when Abraham raised the foundation of the House with Ismail, (Praying) "Our Lord! accept (this service) from us; Verily Thou and Thou (alone) art the All-hearing and All-knowing."   2:127

The Quran again says:

"And remember when we made the House a resort for

mankind and a sanctuary (saying), 'Take ye the station of Abraham a place of prayer (for you); and covenanted with Abraham and Ismail (saying) purify ye two My House for those who make circuit, and for those who prostrate (adoring)." 2: 125

This verse clearly depicts the very purpose of the House, namely it is to be the place of worship and it is pure and sacred. This was also the reason why Abraham housed one of his wives, Hagar, and a son in Mecca near this place which was the House of God. It is said in the Holy Quran:

"O Our Lord! Verily I have housed a part of my offspring in a valley uncultivated, nigh unto Thy Holy House, Our Lord! that they may establish prayer; so make thou the hearts of some of the people yearn unto them! and provide them with fruits, that they may be grateful." 14:37

The following incident shows the Divine protection over the Kaaba. Yaman was then under the rule of the Abyssinians who were Christians, and who had driven out the Jewish Himyar rulers. Abraha Ashram was the Abyssinian Governor or Viceroy. Intoxicated by power and fired by religious fanaticism, he led a big expedition which included large number of elephants against Mecca, intending to destory the Kaaba. His sacrilegious intentions were however defeated by the occurance of a Miracle. No defence was offered by the custodians of the Kaaba as the Abyssinian force was too strong for them. In answer to the fervant prayer of Abd-al-Muttalib a shower of stones, thrown by flocks of birds, destroyed the invading force almost to a man. The stones produced sores and pustules on the skin of the enemy which spread like pestilence. This is the incident referred to in the Surah "Feel" which reads as follows:

"Seest thou not how thy Lord dealt with the companions of the elephant? Did He not make their treacherous plan go astray? And He sent against them flights of birds striking them with stones of baked clay. Then did He make them like an empty field of stalks and straw, (of which the corn) has been eaten up." 105 : 1-5

Formerly the Muslims used to offer their Namaz facing Baitul Muqaddas in Jerusalem. Then the undermentioned Ayat was revealed to the Holy Prophet and ever since the Muslims face towards Kaaba.

"Verily we see the turning of thy face (for guidance) to heaven, so we shall turn 'thee (in prayer) towards a 'Qiblah' thou shalt be pleased with. Turn then thy face towards the Sacred Mosque; and wherever ye be (in prayers) turn ye your faces towards it; verily those who have been given the Book know it is the Truth from their Lord; and Allah is not heedless of what they do"

2:144

Kaaba, the House of God, has been sanctified by the adoration and worship of God taking place inside it by the Prophets and their descendants who were specially appointed by Him to protect it. The last Prophet appointed for this purpose was Hazrat Muhammad Mustafa S.A. who along with his descendants (Progeny) were the guardians of this House. So those who hold fast to them will achieve salvation.

The Prophets
The Angels

Among the highest and greatest of the gifts of God is His Revelation, which is the Criterion by which we may judge between right and wrong—between false and true worship, between the Message that comes from God and the forgeries of men, between the Real in our eternal Future and the fancies by which we are misled. The apostles of God came as men to live among men and guide them.

The Prophets

Hazrat ADAM (A.S.) was the first Prophet, and Muhammad Mustafa (S.A.) was the last of the Prophets, and He WAS SENT AS A MERCY AND A WARNER TO THE WHOLE WORLD "that He may lead you from the depths of darkness into light". He was "The seal of the Prophets".

From amongst the other Prophets were:

1. Hazrat Nooh (A.S.) (Noah)
2. Hazrat Ibraheem (A.S.) (Abraham)
3. Hazrat Moosa (A.S.) (Moses)
4. Hazrat Eesa (A.S.) (Jesus)
5. Hazrat Dawood (A.S.) (David)
6. Hazrat Hud (A.S.)
7. Hazrat Saleh (A.S.)
8. Hazrat Lut (A.S.) (Lot)
9. Hazrat Ismail (A.S.) (Ishmael)
10. Hazrat Ishaq (A.S.) (Issac)
11. Hazrat Yaqoob (A.S.) (Jacob)
12. Hazrat Yousuf (A.S.) (Joseph)
13. Hazrat Suleman (A.S.) (Solomon)
14. Hazrat Zakaria (A.S.) (Zacharias)
15. Hazrat Yahya (A.S.) (John)

25 PROPHETS

1.	Adam	9.	Yunus
2.	Noah	10.	Lut
3.	Ibrahim	11.	Saleh
4.	Ismael	12.	Hud
5.	Isaac	13.	Shu'aib
6.	Jacob	14.	Dawud
7.	Yusuf	15.	Sulayman
8.	Al-Yasa	16.	Dhul-Kifl

60

17. Idriss	22. Musa
18. Elias	23. Harun
19. Zakariya	24. Isa
20. Yahya	25. Muhammad
21. Ayub	

THE HOLY BOOKS:

The TAURAIT (TORAH) was revealed to Hazrat Moosa.
The ZUBOOR (PSALMS) was revealed to Hazrat Dawood.
The INJEEL (EVANGEL) was revealed to Hazrat Eesa.

The QURAN, the last Holy Book, was revealed to our Prophet MUHAMMAD MUSTAFA S.A.

The Angels

Although invisible, they perform innumerable duties assigned to them by God. They offer prayers to God and comply with His Commands. Four of the best known angels are:

1. JIBREEL— The angel who delivers the Commands of God to His Prophets.

2. MIKAEEL— The angel who distributes sustenance to mankind.

3. IZRAEEL— The angel who takes out the soul of human beings, and is known as the angel of death.

4. ISRAFEEL— The angel who will blow the trumpet on Doomsday which will cause death to every living thing. Again he will blow the trumpet, and all the dead will be resurrected before Judgment.

The Mosque

"O Lord keep me firm in Thy religion as long as Thou keepest me alive; and let not my heart deviate, after Thou hast guided me; and let me have mercy from Thee; Verily Thou and Thou alone art the Giver:"

The Mosque

(THE HOUSE OF PEACE ON EARTH)

The Holy Quran says:

"The Mosque of God shall be visited and maintained by such as believe in God and the Last day, establish regular prayers, and practise regular charity, and fear none at all, except God. It is they who are on true guidance."   9 : 18

The Messenger of God has said: "Of all the places the most loved of God is the Mosque."

"The man," said the Holy Prophet, "who having carefully performed his ablution, sets out for the Mosque, has his status raised and his sins effaced at every step, and as long as he stays on the prayer mat, angels continue giving their blessings to Him."

The Mosque is the place where a man finds himself face to face with his Creator and feels himself spiritually elevated and purified.

The atmosphere required for such a house is created by utter simplicity. Perfect equality of status is enjoyed by the worshippers irrespective of birth, wealth or social position. The pinch of misery and poverty, which galls the heart wherever wealth and penury stand contrasted in the day to day dealings, loses its sharpness here. The poor man feels that in the ultimate accounting, worth will be judged by spiritual merits which are not the monopoly of the rich. This gives the place a charm and an attraction for him. Nobody would like to attend a gathering where he is obliged to realise his inferiority and feel himself discarded and looked down upon. Here he finds the meanest at par with the noblest. For instance, if he has arrived first and joined the first row, no dignitary, however great, dare ask him to leave his place. The Mosque discipline enforced by the Holy Prophet removes the indivious contrasts that would be an impediment to attendance by the poor along with the rich. They have to stand shoulder to shoulder with the meanest without leaving a gap. "For, Satan," said the Holy Prophet, "makes his way into your gathering through the gaps." Hence, the man in the row behind is not to hesitate to step forward to fill up the gap in the row ahead, no matter with whom he has to rub his shoulder.

To mantain an atmosphere of serene tranquillity, small children should not be allowed to enter the mosque during prayers. This rule is unfortunately ignored, resulting in small children disturbing the tranquillity which is so essential for prayers and meditation. Worshippers should be permitted to devote themselves to prayers unmolested either by young or old. It must also be remembered that the Mosque is a house of worship of God and it cannot be treated as a place for irrelevant conversation or talk on mercantile dealings.

It is to such a place that we enter, where serene spirituality is lodged in the midst of toil and tumult of life, to an academy where lessons in humility to God are daily rehearsed, when the Muezzin calls us. We fail to respond, perhaps because we are ignorant of the law that makes it incumbent, or perhaps we feel a little embarrassed to mix with the crowd. In the latter case it is doubtful if our prayers at our house will be acceptable to God. Those who attend the Mosque have also to make themselves sure that they do not walk out leaving their faith and fear of God, safely deposited at the Mosque.

Whilst entering the Mosque, one should step in with the right foot and say the following:

"I begin with the name of Allah, and I put my trust in Allah and there is no power save that of Allah".

Whilst leaving the Mosque, one should step out with the left foot and say the following:

"In the name of Allah, I seek protection of Allah, from Satan, the one who is stoned".

The Ahl-ul-Bait

No reward do I ask of you for this except the love of those near of Kin.   *62:23 The Holy Quran*

O Lord confer favour on Prophet Muhammad and the Holy members of his house, whom Thou hast chosen for Thy mission, and whom Thou hast made treasurers of Thy knowledge and guardians of Thy religion and Thy vicegerents in Thy earth, and Thy arguments to Thy creatures, and whom Thou hast of Thy will cleansed of impurity and pollution, with a thorough purification; and whom Thou hast made to be the medium of approaching Thee and the guides to Thy Paradise.

Those who have faith and do righteous deeds, they are the best of creatures. (Khair-ul-Bariyya)
The Holy Quran 98:7

The Holy Quran says:

O ye who believe! Fear God and be with those who are true (in word and deed). 9:19

Verily, verily, Allah intendeth but to keep off from you (every kind of) uncleanliness.

O ye People of the House, and purify you (with) a thorough purification. 33: 33

This Quranic verse is famous as the Ayat-e-Tathir, and is the basis of the Hadis-e-Kissa which points to the Ahl-ul-Bait.

Amir ibne Abi Salma who was brought up by the Holy Prophet relates:

At the revelation of this Ayat, the Holy Prophet S.A. assembled his daughter Fatema, her sons Hasan and Husain, and her husband Ali (who was also the cousin of the Prophet). He covered them including himself under a mantle and addressing Allah said, "O Allah! These constitute my Progeny! Keep them away from every kind of impurity, purified with a perfect purification."

Umme-Salma, the wife of the Holy Prophet in whose house the Prophet was at the time witnessing this marvellous occasion, humbly submitted to the Prophet, "O Messenger of Allah! May I also join this group?" To which the Holy Prophet replied, "No, please remain where thou art."

That they were the Holy Ahl-ul-Bait was further proved on the occasion of the historic event of Mubahala, when the Holy Prophet was commanded by Allah to call the Christians of Najran to a spiritual contest in the presence of Muslims and non-Muslims. The relevent Ayat from the Holy Quran says: "If any one disputes in this matter with thee, now after (full) knowledge hath come to thee. Say: "Come! let us gather together, our sons and your sons, our women and your women, ourselves and yourselves: Then let us earnestly pray and invoke the curse of God on those who lie!" 3;61. In response to this the Holy Prophet came out with his only daughter Fatema, her sons, Husain in his arms, and Hasan holding his hand, and followed by her husband Ali. This simple act of faith was so awe-inspiring and of so solemn a grandeur, that it compelled a spontaneous surrender by the Christians of Najran.

On another occasion the Holy Prophet said:

"The likeness of my Ahl-ul-Bait is that of the Ark of Noah, whoever got into it got saved, and whoever turned away from it got drowned and lost."

That the Ahl-ul-Bait enjoyed an exalted position by the Order of Allah can be seen in the following Ayat of the Holy Quran: "No reward do I ask of you except the love of those near of kin." 62:23

This verse is clear in its meaning that the Holy Prophet is being commanded to ask the believer to love his kith and kin, i.e. the Holy Ahl-ul-Bait. That was the reward the Holy Prophet asked from his followers for having guided them all his life to the right path.

Besides the clear evidence in the Holy Quran about the significance of the status of the Ahl-ul-Bait, there are several authentic sayings of the Holy Prophet. These narrations by the authors of the 'Sehah' and the 'Masaneed' of the Sunni School, support the above statements that none but these five persons were gathered under the 'Shuroot' (Mantle) and that the Holy Prophet pointed out saying "Allahumma haa'oolaaye ahlo-baiti-haa'oollaye itrati" (O Allah! these are the people of my House and these are my Progeny). Tahavi says in his book 'Muskilul Aathaar' that for six or nine months after the revelation of his verse (33:33), the Holy Prophet used to stand at the door of Janab-e-Fatema's house in the morning and in the evening saying, "As salamo Alaikum Ya Ahl-ul-Bait" and then recited this verse of the Tathir.

Allama Zamakshari and Jalaluddin Sooyuti have recorded the following tradition of the Holy Prophet: "He who dies in the love of Aale-Muhammad will be taken to heaven just as the bride is taken to the bridegroom's house; he who dies in the love of Aale-Muhammad, Allah will open two doors of paradise in his grave; he who dies in the love of Aale-Muhammad Allah will make his grave a visiting place for the angels of mercy."

The Four I'ds
I'd-al-Fitr (Ramzan I'd)
I'd-al-Ahza (Bakri I'd)
I'd-al-Ghadir
I'd-al-Mubahala
I'd-z-Milad-un-Nabi

"*Proclaim the Message of God, and pray to him for purity and guidance. God's Revelation carries its own proofs and is recognised by men of wisdom. Its rejectors but lose their own chances of profiting by the Truth, and attaining the Paths that lead to God's own gracious Presence!*"

The Guide (The Holy Prophet) will have to give an account, in the Hereafter, of how the Truth was received which he was charged to proclaim to men.

The Four I'ds

There are four days in a year which bear the name of I'd:

Namely: I'd-al-Fitr   (Ramazan I'd)
         I'd-al-Azha   (Baqri I'd)
         I'd-al-Ghadir
         I'd-al-Mubahala

I'D–UL–FITR AND ITS ORIGIN:

As it is obviously linked with the holy month of Ramazan, the inception of I'd did naturally follow the introduction of fasting in the month of Ramazan from 2 A.H. In veiw of the great significance attached to I'd, numerous traditions consisting of prayers and worship to God on this day have been quoted from the Holy Prophet and his Ahl-ul-Bait.

Taking the solemn bath (Ghusl) on the night preceding the day of I'd is religiously recommended (Sunnat). This is a night of great sanctity and profound virtues, and should preferably be spent in worship and prayer to God.

Imam Zain-ul-Abedin used to devote this whole night to prayers and worship of God and has said "This night is as important as that of Shab-e-Qadr (that is to say, the odd night towards the latter part of Ramazan, when the Holy Quran was first revealed to our Holy Prophet).

It is quoted from the Holy Prophet that "one who offers six 'Rakat' prayers on this night reciting in each Rakat sura 'Al-Hamd' once and Surah 'Qul Huwallah' five times, God will pardon his sins."

Haris Aawar narrates that Ameerul-Momineen, Hazrat Ali, on this night, after Maghrib prayers, used to offer two Rakat prayers. In the first one he used to recite Sura "Al-Hamd" once and sura "Qul Huwallah" one hundred times and in the other both the Suras only once. After completion of the prayers he would bow his head in prostration and recite "Atubo Elallah" (I repent O God) one hundred times and then would comment thus: "I swear by One (God)! who has the sole command over my life." Whoever will, in this way, offer two Rakat prayers, the Beneficent will positively fulfill any wish begged from Him.

The conception of I'd in Islam is not only confined to a celebrational extravagance, luxurious feasts and friendly embraces. The Muslims should rather devote this day to the worship of God and should beseech Him to approve their virtuous deeds and forgive their sins. This is because the doors of God's pardon are kept open this day and His blessings are bountiful.

Once Imam Hasan noticed some folk in a most jovial mood merry-making on the occasion of I'd. He, turning towards his companions, said, "God has made this month of Ramazan, a course of action for His slaves to render their due homage to their Lord and earn His pleasure. Some of them go ahead successfully and reach the goal, i.e. they fast, whilst others linger behind and do not fast. When reward is assured for fasting, how strange it is on the part of those who do not fast to indulge themselves in idle pastimes." "I swear by God, if the curtains of Divination (Ghaib) might be lifted today, both the virtuous and the sinful could visualize the rewards of their good and evil deeds respectively".

It is considered by tradition to be an obligatory (Wajib) prayer, though technically it is an optional prayer with the injunction that it is preferable to offer even if optional (Sunnat Muvakkadah).

Ghusl (purification bath) on I'd day is Sunnat which should preferably be taken under a shelter and not under the open sky.

Before offering I'd prayer it is recommended to have a breakfast of dates. The I'd congregation prayer is preferably held under the open sky. But the natives of Mecca should only offer it within Kaaba. Women are exempted from this prayer. The specified time of I'd prayer is between sunrise and the sun's initial decline (Zawal). If this prayer happens to be missed, it cannot be offered late as 'Qaza'.

It is 'Mustahab' (recommended) to offer I'd prayers with two Kutbas, elaborating the religious rules pertaining to the Zakat-e-Fitr, its conditions, its quantity, the time of its payment, and the person who qualifies to deserve it.

This prayer consists of two 'Rakats'. The 'Niyat' (intention) should be in these words, "I resolve to offer two Rakats I'd prayer, Sunnat, Qurbatan Elallah." This should be followed by The 'Takbeer' (Allah-o-Akbar). In the first 'Rakat' after Sura Al-

Hamd, the Sura Sabbehisma and then five times Dua-e-Qunoot; and in the second Rakat after Sura Al-Hamd, the Sura Washshams and four times Dua-e-Qunoot should be recited. Then after 'Ruku,' 'Sajdah' and 'Tashahhud' the prayer should be completed like morning prayer.

Fitra is compulsory on those who can afford it, and it is a sin not to give it.

Hazrat Imam Jafar-e-Sadiq has said that fasts do not attain perfection without Fitra, just as Namaz is not accepted without invoking the blessings of Allah on Muhammad and his Aal in Tashahhud. Hazrat Imam Jafar-e-Sadiq used to instruct his accountant to take out Fitra for each individual including slaves and servants—male and female—of his household without exception, as he feared that one whose Fitra was not taken out might die within that year.

Fitra is dependant on the major items of food consumed by a person during the year. These may be rice, wheat, barley, dates, etc. In weight Fitra should be three kilograms per person. It is also permissible to pay cash to the value of three kilograms foodgrains.

It is obligatory on the head of the family to give Fitra of all persons (including servants of both sexes of any caste or creed) that take food in his house. Fitra must be given even for an infant who is only fed on milk.

If a guest-Muslim or non-Muslim arrives at one's house before the night of I'd-al-Fitr and dines with his host, it is incumbent on the latter to give the former's Fitra. If the guest arrives after sunset of the night of I'd-al-Fitr, Fitra is not obligatory even if he dines with his host. Even when the guest arriving before sunset does not dine, Fitra is obligatory on the host. In this it is better if both the host and the guest give Fitra.

If one's wife is at her parents' on the night of I'd-al-Fitr, her parents should take out her Fitra.

On the last day of the month of Ramazan, if a person arranges a Majlis which finishes after sunset (Magrib), and if he offers Niyaz or food to his guests, he does not have to give Fitra for them.

71

Fitra should be given to deserving Momins, i.e. one who does not have enough income for the maintenance of his family for the whole year.

Fitra cannot be given to one's dependants. But, it is better to give it to non-dependant deserving relatives; next in order of preference are deserving neighbours and then orphans, widows and other deserving pious persons. Fitra from Syeds can be given to Syeds or non-Syeds. Fitra from non-Syeds cannot be given to Syeds.

If deserving persons are not readily available, Fitra should be sent to places where such persons are found, or the amount should be sent to a Mujtahid who would do the needful in distributing the same.

It is not essential that the recipient of Fitra is an "Aadil' (just), but it is necessary to ensure that it is not given to anyone likely to use it in acts of sin, e.g. drinking liquor, gambling etc.

Although it is permissible to send Fitra to any place, it is preferable if it is distributed to a deserving person locally.

The time for giving Fitra is from the night of I'd-al-Fitr (Ramazan I'd) upto the noon (Zohr) of I'd-al-Fitr. If this is not possible for some reason, the amount of Fitra should be set apart from one's other monies and disbursed when deserving persons are available or it may be sent to a Mujtahid for required distribution.

I'D–AL–AZHA

The word "Azha" literally means sheep, goats or cattle offered in sacrifice. So all the Muslims celebrate this festival by sacrificing cattle in compliance with religion, and God has determined this day as a day of rejoicing.

Id-al-Azha being connected with the historical incident of Hazrat Ibrahim's sacrifice of his son Hazrat Ismail, it is worthwhile to elaborate below some facts concerning both these revered Prophets.

It was almost two thousand seven hundred and ninety-three years before the migration (Hijrat) of Hazrat Muhammad (peace be on him), that in compliance with God's command, Hazrat Ibrahim left Syria accompanied by his wife Janab-e-Hagar and his infant son Hazrat Ismail and alighted on the land of Mecca, which was then a barren and uninhabited desert utterly devoid of water and vegetation for miles together. Glancing at this howling wilderness of the infinite desert, Hazrat Ibrahim prayed to God in the following words:

"O our Lord! Surely I have settled a part of my off-spring in a valley unproductive of fruit near Thy Sacred House. Our Lord! may they keep up prayer: therefore make the hearts of some people yearn towards them and provide them with fruits, haply they may be grateful." (Sura) Ibrahim (verse 37).

Having completed this prayer Hazrat Ibrahim departed from his wife and child entrusting them to God's care and protection.

Janab-e-Hagar, in compliance with God's Will, settled on this land till all the water she had in store was exhausted. Now finding her infant on the verge of perishing of thirst, she climbed the two hills of Safa and Marva seven times each without a stop, in the hope of finding water, but it was in vain. When she returned disappointed to her infant, she found to her thrilling astonishment, a fountain of water rushing forth under the feet of Hazrat Ismail. On viewing the miracle, she burst out with intensive joy, exclaiming, "This is Zamzam." Ever since then, this fountain has come to be known as Zamzam. She thanked God and encompassed the spot with sand.

In the meanwhile, some members of the tribe of Jurhum happened to pass through that vicinity in quest of water. Their attention was attracted by the sight of some fowls hovering above some spot nearby. Tracing out the source they were surprised to see Janab-e-Hagar and her child Ismail being in custody of the fountain. Having gathered the details they stayed at the place "Arafat" with the permission of Janab-e-Hagar.

When Hazrat Ibrahim visited his wife and son he was delighted to learn about the arrival of the tribe of Jurhum and accorded his approval to let them settle down there. 'Bani Jurhum' then encamped themselves near the tent of Janab-e-Hagar and lived on.

73

The people of the tribe grew very much familiar with Hazrat Ismail. They used to present one or two sheep out of their flocks as a gift to him every now and then. Thus, by the time Hazrat Ismail attained maturity, he was the owner of a large number of sheep. He lived a comfortable and contented life along with his mother and used to be visited by Hazrat Ibrahim occasionally.

It is narrated by Imam Jafar-e-Sadiq that one day, while Hazrat Ibrahim was in Mashar-al-Haram along with his wife and son, he saw in a dream that he was slaughtering his son Ismail. As dreams used to constitute one of the mediums of spiritual communion between God and His Prophets, Hazrat Ibrahim took his dream as the very command of His Lord and prepared himself to fulfil it and decided upon the physical slaughter of his son. So he said to his son, "O my son! O my son! surely I have seen in a dream that I am sacrificing you; consider then what you see (what is your opinion)." He said: "O my father, do what you are commanded; if Allah pleases, you will find me among the patient ones." (Sura Saffat: verse 102.) Having heard it, Hazrat Ibrahim took a knife and carried Ismail to a place called 'Mena'.

> "So when they both submitted (prepared for sacri-
> fice) he (father) threw him (son) down upon his
> forehead." (Sura Saffat: verse 103.)

Hazrat Ibrahim then moved the knife across Ismail's neck! At that moment Angel Gabriel replaced Ismail with a sheep whereupon God said:

> "O Ibrahim! you have indeed materialised your
> dream; surely thus do we reward the doers of good. Most
> surely this is a manifest trial. And we ransomed him
> with a great sacrifice. And we perpetuated (praised)
> him among the later generation."
>
> (Sura Saffat, verses 104 to 108)

When Hazrat Ibrahim untied the mask from his eyes he found Ismail standing safe and a slaughtered sheep lying on the ground. He prostrated thankfully before God and took his son to the Kaaba.

74

This devotion and worship of Hazrat Ibrahim earned such a great pleasure of God that all the Muslims were commanded to commemorate the event till dooms-day.

Most of the commentators (Mufassereen) hold the view that the real interpretation of the term Zibh-e-Azeem centres around the person of Imam Husain. The author of the book 'Rauzat-ul-Safa' writes, "The great sacrifice of Hazrat Ismail found its physical conclusion in the Martyrdom of Imam Husain." The same interpretation is confirmed by the verdict of our 'Imams' in respect of Zibh-e-Azeem. This very fact beautifully constitutes the theme of the following couplet of Allama Iqbal:

"Is it not strange that while Muslims regard the observance of the slaughter of a sheep (rather a secondary sacrifice) as one of the religious obligations every year, some extremists among them pass the decree of blasphemy (Bidat) on the commemoration of Imam Husain's Martyrdom which stands as the real picture of the term Zibh-e-Azeem".

Just like I'd-al-Fitr, most of the festive ceremonies remain the same.

The details regarding the prayer of I'd-al-Azha, its time, its importance, etc., are exactly similar to those of I'd-al-Fitr.

The Niyat should be done as follows: "I offer two Rakat prayers of I'd-al-Azha, SUNNAT QURBATAN ELLALLAH". After the prayer the first meal recommended should be with the meat of Qurbani. (Mustahab.)

It is quoted from Imam Jafar-e-Sadiq that Qurbani is obligatory (Wajib) on every Muslim who can afford it. Asked what was his verdict about the dependants, he said: "You may or may not do on behalf of your dependants, but at least you must not neglect it on your own part." Hazrat Umme Salma enquired from the Holy Prophet,

> "O Prophet of God! as I possess no money to purchase cattle for Qurbani (sacrifice), should I borrow for the same?"

"Yes, do so," answered the Holy Prophet, "God will facilitate the return of the loan." If one cannot afford doing it individually, one is allowed to keep from seven to seventy partners to perform Qurbani on a collective basis.

It should be performed preferably on the day of I'd-al-Azha, but it is also permitted on 11th and 12th Zilhajj.

But one, who is in "Mena" can even do it on 13th Zilhajj. If somebody happens to be on a journey and arrives back home upto 12th Zilhajj, he should perform it on the very day.

Camel, ewe, sheep, goat, cow are the livestock religiouslv allowed for being slaughtered in Qurbani. The least permitted ages of various cattle at the time of Qurbani are given below:

Camel	.. ..	5 years
Cow or He-Goat	.. ..	1 year
Ewe, Sheep and She-Goat	.. ..	6 months

Cattle, that are tamed, blind or one-eyed, damaged horn, ear cut off, unhealthy, aged and sick, are not allowed for Qurbani.

The camel should be slaughtered through the process of Nahr and the other cattle through that of Zibh.

It is recommended (Mustahab) to perform Qurbani personally. But if it is not practicable, then the hand should be placed on the hand of the butcher and the prescribed Dua (prayer) should be recited before the act of slaughtering.

The hides of Qurbani (cattle) or its price in cash should be given as alms to poor or should be spent on some philanthropic object. The meat should be divided in three shares. One should be retained for the family, the other should be distributed among neighbours and the third should be given to beggars and destitutes.

I'D-AL-GHADIR

To the Muslims Ghadir-e-Khum is the famous place where the Holy Prophet Muhammad completed his final message to mankind with regard to his succession.

The Arabic word "Ghadir" means a pond, and Khum is the proper name of a particular pond, situated about 90 kilometres north-west of Mecca in the heart of the desert called "Sahra-e-Hujfah".

It was off the beaten track. Once upon a time it might have provided a thirsty traveller with water, but then it had completely dried up, and no caravan was likely to halt there. Its only significance was in its position as a point of dispersal after Hajj, from where the nomads of the desert, returning from the Holy City of Mecca would branch off in different directions, towards the sites of their respective tents and pastures. If the pebbles that lie strewn upon that sandy plain could speak, they would tell us that upto the day before 18th Zilhajj 10 A.H., it was a singularly uninviting and insignificant place. But Destiny had a most unique distinction in store for that very spot, so that today, after the lapse of nearly fourteen centuries, the solitude of Ghadir-e-Khum is the envy of many a populous city, and its desolate wastes the pride of many a green and luxuriant valley.

It had been the general tradition of all the Prophets that they used to nominate their own successors in compliance with the Will and order of God without taking any approval from their Ummat (followers) concerned or subjecting the matter to democratic whims. But when came the turn of Hazrat Muhammad, the last Prophet of God, the appointment of his successor became a subject of controversy among his Ummat in spite of his declaring Hazrat Ali as his successor. A large number of both Islamic and non-Islamic historical books bear testimony to the fact that right from the inception of his prophethood upto his demise the Holy Prophet had on many occasions frequently revealed his view to his associates and followers that he would be succeeded by Hazrat Ali and that it was none but Hazrat Ali who was intended by God to carry on his Mission after his demise. Of those occasions where the Holy Prophet had openly nominated Hazrat Ali as his vicegerent, the first was the meeting of Dawat-e-Asheera (Propagation of Islam among relatives) when the Holy Prophet was ordered to openly invite his kith and kin to embrace Islam. Gibbon picturises the scene of this assembly in these words:

"Friends and kinsmen" said Muhammad to the assembly, "I offer you and I alone can offer the most precious of gifts, the treasures of this world and of the world

77

to come. God has commanded me to call you to His service. Who amongst you will support my burden? Who amongst you will be my companion and my Wazir?"

No one answered. The spell of astonishment and doubt was at length broken by the impatient courage of Ali:

"O Prophet I am the man; whosoever rises against thee, I shall dash out his teeth, tear out his eyes, break his legs, rip up his belly. O Prophet, I will be thy Wazir over them."

Prophet Muhammad accepted his offer with pleasure. Thus, at this very occasion of the introduction of Islam, Hazrat Ali was openly declared by the Holy Prophet as his immediate successor. It was in the month of Zilqad 10 A.H. when the Holy Prophet, under the impression of his approaching end, decided to make a farewell pilgrimage to Mecca. On the 25th of Zilqad, he left Medina with an immense concourse of Muslims ranging from ninety thousand to one lakh and twenty-four thousand. The number of the pilgrims yet kept on swelling more and more on the way. On his arrival at Mecca on the 8th of Zilhajj and before completing all the rites of the pilgrimage, the Holy Prophet addressed the assembled multitude from the top of the Jabal-ul-Arafat in words which yet live in the hearts of the Muslims. Having performed the pilgrimage, the Apostle of God accompanied by the same congregation of Muslims proceeded to Medina. Now as his swift dromedary (camel) sped on and on with its long swinging strides, a life of tireless toil was nearing its end; a mission of mercy and devotion was approaching its culmination; and the seeds of Divine dispensation were about to begin bearing fruit. His mien and bearing showed the signs of a sublime peace, coupled with an overwhelming sense of gratitude and an insatiable yearning for his Creator and Cherisher.

Yet on close scrutiny, his serene features could not have failed to disclose the signs of a ponderous thoughtfulness—as if he were weighing the pros and cons of some momentous decision.

What could be the cause of this restlessness? Had he not accomplished all that he had set his mind to do? The Unity and Justice of God had been convincingly instilled into the

78

hearts of men; the belief in the angels, the scriptures, the prophets, the revival of the dead, and the Day of Judgment had all been authoritatively expounded.

So with the meticulous thoroughness of his genius, Prophet Muhammad realised that the most important part of his task still remained unfulfilled and it was this thought which made him restless in the moment of his greatest triumph. He saw that the sands of time were running out and the cup of life was filled almost to the brim. This being so, the most important task was to ensure the continuity of his life's work after him by someone endowed with all the moral values which he had upheld, or else all his miraculous achievements during the twenty-three years of his Apostolic ministry stood in danger of being irretrievably undone. It was a matter of prime importance that the Divine guidance should continue after him and that the Divine sovereignty should be exercised by the chosen ones of God, to be pointed out by the Prophet.

He had already designated his Ahl-ul-Bait on several occasions, as the Ark of Noah, the strong rope of God, the door of forgiveness, the purified ones and made their love incumbent upon his followers. He had similarly, on many occasions, pointed out Ali as "my brother and successor," "the door of the City of Knowledge," "the most equitable Judge," "the embodiment of Faith," and as having the same position with regard to him as "Aaron had to Moses."

Were these pronouncements going to be forgotten, misinterpreted or ignored by his followers after him? Could the Prophet allow them to be set aside by power-seekers? He knew that he had to make a final and unchallengeable declaration regarding his successor. The choice of the appropriate moment, however, depended not on him but on Divine inspiration. So he thoughtfully marched on towards Medina.

As he arrived at Ghadir-e-Khum, suddenly the signs of revelation appeared. The voice of the Arch-Angel Gabriel coaxed him saying:

"O thou esteemed Messenger, impart the guidance that
has been revealed unto thee";

and in order to impress the urgency of the command, Gabriel went on to say:

79

"For if thou doeth it not, thou hast not imparted His
Message at all"; (Ch. 5 verse 67)
and again in the same breath to allay his fears and misgivings
the angel added:

"God will protect thee from the evil designs of men."

On hearing this imperious command, the Prophet made up
his mind then and there. He motioned the Muezzin Bilal to
stop and recite the Azan with the words, "Hayya'ala Khair
il'amal" (hasten towards the best of deeds), for, surely the
acceptance thereof was to be a crucial event upon which the
perpetuity of the Prophet's work depended. As the Prophet
pulled up his reins, the whole entourage came to a halt. Those
who had gone ahead were summoned back and those who followed gathered round casting inquisitive glances at each other.
The Prophet soon dismounted and ordered his followers to clear
the ground. The pebbles and thorns that lay scattered about,
were promptly brushed aside. Others, on receiving his express
directions, began to untie the saddles from the backs of their
camels, and to pile them one on top of another, so as to make a
pulpit. The arrangements thus completed, the throng squatted
upon the bare ground, some spreading their cloaks underneath
to reduce the discomfort of sitting on the burning sand, others
holding up their handkerchieves to protect their eyes from the
sun's glare, for it was nearly midday.

Then, obeying the divine injunction to the letter, the Prophet of Islam mounted the pulpit made of camel-saddles and
addressed the multitude in the following historic words:

"All praise belongs to God. In Him do I put my faith and
from Him do I crave support. Him do I trust and His protection seek against the malice of our souls and evils of our deeds.
The misguided have no guide save Him, and those who are guided by Him can never go astray. I bear witness that there is no
one worthy of worship save Him and that I, Muhammad, is His
slave and messenger."

"O ye folk, Behold, the All-knowing God hath informed me
that the days of my life are coming to an end and the time is
fast approaching when I shall be called away from your midst
towards the eternal abode. But you and I each one of us must

answer unto God for all the things that are due from us. What then do you say?"

And the listeners answered, "We bear witness that thou hast done thy duty and never stinted to guide and advise us according to the Divine Will."

"Then do ye bear witness," asked the Prophet, "to the Unity of God and the Apostleship of this servant of God who now speaks to you by His command, and do ye not bear witness that the resurrection and judgment, heaven and hell and the life Hereafter are certainties?"

And they all answered "Yea, verily, Yea."

"Now then," continued the Prophet, "Listen to me carefully, for I have been commanded to tell you that I will soon be taken away from your midst, but I leave with you as my legacy two most important things, namely, the Book of God and my Children, the People of the House. Never shall they be separated from one another, and so long as you will adhere unto both of them you will never be led astray after me. Therefore, O ye folk, it is my last Will and Testament unto you that you should always remain faithful to the Quran and my Ahl-ul-Bait as true Muslims until death."

By these portentous words all those who loved their teacher and benefactor were moved to tears.

And he continued, "Do not lag too far behind them and do not walk ahead of them, for in either event you will go astray. But follow them and walk in their footsteps and they will guide you along the straight path."

Then he asked, "Who do you think is more worthy of obedience than your souls?"

And they answered, "God and His messenger know best."

And he continued, "Lo! God is my Master, and am I not worthy of obedience from you?"

And they all said, "Yea, verily, Yea."

Then the Prophet bent down and lifted up Ali in his hands, showing him to the crowds on all sides of the pulpit, and proclaimed, "Just as I am worthy of being obeyed by you, so is Ali the proper object of your obedience." So saying, the Prophet lifted up his hands heavenwards and prayed, "O our God, love those who will love Ali, despise those who will despise him; support those who will support him; and reject those who will reject him."

At the conclusion of this prayer, he asked the congregation, "Have I not truly and faithfully delivered unto you the message?"

And they answered, "Yea, verily, Yea."

Then the Prophet said, "Go now, and let those who have been present here today repeat and convey to those who are absent all that they have seen and heard."

At this moment the Divine Inspiration again descended upon our Lord Muhammad with the memorable words that read,

"This day have I perfected unto you your religion and completed upon you My blessings, and I am well-pleased with Islam as your religion."   (Ch. 5 : verse 3)

The tone and purpose of these two religious revelations— firstly, the verse commanding the Prophet to deliver the Message with the warning that any omission on his part would amount to a complete failure of his mission, and secondly, this last revelation, declaring the Lord's pleasure at the fulfilment of the task—clearly indicate that they relate to some matter of prime importance (and not merely to some abstruse detail of ritual such as the prohibition of ham and pork, or the rules of killing animals for meat). It is only in the light of the Hadith-e-Ghadir that these two passages of the Holy Quran can be properly understood in their true importance and full significance. By consensus of the exegesis these two verses were revealed after the Prophet's last pilgrimage.

The great research scholar, Allama Syed Hamid Hussain Kintoori, has written two volumes of the Abaqat-ul-Anwar on the investigation of the innumerable sources through which the Hadith-e-Ghadir has come down to us. In recent years the eminent Alim-Ayat-Ullah Shaikh Abdul Husain-al-Ameeni of Najaf has listed the names of one hundred and ten companions of the Holy Prophet who have reported this tradition as eye-witnesses and eighty-three Tabe'in who heard it from their elders and

82

three hundred and fifty-nine Ulema of all sects, arranged chronologically through each of the centuries since the time of the Prophet up to the present day, who have recorded the address of Ghadir-e-Khum in their books and acknowledge its authenticity. Ayat-ullah-al-Amini's major opus 'Al-Ghadir,' is a classic of erudition and painstaking research. The book establishes beyond doubt that no matter what criterion of verification may be adopted, the event of Ghadir, which means the nomination of Ali by the Prophet Muhammad as his successor is supported by overwhelming and incontrovertible evidence, and that if ever any tradition is to be believed the Hadith-e-Ghadir holds the first claim to acceptance.

Philosophers, commentators of the Quran, poets, historians and seekers of truth all unanimously acknowledge this vital tradition as an established fact. The valley of Ghadir-e-Khum owes its fame to this single, unique and unforgettable event, upon which the survival of the guidance of Islam depends, and so long as there remains a single grain of sand from that parched and arid wilderness it will rise up and proudly describe how the Prophet of Mercy once trod upon that ground, how he lifted up the worthiest of his disciples and proclaimed him as the Amir-ul-Mominin, for there was no one worthier than him and his descendants, the twelve Imams, to defend, expound and propagate Islam's immortal teachings to the world.

Thus the 18th of Zilhajj is marked as one of the most celebrated and happiest days for Muslims because it commemorates the historical day when the Holy Prophet, in compliance with the Will and Order of God, declared Hazrat Ali as his immediate successor and that the very auspicious day earned God's confirmation of the religion of Islam. The devotees and lovers of the Holy Prophet and his Ahl-ul-Bait do therefore celebrate this day as the day of I'd and call it I'd-al-Ghadir.

It is quoted from Imam Ali Reza, the 8th Holy Imam, that the day of I'd-al-Ghadir is a blessed day. It should be observed by keeping a fast and be devoted to the worship of God. After Ghusul (bath), two rakat prayers, like morning prayers should be offered. The time of this prayer is half an hour before the point of Zawal (decline of sun). After the prayers Shukran

Lillah and Alhamdo-Lillah, both hundred times should be recited in a Sajdah (prostration). The Ziarat of Hazrat Ali should be recited on this day followed by 2 rakats Namaz-e-Ziarat.

I'D–AL–MUBAHALA

In the year 9. A.H., the Holy Prophet sent a letter to the Christians of Najran inviting them to embrace Islam. In response to that letter the Christians counselled among themselves the course of their action and did ultimately send a representative deputation of fourteen members to Medina to study the facts pertaining to Hazrat Muhammad and his Mission. The deputation was headed by three Christian scholars, viz. Abdul Maseeh Aaquib, Saiyed and Abdul Haris. Having reached Medina, the deputation was cordially received by the Holy Prophet who explained to them the righteousness of Islam through various convincing arguments. The Christians, however, continued to argue and asked the Holy Prophet what his verdict was about Jesus Christ. At this stage the discussion was postponed to the next day. Then it was revealed to the Holy Prophet the true position by the following Ayats:

"Surely the likeness of Isa is with Allah as the likeness of Adam;
He created him from dust, then said to him,
"Be, and he was."
"This is the truth from your Lord, so be not of the disputers."   (Al-i-Imran, verse 58-59)

The Holy Prophet recited the above verses before the visiting Christians explaining that Christ was a Prophet like Adam and like Adam, created from dust and therefore could not be the son of God. After this, the Holy Prophet invited them to embrace Islam. The Christians remained obstinate and refused to be convinced by anything. Thereupon the following verse was revealed to the Holy Prophet:

"If anyone disputes in this matter with thee, now after (full) knowledge hath come to thee say: 'Come! let us gather together, our sons and your sons, our women and your women, ourselves and yourselves: Then let us earnestly pray, and invoke the curse of God on those who lie!"   3:60

84

Now the Holy Prophet reproduced the Qur'anic verse before the deputation of the Christians and declared the challenge of 'Mubahala'. The term 'Mubahala' is derived from its Arabic root 'Bahlah' meaning 'curse'. Thus the word 'Mubahala' literally means cursing each other. The Christians consulted each other and ultimately announced their acceptance of the challenge.

Imam Fakhruddin Razi writes in his 'Tafseer-e-Kabeer' (volume 2): "When this verse was revealed to the Holy Prophet, the Christians of Najran accepted the challenge of 'Mubahala' and the Holy Prophet took along with him Imam Husain, Imam Hasan, Janab-e-Fatima and Hazrat Ali to the field of 'Mubahala'."

To quote Allama Zamakhshari in his 'Tafseer-e-Kashshaf': "There can be no more authentic and stronger evidence for the integrity of Ashah-e-Kisa, i.e., Hazrat Ali, Janab Fatima, Imam Hasan and Imam Husain than this Qur'anic verse. For in compliance with the order of God the Holy Prophet summoned his Ahl-ul-Bait, took Husain in his arms, grasped Imam Hasan's hand in his own, asked Janab-e-Fatima to follow him and Hazrat Ali to follow her. This proved that the Holy Ahl-ul-Bait were those to whom the Qur'anic verse was directed."

It is related by Saad Ibne Waqas that:

"When this verse was revealed, the Holy Prophet sent for Hazrat Ali, Janab-e-Fatima, Imam Hasan and Imam Husain and prayed to God thus: "O My God! These are the very Ahl-ul-Bait of mine!" (Sahih Muslim, Vol. 1, Sahih Tirmizi.)

Abdullah Ibne Umar quotes the Holy Prophet to have commented:

"Had there been any soul on the whole earth better than Ali, Fatima, Hasan and Husain, God would have commanded me to take them along with me to 'Mubahala'. But as they were superior in dignity and respect to all human beings, God confined His Choice on them only for participation in 'Mubahala'."

(Tasfeer-e-Baizavi)

However, it was on the morning of 24th Zilhajj that the Holy Prophet emerged from his sacred abode with Imam

85

Husain in his arms and holding Imam Hasan's hand and Janab-e-Fatima followed by Hazrat Ali. The Holy Prophet then directed them to utter "Ameen" when he prayed to God.

No sooner had the sacred caravan of the Holy Prophet appeared to the sight of the opposing group of the Christians of Najran then they were awestruck and spell-bound. Abdul Haris Ibne Alqama, the greatest scholar among them, addressed his people:

"I am beholding such faces among them as can make the mountains move from their spots if they pray to God. So beware! Never try to contest with them, otherwise you will perish and the entire nation of Christians will succumb to extinction!"

Thereupon the Holy Prophet reiterated, "By God! had the Christians of Najran contested with us, they would have been transformed into monkeys and swines. Fire would have rained over them from the sky and they would have been doomed."

When the Christians refrained from 'Mubahala', the Holy Prophet put before them two alternatives: either to embrace Islam or to be prepared to come to terms. But the Christians would not agree till the matter was finally decided by an offer of treaty from their side. Thus a peace treaty was signed on the terms that the Christians of Najran would thereby be committed to pay the Holy Prophet an annual tribute consisting of two thousand costumes—worth: forty thousand Dinars, thirty horses, thirty camels, thirty armours and thirty spears.

(Meraj-un-Nabuwat)

According to some versions it is stated that on the morning of 24th Zilhajj, a large number of people thronged the door of the Holy Prophet, every one anticipating his chance to be selected for the team of 'Mubahala'. But when the Holy Prophet emerged out of his house accompanied by his 'Ahl-ul-Bait'. they were all stunned.

The event of the Mubahala is important for the following reasons:

1. It proved to be a silencing lesson for all the Christians of Arabia who no longer dared any competition with the Holy Prophet.

2. The invitation of 'Mubahala' was directed by God, and it was in compliance with His Command that the Holy Prophet took his Ahl-ul-Bait along with him to the field of 'Mubahala'. This serves to generalise how affairs pertaining to Apostleship and the religion of God are determined by the Will of God; allowing no margin of interference from the common people (Ummat). The matter of Hazrat Ali's succession followed by eleven Imams to the office of religious leadership should be viewed in this perspective.

3. The indispensability of Hazrat Ali, Janab Fatima, Imam Hasan and Imam Husain in following the precepts of the Holy Prophet could no longer be disputed.

4. That notwithstanding their childhood, Imam Hasan and Imam Husain did nevertheless, serve as the active partners of the Holy Prophet in the field of 'Mubahala'. This yields the conclusion that age is no criteria for the greatness of the infallibles (Masoom). They are born adorned with virtues and knowledge.

5. That the Holy Prophet's act of having preferred a few obviously elevates their status above all others.

As Islam had emerged triumphantly against Christianity on the occasion of 'Mubahala', this day assumes the significance of an I'd day in Islamic history.

The Lives of the
Fourteen Masooms
and
Hazrat Abbas and
Janab-e-Zainab

*O ye who believe: Fear God and be with
those who are true (in words and deeds)*

9:119

*Faith leads to humility, avoidance of vanity in word and deed,
charity, continence, faithful observance of trusts and covenants,
devout approach to God,—which are the surest steps to Bliss. Man
carries in himself proofs of God's Providence; the same story is told
if he looks at nature around him; and the long line of Teachers sent
by God shows God's special care of humanity. What though they
were rejected and scorned, maligned and persecuted? Truth won
through, as it always will.*

The Holy Prophet

MUHAMMAD MUSTAFA
Sallallaho Alaihe wa Aalehi wa Sallam.
Name: Muhammad
Title: Al-Mustafa
Kunyat: Abul Qasim
Born at Mecca on Friday, the 17th Rabi-ul-Awwal
Father's name: Abdullah Ibn - Abdul Muttalib

Mother's name: Amina bint-e-Wahab
Died at the age of 63 years on Monday, 28th Safar 11 A.H.
Buried in his apartment adjoining the Mosque at Medina.

In the wake of the seventh century of the Christian era, a youthful man in the prime of his life could be seen walking in the streets of Mecca deep in his own thoughts, yet with a gentle smile, never forgetting to return the salutations of the lowliest, or to pause and speak a few kindly words to children who flocked around him wherever he went.

The young man with deep wistful eyes and a sweet gentle disposition, painfully sensitive about human sufferings, carried with him an air of nobility and grace that inspired love and respect amongst his kinsmen. Even in those days he was known as "Amin" (the truthful and the trusted). In later years, he came to be known as Muhammad, the Prophet of Islam, the last messenger of God.

The word "masoom" in the theological terminology of Islam means "infallible" or "sinless." Mohammed Mustafa, the Messenger of Allah; his daughter, Fatima Zahra; and the twelve Imams in her line, were all Masoomeen. They had to be Masoom because they were charged by Allah with the duty of leading mankind "out of the darkness of error and ignorance" into "the light of True Faith and Knowledge." Allah protected them not only from the sin of disobedience to Him, but also from such human failings as ignorance, stupidity and lapses of memory. They had to be perfect in every sense of the term so they could be examples for the rest of mankind, and each of them was.

Besides these fourteen personages, all the prophets and apostles sent by Allah to this world throughout the ages, were also Masoomeen. If any of them was imperfect—physically, mentally or morally—then the people to whom they were sent, would not even listen to them, much less obey them. Each of them, therefore, was perfect and infallible. In the Islamic tradition, the total number of the prophets and apostles of Allah who came to this world, is given as 124,000. Out of this number, only 25 have been mentioned by name in Quran Majid. May Allah bless them all.

After an interval the Voice from Heaven spoke again "O thou, enwrapped in thy mantle, arise and warn, and glorify thy Lord." This was a signal for him to start preaching the gospel of one God. In the beginning, Muhammad invited only those near him to accept the new faith. The first to embrace Islam amongst women was his wife Khadijah, and the first amongst men was his cousin Ali.

Seeing that the new religion posed a threat to their vested interests, the Quraish tortured Muhammad and all converts to the new faith but the Muslims held fast to their faith in spite of unbearable hostility and suffering.

In the twelfth year of his Prophethood, a delegation from Yathrib (later known as Medina) who had embraced Islam visited the Holy Prophet, and on hearing of the hostility of the people of Mecca against the Prophet and his followers, invited him to come to their city. The Holy Prophet accepted the invitation and ordered his followers to go to Yathrib. He himself stayed back, awaiting a Revelation as to his own course of action.

In the 13th year of his Prophethood occurred the most momentous Night of Hijrat, known as the Night of Flight, from which date the Muslim Era begins. The Prophet was advised by God through Angel Gabriel to leave for Yathrib late that night silently and in utter darkness.

Before he left however, his enemies had made a plan to assassinate him whilst he was sleeping in his bed. God through Angel Gabriel made the Prophet aware of the dastardly intention of his enemies. To make good his escape and to make his enemies believe that he was in bed, he asked Hazrat Ali to lie in his place so as to make his enemies believe that he was asleep. He even asked Hazart Ali to cover himself with his cloak to deceive his enemies.

Later in the night, when the assassins pulled the cioak from the one sleeping in bed, they were astounded to find that it was Hazrat Ali and not the Holy Prophet.

Three days later, Hazrat Ali having fulfilled all the responsibilities entrusted to him, joined the Holy Prophet at Quba (a town in the vicinity of Medina) accompanied by Janab-e-Fatima and other members of the Holy Prophet's family.

At Quba, the Holy Prophet laid the foundation of a Mosque, which is still known as Masjid-e-Quba. This was the first

Mosque ever built. Two days later, they all reached Yathrib (Medina).

A very enthusiastic and cordial welcome awaited the gracious arrival of the Holy Prophet on the soil of Yathrib. On sighting him, multitudes of old and young thronged the way and lined the route with calls of Allaho Akbar (God is Great).

On the day the Holy Prophet set his sacred feet on the soil of Yathrib, the natives named their city Medinat-Un-Nabi, to commemorate that historical day.

The first thing the Holy Prophet did after coming to Medina was purchase a plot of land and lay the foundation of a Mosque.

When the Holy Prophet reached Yathrib and met the followers who had come from Mecca at his call, he immediately appointed for each such follower a person from the people of Yathrib who had accepted his Prophethood, to be a brother to him. This appointment of brothers was an act of great help, for the refugees (known as Muhajireen) could be usefully employed immediately. Hazrat Ali, who was present there, was not appointed as a brother to anyone. On being asked why he had not appointed a brother for Hazrat Ali, the Holy Prophet said, "He (Hazrat Ali) shall be as a brother to me."

The news of the success and glory of Islam kindled the fires of jealousy amongst the idolators of the Quraish in general and the Ommayades in particular. They conspired with the Jews and the Christians to uproot the Muslims. There was widespread treachery all round and the Prophet who had never wielded a weapon, was now compelled to defend Islam by the force of arms. Commencing from the battle of Badr, a series of 80 battles were fought in which the newly formed community defended themselves successfully. None of these battles were of aggression. Each and every one was for the defence of Islam.

Seven years later, the Holy Prophet entered Mecca as a conqueror. He who was once a fugitive in this town, persecuted by his kinsmen, entered to prove the grandeur of Islam with acts of mercy and generosity.

"During the ten years in Madina," writes Amir Ali, "Muhammad presided over the commonwealth of Islam, and a great change had come over the character of the Arab people. By the appointment of delegates to the different tribes and cities, with powers to decide internal as well as tribal disputes, the ancient system of private vendetta was put an end to and impetus given to trade and commerce. The style of living and mode of dress underwent a great change especially among the women. The reckless freedom of heathenism was abandoned, and manners became decorous, almost austere; gambling and drinking were forbidden. Before this there had been no privacy in houses; from this time it became customary to have special apartments for women."

Within a few years Muhammad established order and inspired in his people the belief in One God: prohibited idolatry and made the people ponder not only of this world but the world beyond. He asked them to practise charity, goodness, justice, and universal love. The whole mission was achieved in his life-time.

The Holy Prophet was occupied all the while in looking after the new Islamic State and had no thoughts for his personal welfare. A number of believers therefore requested him to permit them to buy lands and build houses for him. The reply revealed by God was:

> "Say; I do not ask of you any reward, but love for the nearest of my kin;"   42:23

Thereupon the believers asked the Prophet, whose love was made incumbent on them? The Holy Prophet answered, "Love for Ali, Fatima, Hasan and Husain."

Soon after finishing the last Hajj, the Holy Prophet started for Medina. On his way, at Gadir-e-Khum, Angel Gabriel visited him with a message from God and said:

"O Apostle! proclaim the (Message) which hath been sent to thee from thy Lord. If thou didst not, thou wouldst not have fulfilled and proclaimed His Mission. And God will defend thee from men (who mean mischief). For God guideth not those who reject Faith."   5:67

The Holy Prophet immediately ordered Hazrat Bilal to recite the Azan so as to recall the Muslims who had gone ahead, who were behind, and who were proceeding to their homes, to assemble. The Holy Prophet took Hazrat Ali by the hand and said :

"Ali is to me what Haroon was to Musa. Almighty God be a friend to his friend, and be a foe to his foe; help those who help him and frustrate the hope of those who betray him."

All the believers congratulated Ali.

Once again the Voice from Heaven proclaimed: "This day have I perfected your religion and completed my favour on you and chosen for you Islam as a religion."   5:3

WAFAT :

On the Holy Prophet's return to Medina, his strength rapidly failed and the poison administered to him at Khyber by a woman from a hostile Jewish tribe many years ago took its deadly toll. So ended the life dedicated to the service of God and humanity from first to the last. The Prophet, who was sent as a mercy to all mankind, (Rahamatul-lil-Aalamin), died on the 28th Safar eleven years after Hijri.

The humble preacher had risen to be the ruler of Arabia. The Prophet of Islam not only inspired reverence, but love owing to his humility, purity, austerity, refinement and devotion to duty. The master inspired all who came in contact with him. He shared his scanty food with all. He began his meals in the name of God and finished them uttering thanks. He loved the poor and respected them. He would visit the sick and comfort the heart-broken. He commended learning, and has said "To the student who goes forth in quest of knowledge, God will allot a high place in the mansion of Bliss; every step he takes is blessed and every lesson he receives has its reward. The seeker of knowledge will be greeted in Heaven with a welcome from the angels."

The Holy Prophet further preached of the value of knowledge:

"Acquire knowledge, because he who acquires it in the way of the Lord performs an act of piety; who speaks of it, praises the Lord, who seeks it, adores God; who dispenses instructions in it, bestows alms· and who imparts it to its fitting objects, performs an act of devotion to God. Knowledge enables its possessor to distinguish what is forbidden from what is not; it lights the way to Heaven."

Laying great emphasis on the 'Filial duty' among Muslims, the Apostle of God has said, "Revere your mothers as paradise lies under their very feet." Children were very dear to him. He revered his worthy daughter, Janab-e-Fatima to an extent that he would rise on his feet to welcome her whenever she visited him. He looked upon Imam Hasan and Imam Husain as his sons (in conformity with the Quranic Ayat verse 61 Ale Imran) and for whom his love and affection knew no bounds.

His birthday which is known as I'd-e-Milad-un-Nabi is celebrated with great pomp and splendour.

JANAB–E–FATIMA ZAHRA ALAIHAS SALAAM

Name: Fatima
Title: Az-Zahra
Kunyat: Umm-ul-Aimma
Born at: Mecca on Friday, 20th Jamadi-ul-Akhar
Father's name: Holy Prophet Muhammad Ibn-e-Abdulla
Mother's name: Khadija bint-e-Khuwailid
Died at the age 18, at Medina on 14th Jamadi-ul-Awwal
Buried at the graveyard called Jannatul Baqi at Medina

Janab-e-Fatima, the only daughter of the Holy Prophet and Hazrat Khadija, was born on Friday, the 20th Jamadi-ul-Akhar, eight years before Hijrat, in Mecca. The circumstances of her birth are described by Hazrat Khadija as follows. "At the time of the birth of Janab-e-Fatima, I sent for my neighbouring Qurashite women to assist me. They flatly refused, saying that I had betrayed them by supporting Muhammad. I was perturbed for a while, when to my great surprise, I sighted four strange tall women with halos around them, approaching me. Finding me dismayed, one of them addressed me thus, 'O Khadija! I am Sarah, the mother of Ishaq, and the other three are, Mary the mother of Christ, Aasia the daughter of Mazahim, and Umme-Kulsoom, the sister of Moses. We have all been commanded by God to put our nursing knowledge at your disposal.'

Saying this, all of them sat around me and rendered the services of midwifery till my daughter Fatima was born."

The motherly blessings and affection received by Janab-e-Fatima were only for five years, after which Janab-e-Khadija left for her heavenly Home. Hereafter the Holy Prophet brought her up.

MARRIAGE:

When Janab-e-Fatima came of age, there came forward a number of aspirants to ask for her hand in marriage. The Holy Prophet was awaiting a Divine order in this respect, till Hazrat Ali approached him and asked for her hand in marriage.

The Holy Prophet came to Janab-e-Fatima and asked, "My daughter! Do you consent to be wedded to Ali, as I am so commanded by God?"

"Janab-e-Fatima thereupon bowed her head in modesty, and kept quiet in answer to her father's question. A few moments passed and then the Holy Prophet exclaimed: Allaho Akbar," and went out saying: "Fatima's silence is her consent to the marriage."

On Friday 1st Zilhajj in the year 2 A.H., the marriage ceremony took place. All the Muhajireen and Ansar of Medina assembled in the Mosque whilst Hazrat Ali was seated before the Holy Prophet with all the ceremonious modesty of a bridegroom. The Holy Prophet first recited an eloquent sermon and then announced, "I have been commanded by God to get Fatima wedded to Ali, and so I do hereby solemnize the matrimony between Ali and Fatima on a dower of 400 Misquaal." Then he asked Hazrat Ali, "Do you consent to it, O Ali?" "Yes, I do, O Holy Prophet of God!" replied Hazrat Ali. Then the Holy Prophet raised his hands to pray thus: "O my God, bless both of them, sanctify their progeny and grant them the keys of Thy beneficence, Thy Treasures of wisdom and Thy Genius; and let them be a source of blessing and peace to my Ummat."

Her children; Imam Hasan, Imam Husain, Janab-e-Zainab and Janab-e-Kulsum, are well known for their piety, goodness and generosity. Their strength of character and action changed the course of history and fortified Islam which otherwise would have been lost to mankind:

HER ETHICAL ATTRIBUTES:

Janab-e-Fatima inherited the genius and wisdom, the determination and will-power, the piety and sanctity, the generosity and benevolence, the devotion and worship of God, the self-sacrifice and hospitality, the forbearance and patience, and the knowledge and nobility of disposition of her illustrious father, both in words and deeds. "I often witnessed my mother," says Imam Husain, "absorbed in prayer from dusk to dawn." Her generosity and compassion for the poor was such that no destitute or beggar ever returned from her door unattended.

THE PROPERTY OF FADAK:

The Holy Prophet during his life-time gave Janab-e-Fatima a gift of very extensive farm land, known as the Bagh-e-Fidak, which was documented in her name as her absolute property.

The death of the Holy Prophet affected her very much and she was very sad and grief-stricken and wept her heart out crying all the time. She was confronted, after the demise of her father, with the deprivement of the rightful claim of leadership of her husband Hazrat Ali, and the usurpation of her inheritance, the Bagh-e-Fidak. Throughout her life, she never spoke to those who had oppressed her and deprived her of her rightful claims. She requested that her oppressors should be kept away even from attending her funeral.

Her ill-wishers even resorted to physical violence. Once the door of her house was pushed on her, and the child she was carrying was hurt and the baby-boy was still born. Her house was set on fire.

Having been molested and stricken with grief, which crossed all limits of forbearance and endurance, she expressed her sorrows in an elegy composed by herself to mourn her father the Holy Prophet. A couplet of the elegy, with particular reference to her woeful plight, she expressed thus:

"O my father! after your death I was subjected to such tortures and tyranny that if they had been inflicted on the 'Day', it would have turned into 'Night'."

WAFAT:

Janab-e-Fatima did not survive more than seventy-five days after the demise of her father. She breathed her last on the 14th Jamadi-ul-Awwal 11 A.H. Before her demise she bequeathed the following as her will to Hazrat Ali:

1. O Ali, you will personally perform my funeral rites.
2. Those who have displeased me should not be allowed to attend my funeral.
3. My corpse should be carried to the graveyard at night.

Thus Hazrat Ali, in compliance with her will, performed all the funeral rites and accompanied exclusively by her relative and sons carried her at night to Jannat-ul-Baqi, where she was laid to rest and her wishes fulfiled.

THE PROPHET HAS SAID:

"Whoever injures (bodily or sentimentally) Janab-e-Fatima injures me. And whoever injures me injures Allah. And whoever injures Allah practises unbelief."

"O Fatima! If your wrath is incurred, it incurs the wrath of Allah, and if you are happy, it makes Allah happy too".

THE IMAMS

The Holy Prophet Hazrat Muhammad (peace be on him) said, "I shall be succeeded by twelve religious leaders, all of whom will be of Quraish origin." (Sahih Bokhkari).

The twelve Imams are these sacred personages and spiritual leaders about whom the Holy Prophet had prophesied. Pointing them out as the source and means of guidance for mankind, the Holy Prophet remarked, "So long as my twelve successors will continue to govern, this religion (Islam) will exist (in this world)". (Sunan-e-Abu Dawood.)

On a request from his well-known companion, Jabir Ibne Abdullah, the Holy Prophet explained the names of his twelve successors thus, "They are my twelve successors, O Jabir, who will come after me. First of them will be Ali who will be followed, one after the other, by Hasan, Husain, Ali-Ibne-Husain, Muhammad Ibne Ali, Jafar Ibne Muhammad, Moosa Ibne Jafar, Ali Ibne Moosa, Muhammad Ibne Ali, Ali Ibne Muhammad, Hasan Ibne Ali and lastly by Muhammad Mehdi-al-Qaaim (peace be on them)."

THE FIRST IMAM

HAZRAT ALI AL–MURTAZA ALAIHIS SALAAM
AMIR–UL–MOMINEEN

Name: Ali

Title: Al-Murtaza

Kunyat: Abul Hasan

Born in the Holy Kaaba at Mecca on Friday the 13th Rajab

Father's name: Abu Talib-ibne-Abdul Muttalib

Mother's name: Fatima bint-e-Asad

Died at the age of 63 years, at Kufa, on Monday, the 21st Ramazan 40 A.H., murdered by an assassin who mortally wounded him with a poisoned sword in the Mosque at Kufa during morning prayers on the 19th Ramazan.

Buried at Najaf, near Kufa.

Hazrat Ali was the cousin of our Holy Prophet. He was born on Friday, the 13th Rajab in the Kaaba. Providence alone had a hand in bringing his mother towards Kaaba. When his mother came to Kaaba, she felt weighed down by intense pain of pregnancy. She knelt down before the Holy structure and prayed humbly to God. Abbas, son of Abdul Muttalib, saw Hazrat Ali's mother praying to God. No sooner had she raised her head from supplication, then the wall of the sacred House split by a solemn miracle. Fatima entered the Kaaba and that portion returned to its normal position. Abbas and his companions flocked at the gate of the Sacred House which was locked, and tried to open it, but in vain. They then decided to give it up, considering the miraculous nature of the event and the Divine will in action. The news of this miraculous incident soon spread like wildfire in Mecca.

Hazrat Ali was born within the Kaaba with his eyes closed and his body in humble prostration before the Almighty. Fatima stayed in the Kaaba for three days and as the fourth day approached she stepped out, carrying her gem in her arms. To her great surprise, she found the Holy Prophet awaiting to receive the newly-born child in his anxious arms. Imamat feeling the subtle touch of Prophethood, Hazrat Ali opened his eyes and

98

saluted the Divine Prophet "Assalamo Alaika Ya Rasoolallah (Peace be upon you, O Messenger of Allah)."

Hazrat Ali's birth in the Kaaba is unique in the history of the world. Neither a Prophet nor a Divine Saint was ever blessed with such an honour.

He was brought up under the care and affection of the Holy Prophet. As Hazrat Ali says: "The Holy Prophet brought me up in his own arms and fed me with his own morsel. I followed him wherever he went like a baby camel following its mother. Each day a new aspect of his character would beam out of his noble person and I would accept it and follow it as a command." (Nahj-ul-Balagha).

Ten years in the company of the Holy Prophet had kept him so close and inseparable, that he was one with him in character, knowledge, self-sacrifice, forbearance, bravery, kindness, generosity, oratory and eloquence. From his very infancy, he prostrated before God along with the Holy Prophet. As he himself said, "I was the first to pray to God along with the Holy Prophet."

"Hazrat Ali persevered in the footsteps of the Holy Prophet," says Allama Masoodi, "all along his childhood." God created him pure and holy and kept him steadfast on the right path. Though Hazrat Ali is undisputably the first to embrace Islam when the Holy Prophet called upon his listeners to do so, yet by the very fact that since his infancy he was brought up with the Holy Prophet and followed him in every action and deed including prostration before God, he can be said to be born a Muslim.

Hazrat Ali, at all times, accompanied the Holy Prophet to help and protect him from his enemies. He used to write down the verses of the Holy Quran and discuss them with the Prophet as soon as they were revealed by the Holy Messenger, the Angel Gabriel. He was so closely associated with the Holy Prophet that as soon as a verse was revealed to him during the day or night, Hazrat Ali was the first to hear it.

The Prophet has said of Hazrat Ali:

"O Ali, you are my brother in this world as well as the Hereafter".

"I am the city of knowledge and Ali is the gate."
"Nobody knows Allah except I and Ali.
Nobody knows Ali except Allah and I.
Nobody knows me except Allah and Ali."

"If you want to see the knowledge of Adam, the piety of Noah, the devotion of Abraham, the awe of Moses, and the service and abstinence of Christ, look at the bright face of Ali."

When the Holy Prophet reached Yathrib (Medina) and met his followers who had come from Mecca at his call, he immediately appointed for each such follower a person from the people of Yathrib who had accepted his prophethood to be a brother to him. His appointment of brothers was a great act of help for the refugees (known as Ansars), who had left their home and come to Yathrib. He made brothers of people who followed the same trade so that the Ansars could be usefully employed immediately. While the Prophet was appointing an Ansar a brother to a Muhajarin (converts of Yathrib), Hazrat Ali who was present there, was not appointed as a brother to any Muhajarin. On being questioned as to why he had not appointed a brother for Hazrat Ali, the Prophet said: "He shall be a brother to me."

The character and calibre of Ali as judged by Allama Masoodee is, "If the glorious name of being the first Moslem, a comrade of the Prophet in exile, his faithful companion in the struggle for faith, his intimate associate in life, and his kinsman; if a true knowledge of the spirit of his teachings and of the Book; if self-abnegation and practice of justice; if honesty, purity, and love of truth; if a knowledge of law and science, constitute a claim to pre-eminence, then all must regard Ali as the foremost Moslem. We shall search in vain to find, either among his predecessors (save one) or among his successors, those attributes."

Gibbon says "The birth, the alliance, the character of Ali which exalted him above the rest of his countrymen, might justify his claim to the vacant throne of Arabia. The son of Abu Taleb was in his own right the chief of Bani Hashim and the hereditary prince or guardian of the city and temple of Mecca.

Hazrat Ali had the qualifications of a poet, a soldier, and a saint; his wisdom still breathes in a collection of moral and religious sayings; and every antagonist, in the combats of the tongue or of the sword, was subdued by his eloquence and valour. From the first hour of his mission to the last rites of his funeral, the Apostle was never forsaken by a generous friend, whom he delighted to name his brother, his vicegerent, and the faithful Aaron of a second Moses."

MARRIAGE:

Under Divine instruction, the Apostle of Allah married his beloved daughter Fatima to Aii, though others vainly tried for her hand.

Among their children, Imam Hasan, Imam Husain, Janab-e-Zainab and Ume-Kulsum have left their marks on the history of the world.

After the death of Janab-e-Fatima, Hazrat Ali married Ummul Banin. Hazrat Abbas was born out of this wedlock and was so handsome that he was fondly called Qamar-e-Bani Hashim. He personified loyalty and bravery and proved it in the battlefield at Kerbala.

WAFAT:

In the 40th year of Hijri, in the small hours of the morning of 19th Ramazan, Hazrat Ali was struck with a poisoned sword by a Kharejite while offering his prayers in the Mosque at Kufa. He died on the 21st day of Ramazan 40 A.H. and was buried in Najaf-ul-Ashraf. He was born in the House of God, the Kaaba and martyred in the House of God, the Masjid-e-Kufa. The Lion of God, the most brave-hearted and gentle Moslem that ever lived began his glorious life with devotion to Allah and His Apostle and ended it in the service of Islam.

"And do not speak of those who are slain in
Allah's way as dead; nay they are alive but you
do not perceive." 11 : 154

THE SECOND IMAM
IMAM HASAN ALAIHIS SALAAM

Name : Hasan

Title : Al-Mujtaba

Kunyat : Abu Muhammad

Born at Medina on Tuesday, 15th Ramazan 3 A.H.

Father's name : Ali-ibne-abi-Talib

Mother's name : Fatima (daughter of the Holy Prophet)

Died at the age of 46 years, at Medina, on Thursday, 28th Safar, 50 A.H.

Buried at Jannat-ul-Baqi in Medina.

Imam Hasan, the elder son of Hazrat Ali and Janab-e-Fatima, was born on 15th Ramazan 3 A.H. in Medina. Having received the happy news of his grandson's birth, the Holy Prophet came to the house of his beloved daughter, took the newly born in his arms, recited "Azan and Eqamat" (calls for prayers) in his right and left ears respectively, and in compliance with God's command, named him 'Hasan'.

CHILDHOOD :

The first phase of seven years of his infancy was blessed with the gracious patronage of the Holy Prophet, who gifted him all his great qualities and adorned him with Divine knowledge to such an extent that he was outstanding in his knowledge, tolerance, intelligence, bounty and valour. Being infallible by birth and decorated with Heavenly knowledge by God, his insight had an access to Lauh-e-Mahfooz (the Guarded tablet on which the transactions of mankind have been written by God for all eternity).

The Holy Imam immediately became conversant with all the contents of any 'Wahi' (Quranic verse) revealed when the Holy Prophet would disclose it to his associates. To the great surprise of the Holy Prophet, Janab-e-Fatima would often recite the exact text of a newly revealed 'Wahi' before he disclosed it personally to her. When he inquired, she would inform him that it was Hasan through whom she had learned the Revelation.

102

REMEMBRANCE OF GOD :

The Holy Imam devoted himself to prayers in such abundance, that all the limbs employed in prostration bore scars and impressions of his "Sajda". Most of the nights were spent on the prayer-carpet. The sense of his absorption and humiliation in prayers to God were in such earnest that he would shed tears profusely out of fear of God. While performing ablution, he trembled with the fear of God and his face grew pale at the time of prayers. His earnest meditation in the offering of prayers and his extreme absorption in communion with God would render him entirely unconscious of his environments.

HIS PIOUSNESS AND CONTENTMENT :

Imam Hasan had the worldly possessions at his disposal and could have well enjoyed a luxurious life, but he utilised all of it in the betterment of the condition of the poor.

He was so courteous and humble that he never hesitated to sit along with the beggars in the lanes and on the thoroughfares of Medina to reply to some of their religious queries. Through his cordial attitude and hospitality he never let the poor and the humble feel inferior to him when they visited his abode.

IMAMAT :

The demise of the Holy Prophet was followed by an eventful era when the Islamic world came in the grip of the fever of expansionism and conquest. But even under such a revolutionary phase, Imam Hasan kept devoting himself to the sacred mission of peacefully propagating Islam and the teachings of the Holy Prophet along with his great father Hazrat Ali.

The martyrdom of Hazrat Ali on the 21st of Ramazan marked the inception of Imam Hasan's Imamat. The majority of Muslims pledged their allegiance to him and finalised the formality of "Baiat" (Oath of Allegiance). No sooner had he taken the reins of leadership into his hands than he had to meet the challenge of Muawiya, the Governor of Syria, who declared a war against him. In compliance with the Will of God and with a view to refrain from causing the massacre of Muslims however, he entered into a peace treaty with Muawiya on terms which saved Islam and stopped a civil war. But this peace treaty was never meant as a surrender by him of the permanent leadership to Muawiya. It was meant only as an interim transfer of the administration of the Islamic Kingdom, subject to the condition that the administration would be surrendered back to Imam Hasan after Muawiya's death and then it would in turn be inherited by Imam Husain. Having relieved himself of the administrative responsibilities, Imam Hasan kept the religious leadership with himself and devoted his life to the propagation of Islam and the teachings of the Holy Prophet in Medina.

MARTYRDOM :

Muawiya's malice against Imam Hasan led him to conspire with the Imam's wife Juda, the daughter of Ashas. She was made to give the Imam some poison which affected his liver. Imam Hasan thus succumbed to Muawiya's fatal mischief and attained his martyrdom on 28th Safar 50 A.H. His funeral was attended by Imam Husain and the members of the Hashimite family. His bier whilst being taken for burial to the Prophet's tomb was shot at with arrows by his enemies, and it had to be diverted for burial to the Jannat-ul-Baqi at Medina. His tomb was demolished, along with others in 1925 A.D. (English Calendar).

The terms of the peace treaty were soon violated, but earned only a short-lived glory for Muawiya. Its aftermath proved disastrous and doomed the fate of his son Yezid and dealt a fatal blow to the entire family of Ummayyads. After the death of Muawiya, Imam Husain emerged as the insurmountable mountain of truth and determination. In the gruesome tragedy of Kerbala, by sheer force of numbers, and by isolating the 72 members of Imam Husain's party and stopping them from even getting water to drink for three days, Yezid succeeded in annihilating the seventy two persons including members of the Imam's family who were with him.

This dastardly success of Yezid was, however, short lived. The Muslims turned against him on learning of the heinous act he had committed and this resulted in the downfall of Yezid and the extinction of the Ummayyad power from the face of the earth.

THE THIRD IMAM

IMAM HUSAIN ALAIHIS SALAAM

Name : Husain

Title : Saiyid-ush-Shohada

Kunyat : Abu Abdullah

Born at Medina on Thursday, 3rd Shaban 4 A.H.

Father's name : Ali-ibne-Abi Talib

Mother's name : Fatima (daughter of the Holy Prophet)

Martyred at Kerbala aged 57 years on Monday, 10th Moharram 61 A.H. and buried there.

In the house of the Holy Prophet, which presented the best image of both the worlds—the heaven and the earth—a child who benefited humanity as if he was a Divine Impression reflecting the earth, was born on one of the nights of the month of Shaban. His father was Hazrat Ali, the best model of kindness towards his friends and the bravest against the enemies of Islam, and his mother was Janab-e-Fatima, the only daughter and child of the Holy Prophet, who had as universally acknowledged, inherited the qualities of her father.

Imam Husain, the third Apostolic Imam as the child came to be known, was born on 3rd of Shaban 4 A.H. in Medina. When the good news of his birth reached the Holy Prophet, he came to his daughter's house, took the newly-born child in his arms, recited the Azan and the Eqamat (calls of prayer) in his right and left ears respectively, and on the 7th day of his birth, after performing the rites of Aqeeqa, named him Husain, in compliance with God's command.

Abdulla Bin Abbas relates: "On the very day when Imam Husain was born, God ordered Angel Gabriel to descend and congratulate the Holy Prophet on His behalf and on his own. While descending, Gabriel passed over an island where the angel 'Fitrus' had been banished due to his delay in executing a commission assigned by God. He was deprived of his wings and expelled to the island, where he remained for several years praying and worshipping God and asking for his forgiveness.

When the angel Fitrus saw Gabriel, he called out, "Where are you going, O Gabriel?" To this he replied, "Husain, the

105

grandson of Muhammad is born, and for this very reason God has commanded me to convey His congratulations to His Apostle." Thereupon, the angel said, "Can you carry me also along with you? May Muhammad recommend my case to God." Gabriel took the angel along with him, came to the Holy Prophet, offered congratulations to him on behalf of God and himself and referred the case of the angel to him. The Holy Prophet said to Gabriel, "Ask the angel to touch the body of the newly-born child and return to his place in Heaven." On doing this, the angel re-obtained his wings instantly and praising the Holy Prophet and his newly-born grandson, ascended towards Heaven.

Hasan and Husain, the two sons of the Holy Imam Ali-Ibne-Abi-Talib and Janab-e-Fatima, our Lady of Light, were respected and revered as the Leaders of the Youths of Paradise as stated by the Holy Prophet.

The Holy Prophet Muhammad had openly prophesied that the faith of Islam would be rescued by his second grandson Husain, when Yezid, son of Muawiya, would endeavour to destroy it.

Yezid was known for his devilish character and brutish conduct. He was known as the most licentious of men. The people having known and understood the character of Yezid, formed a covenant by which Muawiya could not appoint Yezid as his successor. There however existed an undertaking known to a few, whereby Muawiya had pledged to appoint Imam Husain as his successor. This undertaking was given by Muawiya to Imam Hasan from whom Muawiya had snatched power. Muawiya violated this undertaking and nominated Yezid who succeeded his father.

Immediately as he came to power, Yezid began acting in full accordance with his known character. He started interfering in the fundamentals of the faith and practised every vice and wickedness freely with the highest degree of impunity and yet held himself out as the successor of the Holy Prophet, demanding allegiance to himself as the leading guide of the faith. Paying allegiance to Yezid was nothing short of acknowledging the devil as God. If a divine personality like the Holy Imam Husain had agreed to his authority, it would be actually recommending the devil to humanity in place of God. Yezid demanded allegiance from the Holy Imam Husain, who could have never agreed to it at any cost. The people fearing death and destruction at the hands of the tyrant had yielded to him out of fear. Imam Husain said that come whatever may, he would never yield to the devil in place of God and undo what his grandfather, the Holy Prophet had established.

The refusal of the Holy Imam to pay allegiance to this fiend marked the start of the persecution of the Holy Imam. As a result he had retired to Medina where he led a secluded life. Even here he was not allowed to live in peace, and was forced to seek refuge in Mecca—where also he was badly harassed and Yezid plotted to murder him in the very precincts of the great sanctuary of Kaaba.

In order to safeguard the great sanctuary Imam Husain decided to leave Mecca for Kufa just a day before the Hajj pilgrimage. When asked the reason for the mysterious departure from Mecca foregoing the pilgrimage which was only the next day, Imam Husain said that he would perform the year's pilgrimage at Kerbala, offering the sacrifice not of any animals, but of his kith and kin and some faithful friends. He enumerated the names of his kith and kin who would lay down their lives with him in the great sacrifice at Kerbala.

The people of Kufa getting tired of the tyrannic and satanic rule of Yezid, had written innumerable letters and sent emissaries to Imam Husain to come over and give them guidance in faith. Although Imam Husain knew the ultimate end of the invitations, he as the divinely chosen Imam could not refuse to give the guidance sought for. When the Holy Imam with his entourage had reached Kerbala his horse mysteriously stopped and would not move any further. Upon this the Holy Imam declared: "This is the land, the land of sufferings and tortures." He alighted from his horse, and ordered his followers to encamp there saying, "Here shall we be martyred and our children be killed. Here shall our tents be burned and our family arrested. This is the land about which my grandfather the Holy Prophet had foretold, and his prophecy will certainly be fulfilled."

On the 7th of Muharram water supply to the Imam's camp was cut and the torture of thirst and hunger started. The Holy

Imam's camp consisted of ladies, innocent children including babies and some male members of the Holy Prophet's family; along with a small band of some faithful friends of Imam Husain who had chosen to die with the Holy Imam, fighting against the devil for the cause of God.

THE DAY OF AASHURA (10TH OF MUHARRAM):

At dawn the Imam glanced over the army of Yezid and saw Ibne-Saad ordering his forces to march towards him. He gathered his followers and addressed them thus: "Allah has, this day, permitted us to be engaged in a Holy War and He shall reward us for our Martyrdom. So prepare yourselves to fight against the enemies of Islam with patience and resistance. O sons of the noble and self-respecting persons, be patient! Death is nothing but a bridge which you must cross after facing trials and tribulations so as to reach Heaven and its joys. Which of you do not like to go from this prison (world) to the lofty palaces (Paradise)?"

Having heard the Imam's address, all his companions were overwhelmed and cried out, "O our Master! We are all ready to defend you and your Ahl-ul-Bait, and to sacrifice our lives for the cause of Islam."

Imam Husain sent out from his camp one after another to fight and sacrifice their lives in the way of the Lord. Lastly when all his men and children had laid down their lives, Imam Husain brought his six-month old baby son Ali-Azghar, and offering him on his own hands, demanded some water for the baby, dying of thirst. The thirst of the baby was quenched by a deadly poisoned arrow from the brute's forces, which pinned the baby's neck to the arm of the helpless father. At last when the six-month old baby also was killed, Imam Husain addressed God: "O Lord! Thy Husain has offered in Thy way, whatever Thou hath blessed him with. Bless Thy Husain, O Lord, with the acceptance of this sacrifice. Everything Husain could do till now was through Thy help and by Thy Grace." Lastly Imam Husain came into the field and was killed, the details of which merciless slaughter are heart rending. The forces of Yezid having killed Imam Husain, cut and severed his head from his body and raised it on a lance. The severed head of the Holy Imam began glorifying God from the point of the lance saying 'Allaho Akbar'. "All glory be to God Who is the Greatest!"

After the wholesale, merciless and most brutal slaughter of the Holy Imam with his faithful band, the helpless ladies and children along with the ailing son of Imam Husain, Imam Zain-ul-Abedin, were taken captives.

SOME SAYINGS OF THE HOLY PROPHET DURING HIS LIFE TIME WITH REFERENCE TO IMAM HUSAIN:

1. Hasan and Husain are the Leaders of the youths of paradise.

2. Husain is from me and I am from Husain, God befriends those who befriend Husain and He is the enemy of those who bear enmity to him.

3. Whosoever wishes to see such a person who lives on earth but whose dignity is honoured by the Heaven-Dwellers, should see my grandson Husain.

4. O my son! thy flesh is my flesh and thy blood is my blood; thou art a leader, the son of a leader and the brother of a leader; thou art a spiritual guide, the son of a spiritual guide and the brother of a spiritual guide; thou art an Apostolical Imam, the son of an Apostolical Imam and the brother of an Apostolical Imam; thou art the father of nine Imams, the ninth of whom would be the Qaim (the last infallible spiritual guide).

5. The punishment inflicted on the murderer of Husain in hell would be equal to half of the total punishment to be imposed on the entire sinners of the world.

6. When the Holy Prophet informed Janab-e-Fatima of the Martyrdom in store for his grandson, she burst into tears and asked "O my father! when would my son be martyred?" "In such a critical moment," replied the Holy Prophet, "when neither I nor you, nor Ali would be alive." This accentuated her grief and she inquired again, "Who then, O my father, would commemorate Husain's Martyrdom"? The Holy Prophet said, "The men and the women of a particular sect of my followers, who will befriend my Ahl-ul-Bait, will mourn for Husain and commemorate his martyrdom each year in every century."

IBEN SAAD NARRATES FROM SHABI:

Hazrat Ali while on his way to Siffin, passed through the desert of Kerbala, there he stopped and wept very bitterly. When interrogated regarding the cause of his weeping, he commented that one day he visited the Holy Prophet and found him weeping. When he asked the Apostle of God as to what was the reason which made him weep, he replied, "O Ali, Gabriel has just been with me and informed me that my son Husain would be martyred at Kerbala, a place near the bank of the Euphrates. This moved me so much that I could not help crying."

ANAS BIN HARRIS NARRATES:

One day the Holy Prophet ascended the pulpit to deliver a sermon to his associates while Imam Husain and Imam Hasan were sitting before him. When his address was over, he put his left hand on Imam Husain and raising his head towards heaven, said: "O my Lord! I am Muhammad, Thy slave and Thy Prophet, and these two are the distinguished and pious members of my family who would fortify my cause after me. O my Lord! Gabriel has informed me that my son Husain would be killed. O my Lord! bless my cause in recompense for Husain's Martyrdom, make him the leader of the martyrs, be Thou his helper and guardian and do not bless his murderers."

SIR MOHAMED IQBAL SAYS:

Imam Husain uprooted despotism forever till the day of resurrection. He watered the dry garden of freedom with the surging wave of his blood, and indeed he awakened the sleeping Muslim nation.

If Imam Husain had aimed at acquiring a worldly empire, he would not have travelled the way he did (from Medina to Kerbala). Husain weltered in blood and dust for the sake of truth. Verily he therefore, became the bed-rock (foundation) of the Muslim creed; La Ilaha Illallah.

KHAJA MOINUDDIN CHISTI SAYS:

He gave his head, but did not put his hand into the hands of Yezid. Verily Husain is the foundation of La Ilaha Illallah. Husain is Lord and the Lord of Lords.

Husain himself is Islam and the shield of Islam. Though he gave his head (for Islam) but never pledged Yezid. Truly Husain is the founder of "There is no Deity except Allah."

BROWNE IN HIS 'LITERARY HISTORY OF PERSIA' WRITES:

As a reminder, the blood stained field of Kerbala where the grandson of the Apostle of Allah fell at length, tortured by thirst and surrounded by the bodies of his murdered kinsmen, has been at any time since then sufficient to evoke, even in the most lukewarm and heedless, the deepest emotion, the most frantic grief and the exaltation of spirit before which pain, danger, and death shrink to unconsidered trifles. Verily on the tenth of Muharram, the tragedy is rehearsed in Persia, in Turkey, in Egypt, wherever a Shia community or colony exists. As I write, it all comes back; the wailing chant, the sobbing multitudes, the white raiment red with blood from self-inflicted wounds, the intoxication of grief and sympathy.

THE FOURTH IMAM

IMAM ZAIN–UL–ABEDIN ALAIHIS SALAAM

Name: Ali-ibn-ul Husain

Title: Zain-ul-Abedin

Kunyat: Abu Muhammad

Born at Medina, on Saturday, 15th Jamadi-ul-Awwal 37 A.H.

Father's Name: Imam Husain Ibne-Ali

Mother's Name: Shahr Banoo, daughter of King Yazdjard II Died aged 58 years, at Medina, poisoned by Waleed bin Abdul Malik Marwan, on 25th Muharram 95 A.H.

Buried at Jannat-ul-Baqi in Medina.

The fourth Holy Imam, Ali-Zain-ul-Abedin was born in Medina on 15th Jamadi-ul-Awwal 37 A.H. (658 A.D.). His epithet was Abu Muhammad and was popularly titled as "Zain-ul-Abedin". The mother of this Holy Imam was the royal personage, Shahr Banoo, the daughter of King Yazdjard, the last pre-Islamic Ruler of Iran.

111

The Holy Imam Zain-ul-Abedin spent the first two years of his infancy in the lap of his grandfather Ali Ibne Abi Talib and then for twelve years he had the gracious patronage of his uncle, the second Holy Imam Hasan Ibne Ali. In 61 A.H. he was present in Kerbala, at the time of the gruesome tragedy of the wholesale massacre of his father, his uncles, his brothers, his cousins and all the godly comrades of his father; and suffered a heartless captivity and imprisonment at the hands of the devilish forces of Yezid.

When Imam Husain had come for the last time to his camp to bid good-bye to his family, Ali Zain-ul-Abedin was lying semi-conscious in his sick-bed and hence he escaped the massacre at Kerbala. Imam Husain could only manage a very brief talk with the inmates of his camp and departed nominating his sick son as Imam.

The Holy Imam Zain-ul Abedin lived for about 34 years after his father and all his life he passed in prayers and supplication to God and in remembrance of his martyred father. It is for his ever being in prayers to God, mostly lying in prayerful prostration, that this Holy Imam was popularly called "Sajjad".

The Knowledge and piety of this Holy Imam was matchless. Zohri, Waqidi and Ibne Ainiyah say that they could not find any one equal to him in piety and godliness. He was so mindful of God that whenever he sat for ablution for prayers, the complexion of his face would change and when he stood at prayer his body was seen trembling. When asked why this was, he replied, "Know ye not before whom I stand in prayers, and with whom I hold discourse?"

Even on the gruesome day of Ashura when Yezid's forces had massacred his father, his kith and kin and his comrades and had set fire to the camp, this Holy Imam was engrossed in his supplications to the Lord.

When the brutal forces of Yezid's army had taken the ladies and children as captives, carrying them seated on the bare back of the camels, tied in ropes; this Holy Imam, though sick, was put in heavy chains with iron rings round his neck and his ankles, and was made to walk barefooted on the thorny

112

plains from Kerbala to Kufa and to Damascus; and even then this godly soul never was unmindful of his prayers to the Lord and was always thankful and supplicative to him.

His charity was unassuming and hidden. After his passing away, the people said that hidden charity ended with the departure of this Holy Imam. Like his grandfather Ali Ibne Abi Talib, Ali-e-Zain-ul-Abedin used to carry on his own back at night bags of flour and bread for the poor and needy families in Medina and he so maintained hundreds of poor families in the city.

The Holy Imam was not only hospitable even to his enemies but also used to continually exhort them to the right path.

The Holy Imam along with the Ahl-ul-Bait passed through dreadful and very dangerous times, for the aggressions and atrocities of the tyrant rulers of the age had reached a climax. There was plunder, pillage, and murder everywhere. The teachings of Islam were observed more in their breach. The heartless tyrant Hajjaj bin Yousuf was threatening every one who professed allegiance or devotion to the Ahl-ul-Bait; and those caught were mercilessly put to death. The movement of the Holy Imam was strictly restricted and his meeting with any person was totaly banned. Spies were employed to trace out the adherents of the Ahl-ul-bait. Practically every house was searched and every family scrutinised.

The Holy Imam was not given the time to offer his prayers peacefully, nor could he deliver any sermons. This God's Vicegerent on earth therefore adopted a third course which proved to be very beneficial to his followers. This was in compiling supplicative prayers for the daily use of man in his endeavour to approach the Almighty Lord. The invaluable collection of his edited prayers are known as "Sahifa-e-Kamila" or "Sahifa-e-Sajjadiah", known also as "Zaboor-e-ale Muhammad". The collection is an invaluable treasury of wonderfully effective supplications to the Lord in inimitably beautiful language. Only those who have ever come across those supplications would know the excellence and the beneficial effect of these prayers. Through these prayers the Imam gave all the necessary guidance to the faithful during his seculsion.

On the 25th of Moharram A.H. when he was in Medina, Waleed bin Abdul Malik Marwan, the then ruler got this Holy Imam martyred by poison. The funeral prayers for this Holy Imam were conducted by his son the fifth Imam, Muhammad-al-Baqir and his body was laid to rest in the cemetery Jannat-ul-Baqi" in Medina.

THE FIFTH IMAM

IMAM MUHAMMAD–AL–BAQIR ALAIHIS SALAAM

Name: Muhammad

Title: Al-Baqir

Kunyat: Abu Jafar

Born at Medina, on Tuesday, 1st Rajab 57 A.H.

Father's name: Imam Zain-ul-Abedin.

Mother's name: Fatima Bint Hassan, known as Umm-e-Abdulla.

Died: Aged 59 years, at Medina on Monday, 7th Zilhajj 116 A.H. Poisoned by Hisham bin Abdul Malik.

Buried at Jannat-ul-Baqi at Medina.

The fifth Imam Muhammad-Al-Baqir was born in Medina on first Rajab 57 A.H. (677 A.D.). His epithet was Abu Jafar and he was popularly titled "Al-Baqir." His father was Ali-Zain-ul-Abedin, the son of Imam Husain, and his mother was Fatema, the daughter of Imam Hasan. Thus he was the only Imam who was connected with Janab Fatema-Zahra both from his paternal and maternal sides.

Imam Muhammad-al-Baqir was brought up in the holy lap of his grandfather Imam Husain, for three years. For 34 years he was under the gracious patronage of his father, Ali-Zain-ul-Abedin.

The Holy Imam was present in Kerbala at the time of the gruesome tragedy of the wholesale massacre of his grandfather Imam Husain and his companions. He also suffered with his father and the ladies of the house of the Prophet (Ahl-ul-Bait) the heartless captivity and imprisonment at the hands of the devilish forces at the command of Yezid Ibne Muawiya. After

114

the tragedy of Kerbala, the Imam passed his time peacefully in Medina praying to God and guiding the people to the right path.

The downfall of the Ummayyads had begun since Yezid the son of Muawiya who had slaughtered Imam Husain. Yezid himself had completely realised the evil consequences of his deeds even during the short period of his rule. His son Muawiya the second, refused to accept the Caliphate saying:

"I cannot favour such a throne which has been erected on the basis of oppression and tyranny."

Allama Ibne Hajar, a famous scholar belonging to the Sunnite says: "Imam Muhammad-Al-Baqir has disclosed the secrets of knowledge and wisdom and unfolded the principles of spiritual and religious guidance. Nobody can deny his exalted character, his God given knowledge, his divinely-gifted wisdom and his obligation and gratitude towards spreading of knowledge. He was a sacred and highly talented spiritual leader and for this reason he was popularly titled "Al-Baqir" which means "the expounder of knowledge." Kind of heart, spotless in character, sacred by soul and noble by nature, the Imam devoted all his time in submission to God (and in advocating the teachings of the Holy Prophet and his descendants). It is beyond the power of a man to count the deep impression of knowledge and guidance left by the Imam on the hearts of the faithful. His sayings in devotion and abstinence, in knowledge and wisdom, and in religious exercise and submission to God are so great in number that the volume of this book is quite insufficient to cover them all." (Sawayed-e-Mohreqa, p. 120).

The Holy Imam managed to collect the teachings and reforms of the Holy Prophet and his Ahl-ul-Bait in the form of books. His pupils compiled books on different branches of science and arts under his instructions and guidance.

In the excellence of his personal purity and godly traits, the Holy Imam Muhammad al-Baqir was a model of the Holy Prophet and his great grandfather, Ali Ibne Abi Talib. His admonitions created a spiritual sensation among the Muslims in general. He was not only hospitable even to his worst enemies but also used to continually exhort them to the right path. He urged people to earn their livelihood by their own hard work.

The Holy Imam gave much importance to convening Majalıs' (meetings) in commemoration of the martyrdom of Imam Husain. Kumail Ibne Zaid, one of the most famous and highly talented poets of that time, used to recite the elegy of Imam Husain in those Majalis' (meetings). Such type of Majalıs' (meetings) were also greatly encouraged by Imam Jafar-as Sadiq and Imam Ali-al-Reza, the sixth and the eighth Imams.

The Holy Imam continued his preaching peacefully till 114 A.H. On the 7th Zilhajj when he was 57 years old, Hisham Ibne Abdul Malik, the then ruler, got him martyred through poison. The funeral prayers for this Holy Imam were conducted by his son Imam Jafar-as-Sadiq, the sixth Imam, and his body was laid to rest in Jannat-ul-Baqi in Medina.

THE SIXTH IMAM
IMAM JAFAR–AS–SADIQ ALAIHIS SALAAM

Name: Jafar

Title: As-Sadiq

Kunyat: Abu Abdulla

Born at Medina on Monday the 17th Rabi-ul Awwal 83 A.H.

Father's name: Imam Muhammad Baqir

Mother's name: Umme-e-Farwah

Died aged 65 years at Medina on Monday, 15th Rajab 148 A.H. Poisoned by Mansur Dawaneeqi the Abbaside.

Buried at Jannat-ul-Baqi at Medina.

The Holy Imam Jafar-as-Sadiq was the sixth in the succession of the twelve Holy Imams. His epithet was Abu Abdullah and his famous titles were as-Sadiq, al-Fazil and al-Tahir. He was the son of Imam Muhammad-al-Baqir, the fifth Imam and his mother's name was Umm-e-Farwah, the daughter of Qasim Ibne Muhammad Ibne Abu Bakr.

Born on Friday the 17th Rabi-ul-Awwal 83 A.H. at Medina, he was brought up by his grandfather, the Holy Imam Zain-

116

ul-Abedin for 12 years and then remained under the sacred patronage of his father the Holy Imam Muhammed-al-Baqir, for a period of nineteen years.

IMAMAT:

After the death of his holy father in 114 A.H., he succeeded him as the sixth Imam, and thus the sacred trust of Islamic mission and spiritual guidance was relayed down to his custody right from the Holy Prophet through the succession of preceding Imams.

POLITICAL CONDITION:

The period of his Imamat coincided with the most revolutionary and eventful era of Islamic history which saw the downfall of the Ummayyad Empire and the rise of the Abbaside Caliphate. The internal wars and political upheavals were bringing about speedy reshufflements in government. Thus the Holy Imam witnessed the reigns of various kings starting from Abdul Malik down to the Ummayyad ruler Marwan-e-Hemar. He further survived till the time of Abul Abbas Al Saffah and Mansoor among the Abbasides. It was due to the political strife between two groups viz. the Ummayyads and the Abbasides for power that the Imam was left alone undisturbed to carry out his devotional duties and peacefully carry on his mission to propagate Islam and spread the teachings of the Holy Prophet.

In the last days of the Ummayyad rule, their Empire was tottering and was on the verge of collapse, and a most chaotic and demoralised state of affairs prevailed throughout the Islamic State. The Abbasides exploited such an opportunity and availing themselves of this political instability, assumed the title of "Avengers of Bani-Hashim". They pretended to have stood for the cause of taking revenge on the "Ummayyads" for shedding the innocent blood of the Holy Imam Husain.

The common people who were groaning under the yoke of the Ummayyads, were fed up with their atrocities and were secretly yearning for the progeny of the Holy Prophet to take power. They realised that if the leadership went to the Ahl-ul-Bait, who were its legitimate heir, the prestige of Islam would be

117

enhanced and the Prophet's mission would be genuinely propagated. However, a group of Abbasides secretly dedicated their lives to a campaign for seizing power from the hands of the Ummayyads on the pretext that they were seizing it only to surrender it to the "Bani-Hashim." Actually they were plotting for their own ends. The common people were thus deceived into supporting them and when these Abbasides did succeed in snatching power from the Ummayyads, they turned against the Ahl-ul-Bait.

RELIGIOUS CONDITION:

The downfall of the Ummayyads and the rise of the Abbasides constituted the two principal plots in the drama of Islamic history. This was a most chaotic and revolutionary period when the religious morals of Islam had gone down and the teachings of the Holy Prophet were being neglected, and a state of anarchy was rampant. It was amidst such deadly gloom that the virtuous personage of Imam Jafar-as-Sadiq stood like a beacon of light shedding its lustre to illuminate the ocean of sinful darkness around. The world got inclined towards his virtuous and admirable personality. Abu Salma Khallal also offered him the throne of the Caliphate. But the Imam keeping up the characteristic tradtion of his ancestors flatly declined to accept it, and preferred to content himself with his devotional pursuits and service to Islam. On account of his great learning he was always triumphant in his many debates with the priests of rival orders like Atheists, Christians, Jews, etc.

TEACHINGS:

The versatile genius of Imam Jafar-as-Sadiq in all branches of knowledge was acclaimed throughout the Islamic world, which attracted students from far-off places towards him till the strength of his disciples had reached four thousand. The scholars and experts in Divine Law have quoted many traditions (Ahadis) from Imam Jafar-as-Sadiq. His disciples compiled hundreds of books on various branches of science and arts. Other than 'Fiqha' (religious laws), 'Hadis' (tradition); 'Tafsir' (commentary), etc. the Holy Imam also imparted mathematics and chemistry to some of his disciples. Jabir Ibne Hayyan Tartoosi, a famous scholar of mathematics, was one of the

118

Imam's disciples who benefited from the Imam's knowledge and guidance and was able to write 400 books on different subjects.

It is an undeniable historical truth that all the great scholars of Islam were indebted for their learning to the very presence of the Ahl-ul-Bait who were the fountain of knowledge and learning for all.

Allama Shibli writes in his book "Seerat-un-Noman": "Abu Hanifa remained for a considerable period in the attendance of Imam Jafar-as-Sadiq, acquiring from him a great deal of precious research on Fiqha and Hadis. Both the sects— Shia and Sunni—believe that the source of Abu Hanifa's knowledge was mostly derived from his association with Imam Jafar-as-Sadiq."

The Imam devoted his whole life to the cause of religious preaching and propagation of the teachings of the Holy Prophet and never strove for power. Because of his great knowledge and fine teaching, the people gathered around him, giving devotion and respect that was his due. This excited the envy of the Abbaside ruler Mansur Dawaneeqi, who fearing the popularity of the Imam, decided to do away with him.

DEATH:

On 15th Rajab 148 A.H., the Governor of Medina by the order of Mansur, got the Imam martyred through poison. The funeral prayer was conducted by his son Imam Moosa al-Kazim, the seventh Imam, and his body was laid to rest in the cemetery Jannat-ul-Baqi in Medina.

THE SEVENTH IMAM

IMAM MOOSA-E-KAZIM ALAIHIS SALAAM

Name: Moosa

Title: Al-Kazim

Kunyat: Abu Ibrahim

Born at Abwa (between Mecca and Medina) on Sunday the 7th Safar 128 A.H.

Father's name: Imam Jafar-as-Sadiq

Mother's name: Hamida Khatoon

Died aged 55 years at Baghdad on Friday, 25th Rajab 183 A.H.

Poisoned by Harun-al-Rashid.

Buried at Kazmain, Baghdad.

NAME EPITHET AND TITLES:

Name 'Moosa', epithet Abul Hasan and his famous title was Kazim. His matchless devotion and worship of God has also earned him the title of "Abd-e-Saleh" (virtuous slave of God). Generosity was synonymous with his name and no beggar ever returned from his door empty handed. Even after his death, he continued to be obliging and was generous to his devotees who came to his Holy tomb with prayers and behests which were invariably granted by God. Thus, one of his additional titles is also "Bab-e-Qaza-ul-Hawaij" (the door to fulfilling needs).

PARENTS:

The Holy Imam Moosa-e-Kazim was the son of Imam Jafar-as-Sadiq the sixth Imam. The name of his mother was Hamida who was the daughter of a noble man named Saed, hailing from the country of Berber.

BIRTH:

The Holy Imam was born on 7th Safar 128 A.H. at a place called Abwa, situated between Mecca and Medina.

CHILDHOOD:

Imam Moosa-e-Kazim passed 20 years of his sacred life under the gracious patronage of his Holy father. His inherent genius and gifted virtues combined with the enlightened guidance and education from the Holy Imam Jafar-as-Sadiq, showed in the manifestation of his future personality. He was fully versed with Divine knowledge even in his childhood.

Allama Majlisi relates that once Abu Hanifa happened to call upon the holy abode of Imam Jafar-as-Sadiq to ask him about some religious matters (Masail). The Imam was asleep and so he was kept waiting outside till the Imam's awakening.

Meanwhile Imam Moosa Kazim, who was then 5 years old, came out of his house. Abu Hanifa, after offering him his best compliments, enqired:

"O the son of the Holy Prophet! what is your opinion about the deeds of a man? Does he do them by himself or does God makes him do them?"

"O Abu Hanifa", the five year old Imam replied at once, in the typical tone of his ancestors. "The doings of a man are confined to three possibilities. First, that God alone does them while the man is quite helpless. Second, that both God and the man do equally share the commitment. Third, that man does them alone. Now if the first assumption is true, it obviously proves the unjustness of God who punishes His creatures for sins which they have not committed. And if the the second condition be acceptable, even then God becomes unjust if He punishes the man for the crimes in which he is equally a partner. But the undesirability of both these conditions is evident in the case of God. Thus we are naturally left with the third alternative to the problem that men are absolutely responsible for their own doings."

IMAMAT:

The Holy Imam Jafar-as-Sadiq breathed his last on 15 Rajab 148 A.H. and with effect from the same date Imam Moosa-e-Kazim succeeded the Holy Office of Imamat as the seventh Imam. The period of his Imamat continued for 35 years. In the first decade of his Imamat, Holy Imam Moosa Kazim could afford a peaceful execution of the responsibilities of his sacred office and carried on the propagation of the teachings of the Holy Prophet. But soon after, he fell a victim to the ruling kings and a greater part of his life passed in prison.

POLITICAL CONDITION:

Imam Moosa-e-Kazim lived under the most crucial times in the regimes of the despotic Abbaside kings who were marked for their tyrannical and cruel administration. He witnessed the reigns of Mansur-e-Dawaniqi, Medhi and Haroon-al-Rashid. Mansur and Haroon were the despotic kings who put a multitude of innocent descendants of the Holy Prophet to the sword.

Thousands of these martyrs were buried alive inside walls or put into horrible dark prisons during their lifetime. These depraved Caliphs knew no pity or justice and they killed and tortured for the pleasure they derived from human sufferings.

The Holy Imam was saved from the tyranny of Mansur because the king, being occupied with his project of constructing the new city of Baghdad, could not get time to turn towards victimising the Imam. By 157 A.H. the city of Baghdad was built. This was soon followed by the death of its founder a year later. After Mansur, his son Mehdi ascended the throne. For a few years he remained indifferent towards the Imam. When in 164 A.H. he came to Medina and heard about the great reputation of the Imam, he could not resist his jealousy and the spark of his ancestral malice against the Ahl-ul-Bait was rekindled. He somehow managed to take the Imam along with him to Baghdad and got him imprisoned there. But after a year he realised his mistake and released the Imam from jail. Caliph Mehdi was succeeded by Hadi who lived only for a year. Now in 170 A.H., the most cruel and tyrannical king Haroon-al-Rashid appeared at the head of the Abbaside Empire. It was during his reign that the Holy Imam passed the greater part of his life in a miserable prison till he died.

MORAL AND ETHICAL EXCELLENCE:

As regards his morality and ethical excellence, Ibne-Hajar remarks, "The patience and forbearance of Imam Moosa-e-Kazim was such that he was given the title of Al-Kazim (one who swallows down his anger). He was the embodiment of virtue and generosity. He devoted his nights to the prayers of God and his days to fasting. He always forgave those who did wrong to him."

His kind and generous attitude towards the people was such that he used to patronise and help the poor and destitutes of Medina and provide for them cash, food, clothes and other necessities of sustenance secretly. It continued to be a riddle for the receivers of gifts throughout the Imam's life-time as to who their benefactor was, but the secret was not revealed until after his death.

LITERARY ATTAINMENTS:

Time and circumstances did not permit the Holy Imam Moosa-e-Kazim to establish institutions to impart religious knowledge to his followers as his father, Imam Jafar-as-Sadiq and his grandfather, Imam Muhammad-al-Baqir had done. He was never allowed to address a congregation. He carried on his mission of preaching and guiding people quietly. He also became the author of a few books of which the most famous is "Musnand of Imam Moosa-e-Kazim".

DEATH:

In 179 A.H. King Haroon-al-Rashid visited Medina. The fire of malice and jealousy against the Ahl-ul-Bait was kindled in his heart when he saw the great influence and popularity which the Holy Imam enjoyed amongst the people there. He got the Imam arrested while he was busy in prayer at the tomb of the Holy Prophet and kept him in prison in Baghdad for a period of about 4 years. On the 25th of Rajab 183 A.H., he got the Imam martyred by poison. Even his corpse was not spared humiliation and was taken out of the prison and left on the Bridge of Baghdad. His devotees however, managed to lay the Holy body of the Imam to rest in Kazmain (Iraq).

THE EIGHTH IMAM

IMAM ALI REZA ALAIHIS SALAAM

Name : Ali Ibne Moosa

Title : Ar-Reza

Kunyat : Abul Hasan

Born at Medina on Thursday, 11th Zil-kad 148 A.H. (765 A.D.).

Father's name : Imam Moosa-e-Kazim

Mother's name : Ummul Baneen Najma

Died aged 55 years at Meshad in Khorasan on Tuesday the 17th Safar 203 A.H. (818 A.D.)

Poisoned by Mamoon the Abbaside Caliph.

Buried at Meshad (also called Toos), Iran.

Hazrat Imam Ali-ar-Reza was born at Medina on 11th Zil-kad 148 A.H. He was also known as Abul Hasan.

TRAINING AND EDUCATION :

Imam Ali-ar-Reza was brought up under the Holy guidance of his father for 35 years. His own insight and brilliance in religious matters combined with the excellent training and education given by his father made him unique in his spiritual leadership. Imam Reza was a living example of the piety of the great Prophet and the chivalry and generosity of Hazrat Ali.

SUCCESSION:

Imam Moosa-e-Kazim was well aware of the aggressive designs of the government in power against the Imamat and therefore during his life-time he declared Imam Reza as his successor in the presence of 171 prominent religious divines and called upon his sons and his family to submit to him and refer to him in all matters after him. He also left behind a written document declaring the succession of Imam Reza duly signed and endorsed by not less than 16 prominent people. All these necessary steps were taken by the Great Imam to avoid any confusion that may have arisen after his death.

IMAMAT:

Imam Moosa-e-Kazim was poisoned while he was still in prison and expired on 25th Rajab 183 A.H., and the same day Imam Reza was declared the 8th Imam of the Muslim World. Imam Reza had the great task before him of coming out with the correct interpretation of the Holy Quran; specially under the most unfavourable circumstances prevailing under the Government of Haroon-al-Rashid. Many belonging to the faith were imprisoned and those who were free and could not be jailed faced untold atrocities and sufferings. Imam Reza ofcourse stamped his impression upon his age by carrying on the mission of the Great Prophet in a peaceful manner even during the most chaotic periods, and it was mostly due to his efforts that the teachings of the Holy Prophet and his descendants became widespread.

Imam Reza had inherited great qualities of head and heart from his ancestors. He was a versatile person and had full com-

mand over many languages. Ibne-Asir Jazeri penned very right-
ly that Imam Reza was undoubtedly the greatest sage, saint and
scholar of the second century (A.H.).

Once, on his way to Khorasan from Medina he arrived on
horseback at Nishapur. Myriads of people gathered round him
and all roads were overcrowded as they had come to meet and
see their Great Imam. Abu-Zare-Razi and Muhammad Ibne
Aslam Toosy, the two great scholars of the day, stepped out of
the crowd and begged the Imam to halt there for a moment so
that the faithful may be able to hear his voice. They also requested the Imam to address the gathering. The Imam granted
the request and in his brief address told the mammoth gathering
the real interpretation of "La-Illaha-Illal-Lah". Quoting God, he
continued to say that the Kalema is the fortress of God and
whoever entered the fortress saved himself from His wrath.

He paused for a moment and continued that there were also
a few conditions to entitle the entrance to the fortress and the
greatest of all conditions was sincere and complete submission
to the Imam of the day; and very boldly and frankly explained
to the people that any disloyalty to the Prophet and his
descendants would withdraw the right of the entrance to the
fortress. The only way to earn Almighty God's pleasure was to
obey the Prophet and his progeny and that was the only path
to salvation and immortality.

The above-mentioned incident speaks clearly of the great
popularity of Imam Reza, and the love, loyalty and respect the
Muslims gave their beloved Imam. Mamoon-ul-Rashid, the
king, was conscious of the fact that he would not survive for
long if he also did not express his loyalty to the great leader
and his intelligence department had made it clear to him that
the Iranian people were truly and sincerely loyal to the Imam
and he could only win them over if he also pretended to give
respect and sympathetic consideration to Imam Ali Reza.
Mamoon was a very shrewd person. He made a plan to invite
Imam Reza and to offer him the heirship to the throne. The
Imam was summoned by a royal decree and was compelled,
under the circumstances, to leave Medina—where he was living
a quiet life—and present himself at the royal court of Mamoon.

On his arrival, Mamoon gave him a royal reception and offered him the heirship, commenting in no uncertain terms that he (Mamoon) was a usurper of the rights of the Imam, and begged him to accept the offer.

The Imam at first rejected the offer saying that he was not interested in holding worldly power and he was quite satisfied in carrying on the missionary work and living a quiet life in Medina. Mamoon knew that the final rejection of his offer by the Imam would lead him to extreme unpopularity and pestered the Holy Imam to accept. Imam Reza then very reluctantly agreed to the demand and wrote the following remarks on the document of succession: "I accept the heirship of Mamoon on the condition that he admits our rights to the direct succession of the Prophet. I can foresee that there is a catch in it but do not want to disappoint the mover of the proposal until he proves to be unworthy of his commitment."

Quoting Allama Shibly from his book "Al-Mamoon" we get a very clear picture of how Mamoon decided to offer his leadership to Imam Reza:

"Imam Reza was the 8th Imam and Mamoon could not help holding him in great esteem because of the Imam's piety, wisdom, knowledge, modesty, decorum and personality. Therefore he decided to nominate him as the rightful heir to the throne. Earlier in 200 A.H. he had summoned the Abbasides. Thirty three thousand Abbasides responded to the invitation and were entertained as royal guests. During their stay at the capital he very closely observed and noted their capabilities and eventually arrived at the conclusion that not one of them deserved to succeed him. He therefore spoke to them all in an assembly in 201 A.H. telling them in categorical terms that none of the Abbasides deserved to succeed him. He demanded allegiance to Imam Reza from the people in this very meeting and declared that royal robes would be green in future, the colour which had the unique distinction of being that of the Imam's dress. A royal decree was published saying that Imam Reza will succeed Mamoon and his title will be Ali-Reza-Min-Ale-Muhammad.

Even after the declaration of succession when there was every opportunity for the Imam to live a splendid worldly royal life, he did not pay any heed to material comforts and devoted himself completely to imparting the true Islamic conception of the Prophet's teachings and the Holy Quran. He spent most of his time praying to God and serving the people.

Taking full advantage of the concessions given to him by virtue of his elevated position in the royal court, he organised the Majlis' (meetings) commemorating the martyrdom of the Shahids of Kerbala. These Majlis' were first held during the days of Imam Muhammad Baqir and Imam Jafar-as-Sadiq but Imam Reza gave the Majlis' a new impetus by encouraging those poets who wrote effective poems depicting the moral aspects of the tragedy and the suffering of Imam Husain and his companions.

Mamoon had been very scared of the growing popularity of the Imam and he had appointed him as his heir to the throne only for the fulfilment of his own most ambitious and sinister designs and getting the Imam's endorsement to his tricky plans. But the Imam naturally refused to give his endorsement to any such plans which were against the teaching of Islam. Mamoon therefore became very disappointed with him and decided once and for all to check his growing popularity and ensuring his own survival by acting according to the old traditions of killing the Imam. Wanting to do it in a more subtle manner, he invited the Imam to dinner, and fed him poisoned grapes. The Imam died on 17th Safar 203 A.H. he was buried in Toos (Meshad) and his Grand Shrine speaks well for the great personality the Imam possessed. Myriads of Muslims visit his shrine every year to pay their homage to this Imam.

THE NINTH IMAM
IMAM MUHAMMAD TAQI ALAIHIS SALAAM

Name : Muhammad Ibne-Ali

Title : Taqi and Al-Jawad

Kunyat : Abu Jafar

Born at Medina on Friday the 10th Rajab 195 A.H. (811 A.D.).

Father's name : Imam Reza A.S.

Mother's name : Khaizuran.

Died at the age of 25 years at Kazmain on Wednesday the 29th Zilqad. 220 A.H. (835 A.D.) poisoned by Mu'tasin the Abbaside Caliph.

Buried at Kazmain, Baghdad, (Iraq)

EPITHET AND TITLES:

The epithet of the Imam was Abu Jafar and his famous titles were al-Taqi and al-Jawad. Since Imam Muhammad al-Baqir, the fifth Imam was called Abu Jafar historians have mentioned this Imam as Abu Jafar the second.

CHILDHOOD:

Imam Muhammad Taqi was brought up by his Holy father Imam Ali Reza for 4 years. Under the force of circumstances Imam Ali Reza had to migrate from Medina to Khorasan (Iran), leaving his young son behind him. The Imam was fully aware of the treacherous character of the ruling king and was sure that he would return to Medina no more. So before his departure from Medina he declared his son Muhammad-al-Taqi his successor, and imparted to him all his stores of Divine knowledge and spiritual genius.

IMAMAT:

Imam Ali Reza was poisoned on the 17th Safar 203 A.H. and with effect from the same date Imam Muhammad al-Taqi was commissioned by God to hold the responsibility of Imamat. At the tender age of eight there was no apparent chance or means of the young Imam reaching great heights of knowledge and practical achievements. But after a few days he is known not only to have debated with his contemporary scholars on subjects pertaining to Fiqh (Jurisprudence), Hadith (tradition) Commentary (Tafsir), etc. and outwitted them but also to exhort their admiration and acknowledgement of his learning and superiority. Right from then the world realised that he possessed Divine knowledge and that the knowledge commanded by Holy Imams was not acquired, but granted by God.

LITERARY ATTAINMENTS AND EXCELLENCE:

The span of the life of Imam Muhammad Taqi was shorter than that of his predecessors as well as his successors. He became Imam at the age of 8 years and was poisoned at the age of 25; yet his literary attainments were many and he commanded great respect and esteem.

The Holy Imam was the symbol of Hazrat Muhammad's affability and Hazrat Ali's attainments. His hereditary qualities comprised of gallantry, boldness, charity, learning, forgiveness and tolerance. The brightest and most outstanding phases of his nature and character were to show hospitality and courtesy to all without discrimination, to help the needy; to observe equality under all circumstances, to live a simple life; to help the orphans, the poor and the homeless; to impart learning to those interested in the acquisition of knowledge and guide the people to the Right Path.

MIGRATION TO IRAQ:

For the consolidation of his empire, it was realised by Mamoon, the Abbaside Emperor, that it was necessary to win the sympathy and support of the Iranians who had always been friendly to the Ahl-ul-Bait. Consequently Mamoon was forced, from a political point of view, to establish contacts with the tribe of Bani Fatima at the expense of the ties with Bani Abbas and thereby win the favour of the Shias. Accordingly he declared Imam Ali Reza as his heir even against the Imam's will and got his sister Umme-Habiba married to him. Mamoon expected that Imam Ali Reza would lend him his support in political affairs of the State. But when he discovered that the Imam was little interested in political matters and that the masses were more and more submitting themselves to him due to his spiritual greatness, he got him poisoned. Yet the exigency which directed him to nominate Imam Ali Reza as his heir and successor still continued. Hence he desired to marry his daughter Umm-ul-Fazl to Muhammad-al-Taqi, the son of Imam Ali Reza and with this object in view summoned the Imam from Medina to Iraq.

129

The Bani Abbas were extremely disconcerted when they came to know that Mamoon was planning to marry his daughter to Imam Muhammad-al-Taqi. A delegation of some leading persons waited on him in order to dissuade him from his intention. But Mamoon continued to admire the learning and excellence of the Imam. He would say that though Imam Muhammad al-Taqi was still young, yet he was a true successor to his father in all his virtues and that the profoundest scholars of the Islamic world could not compete with him. When the Abbasides noticed that Mamoon attributed the Imam's superiority to his learning they chose Yahya Ibne Aksam, the greatest scholar and juror of Baghdad, to contend with him.

Mamoon issued a proclamation and organised a grand meeting for the contest which resulted in a huge gathering of people from all parts of the kingdom. Apart from noble and high officials, there were as many as nine hundred chairs reserved for scholars and learned men only. The world wondered how a young child could contest with the veteran Judge in religious laws (Qazi-ul-Quzat) and the greatest scholar of Iraq.

Imam Muhammad-al-Taqi was seated beside Mamoon on his throne face to face with Yahya Ibne Aksam, who addressed the Imam thus:

"Do you permit me to ask you a question?"

"Ask me whatever you wish," said the Imam in the typical tone of his ancestors.

Yahya then asked the Imam, "What is your verdict about a man who indulges in hunting while he is in the state of "Ehram". (In the code of religious law hunting is supposed to be forbidden for a pilgrim).

The Imam at once replied, "Your question is vague and misleading. You should have definitely mentioned whether he hunted within the jurisdiction of the Kaaba or outside; whether he was literate or illiterate; whether he was a slave or a free citizen; whether he was a minor or a major; whether it was for the first time or he had done it previously; also whether, that victim was a bird or some other creature; whether the prey was small or big; whether he hunted in the day or at night;

130

whether the hunter repented for his action or persisted in it; whether he hunted secretly or openly; whether the "Ehram" was for Umra or for Haj. Unless all these points are explained no specific answer can be given to this question."

Qazi Yahya was staggered in listening to these words of the Imam and the entire gathering was dumbfounded. There was no limit to Mamoon's pleasure. He expressed his sentiments of joy and admiration thus, "Bravo! well done! O Abu Jafar! (Ashanta Ashanta ya Abu Jafar), your learning and attainments are beyond all praise."

As Mamoon wanted that the Imam's opponent be fully exposed, he said to the Imam, "You may also put some question to Yahya Ibne Aksam."

Then Yahya also reluctantly said to the Imam, "Yes you may ask me some question. If I know the answer, I will tell it; otherwise I shall request you to give its answer."

Thereupon the Imam asked a question to which Yahya could not reply. Eventually the Imam answered his question.

Then Mamoon addressed the audience thus: "Did I not say that the Imam comes of a family which has been chosen by Allah as the repository of knowledge and learning? Is there any one in the world who can match even the children of this family?"

All of them shouted, "Undoubtedly there is no one parallel to Muhammad ibne-Ali-al-Taqi."

At the same assembly Mamoon wedded his daughter, Umm-ul-Fazl to the Imam and liberally distributed charity and gifts among his subjects as a mark of rejoicing. One year after his marriage the Imam returned to Medina from Baghdad with his wife and there he set about preaching the commandments of Allah.

DEATH:

When after the death of Mamoon, Motasim Billah ascended the throne, he got an opportunity to persecute the Imam and to ventilate spite and malice against him. He summoned the Imam to Baghdad. The Imam arrived at Baghdad on the 9th of

Muharram 220 A.H. and Motasim got him poisoned in the same year. He died on the 29th Zilqad 220 A.H. and was buried beside his grandfather, Imam Moosa-al-Kazim the seventh Imam, at Kazmain in the suburb of Baghdad.

THE TENTH IMAM

IMAM ALI NAQI ALAIHIS SALAAM

Name : Ali Ibn-e-Muhammad

Title : An-Naqi and Al-Hadi

Kunyat : Abul Hasan

Born at Surba in the environs of Medina, on Friday 15th Zilhajj 212 A.H.

Father's name : Imam Muhammad Taqi

Mother's name : Summana Khatoon

Died aged 42 years at Samarra on Monday 26th Jamadi-ul-Akhar 254 A.H. poisoned by Mutaz the Abbaside.

Buried at Samarra near Baghdad, Iraq.

The tenth Holy Imam like his father, was also elevated to the rank of Imam in his childhood. He was six years old when his father Imam Muhammad Taqi died. After the death of Mamoon-al Rashid, Mutasin succeeded him, and was later followed by the Caliph Wasiq Billah. In the first five years of the reign of Wasiq, Imam Ali Naqi lived peacefully. After Wasiq Billah, Motawakkil came to power. Being too occupied in state affairs, Motawakkil did not get any time to harass the Imam and his followers for four years. But as soon as he freed himself from state affairs he started to molest the Imam. The Holy Imam devoted himself to the sacred mission of preaching in Medina and did thus earn the faith of the people as well as their allegiance and recognition of his great knowledge and attributes. This reputation of the Imam evoked the jealousy and malice of Mutawakkil against him.

The Governor of Medina wrote to Mutawakkil that Imam Ali Naqi had been manoeuvring a coup against the government and a multitude of Shiaites were pledged to his support. Although enraged by this news Mutawakkil still preferred the diplomacy of not arresting the Holy Imam. Under the garb of pretended respect and love towards the Imam, he planned to put him under life-imprisonment after inviting him to his place.

Prior to his imprisonment, in a series of correspondence with the Imam, he expressed the view that he was convinced of all the claims of the Imam and was ready to settle them amicably. He wrote to the Imam that having been acquainted with his great personality, his matchless knowledge and his peerless attributes, he was impatiently looking forward to the honour of seeing him, and he most cordially invited him to Samarra. Although the Imam was well aware of Mutawakkil's treacherous intentions, he, anticipating the fatal consequences of refusing the offer, reluctantly decided to leave Medina. But when the Imam arrived at Samarra and Mutawakkil was informed about it, he took no notice of the Imam's arrival. When asked about where the Imam should stay, he ordered that the Imam should be put up in the inn meant for beggars, destitutes and homeless people.

Mutawakkil who was a deadly enemy of the Ahl-ul-Bait, removed the Imam from this inn and entrusted him to the custody of a stone-hearted brute named Zarraqui. But, by the grace of God, his enmity was in a short time transformed into love and devotion for the Imam. When Mutawakkil learnt about it, he shifted the Imam into the custody of another cruel man called Sayeed. The Imam remained under his strict vigilance for a number of years, during which he was subjected to boundless tortures. But even in this miserable imprisonment, the Imam kept devoting himself at all times to the worship of God. The watchman of the prison used to comment that Imam Ali-an-Naqi seemed to be an angel in human garb.

When Fateh Ibne Khaqan became the Wazir of Mutawakkil he, being a Shia, could not stand the idea of the Imam's captivity. He endeavoured to have him released from imprisonment and arranged for his comfortable residence in a personally purchased house at Samarra. Still Mutawakkil could hardly refrain from his antagonism to the Imam and he appointed spies to watch the Imam and his connections. But, through all these attempts, his hope of creating some fabrication to prove the Imam's activity against himself could not be realised.

In the time of Mutawakkil there was a woman named Zainab who claimed to be a descendent of Imam Husain. Mutawakkil sought the confirmation of Zainab's claim from the Imam and said "That as the beasts are prohibited to eat the flesh of the descendents of Imam Husain he would throw Zainab to the beasts and test her claim." On hearing this, Zainab began to tremble and confessed that she was a fake. Mutawakkil then ordered the Imam to be thrown to the beasts to test the claim. To his great surprise, he witnessed the beasts prostrating their heads before the Imam.

Once Mutawakkil happened to suffer from a serious malady which was eventually declared incurable by his physicians. When the Imam was approached for some remedy, he prescribed an application which resulted in a spontaneous cure.

Once Mutawakkil was informed that the Imam was preparing a revolt against him. Thereupon he ordered a detachment of the army to launch a raid on the Imam's residence. When the soldiers entered his house, they found him sitting on a mat, reciting the Holy Quran.

Not only Mutawakkil, but his successors' opposition to the Imam was fierce. After the death of Mutawakkil, Mustansir Billah, Mustain Billah and Mutaz Billah carried on the same mission of harassment against the family of the Imam.

Mutaz, understanding the uncontrollable and intense devotion of the people towards the Imam, eventually contrived the Imam's assassination. He got him poisoned through an ambassador which resulted in the Imam's death within a few hours. The martyrdom occurred on 26th Jamadi-ul-Akhar 254 A.H., and his funeral prayer was conducted by his son, Imam Hasan-al-Askari. The Imam was only forty-two years old at the time of death. The period of his Imamate was thirty-five years. He was buried in Samarra, (Iraq).

THE ELEVENTH IMAM

IMAM HASAN ASKARI ALAIHIS SALAAM

Name : Hasan

Title : Al-Askari

Kunyat : Abu Muhammad

Born at Medina, on Monday, 8th Rabi-ul-Akhar 232 A.H.

Father's name : Imam Ali Naqi

Mother's name : Saleel

Died, aged 28 years, at Samarra (Iraq), on Friday, 8th Rabi-ul-Awwal 260 A.H. poisoned by Mo'tamad, the Abbaside ruler.

Buried at Samarra.

The Holy Imam Hasan-al-Askari spent twenty-two years of his life under the patronage of his father the Holy Imam Ali Naqi after whose martyrdom he became his divinely commissioned Imam.

During his times the Abbaside rulers were entangled in political tussles. They however very much dreaded the existence of the rightful and divinely ordained Imam of the Holy Prophet, the Holy Imam Hasan Askari and knew that the son of this Holy Imam would be the "Mehdi" or "Guide" to humanity for all times until the Day of Judgment. So these rulers inflicted all sorts of calamities on the Holy Imam and hence the greater part of his life passed in prison and many restrictions were placed on his movements. In spite of this he always discharged the duties of Imamat with cheer and matchless perseverance.

The Holy Imam was ever busy in imparting religious knowledge and guiding people towards the straight path. History shows that the commentators of the Holy Quran have often quoted the interpretation of the Ayats of the Holy Quran from this Holy Imam.

Mo'tamad, the Abbaside ruler of the time realising that the world was ringing with the praises of this Holy Imam became restless with envy, and dreading that the people would openly declare their allegiance to the Imam, had him martyred.

Thus, on Friday the 8th Rabi-ul-Awwal 260 A.H., the Holy Imam departed from this world and was buried besides his father Imam Ali Naqi, in Samarra (Iraq).

THE TWELFTH IMAM

IMAM MEHDI ALAIHIS SALAAM

Name : Muhammad

Title : Al-Mehdi, Saheb-ul-Asr and Al-Hujjat

Kunyat : Abul Qasim

Born at Samarra, on Friday, the 15th Shaban 255 A.H.

Father's name : Imam Hasan-al-Askari

Mother's name : Nargis Khatoon

He is still living and will appear before the end of the world.

1st Heavenly concealment : 8th Rabi-ul-Awwal 260 A.H.

Final Heavenly concealment : 10th Shawwal, 328 A.H. (939 A.D.)

There existed a good deal of harmony and uniformity between the aspects pertaining to the births of Prophet Muhammad, the last Apostle of God and Imam Mehdi, the last Apostolical Imam. Just as the coming of the Holy Prophet was prophesied well in advance by the preceding Prophets, similarly the impending news of the gracious birth of Imam Al-Mehdi was foretold by the Holy Prophet.

Innumerable traditions in this context, quoted right from the Holy Prophet, from the glowing contents of many books of Masanid, Sehan and Akhbar, and of Shia scholars (Ulama) existed. Many Sunni scholars have accumulated these traditions in complete volumes also, e.g.: "Albayan fi Akhbar-e-Sahib-al-Zaman" by Hafiz Muhammad Ibne Yusuf Shafeyee and "Zikrenat ul-Mehdi" by Hafiz Abu Nayeem Ispahani, as well as ',Sehah-e-Abudaud" and "Sunan Ibne-e-Maja". All of the above books record the traditions bearing evidence of the coming of this Holy Imam. Out of those traditions two are quoted below:

136

PROPHECIES:

1. Abdullah Ibne Masood quotes the Holy Prophet as having said, "Even when the entire time of the world's existence will have been already exhausted and one solitary day left to embrace the eve of Doomsday, God will expand and make that very day swell to such a length of time as to accomodate the ultimate reign of a person out of my holy progeny who will be called after my name. He will then make the earth abound with peace and justice as it will have been fraught with injustice and tyranny before him."

2. Hazrat Abdullah Ibne Abbas narrates that the Holy Prophet said, "I am the leader of all the Prophets while Ali is the leader of all the Imams (Successors of the Prophets). I will be followed by twelve successors, the first amongst them being Ali and the last one Mehdi." (Behar-Ul-Anwar). The above tradition vouches well for the fact that the twelfth Imam is the last Imam of the Holy Prophet, and stands as the final Divine Authority (Hujjat) on earth. His Apostolical career is divided into three important phases, i.e. the period of his childhood, the period of his "Ghaibat" (concealment) and the period of his "Zuhor" (Re-appearance).

NAME EPITHET AND TITLES:

The name of our twelfth Imam is Muhammad, epithet Abdul-Qasim and his well-known titles are 'Alqaim', 'Al-Hujjat', 'Al-Muntazer', 'Al-Mehdi' and 'Sahbe-uz-Zaman'.

BIRTH:

He was born on 15th Shaban 255 A.H. in the city of Samarra. The momentous and singular aspects of his birth greatly resembled those under which the Prophet Moosa (Moses) was born. The birth of Hazrat Moosa had signalled the downfall and extinction of the empire of Pharoah, who had ordered the slaying of all the newly born children of Bani-Israel. The Abbaside kings were similarly apprehensive of the continuous traditions of the Holy Prophet about the birth of Imam Mehdi, who was to bring about a curse to their (Abbaside) very empire. They were, therefore, laying in ambush to discover the birth of the Imam and to put an end to his life. But the event of the Imam's birth was enveloped and shielded by the same Divine protection and miraculous phenomena which had marked the historical birth of Prophet Moosa. His birth remained strictly confidential and his nursery shrouded in secrecy except to a few devotees.

The Imam's birth had coincided with the reign of Al-Mutamad, the well-known Abbaside king. He, being aware of the the prophecy of the twelfth Imam's birth occurring in his reign, was extremely worried and anxious to trace him out. But on the death of Imam Hasan Askári, when he was informed about the Imam's funeral prayer having been conducted by his four year old son, his perplexity knew no bounds.

It struck his mind that this very boy must be the Imam, but he managed to hide his inner concern at the news of the existence of the young Imam. In order to get confirmation that the young Imam did in fact exist, he ordered the arrest of the Imam's mother, Janab-e-Nargis Khatoon.

THE ARREST OF JANAB-E-NARGIS KHATOON:

When Janab-e-Nargis was brought before Al-Mutamad and inquiries made about the birth of the twelfth Holy Imam, she, in order to safeguard her own life as well as to protect her son, replied that she had never felt the symptoms of maternity and labour pain; so, for the moment, he did not harass her, but did put her under the most strict surveillance of Qazi Abu Shorab, entrusting him with the task of killing any child born to her.

Soon after this incident, the Abbaside kingdom passed through a revolutionary phase which greatly bewildered Al-Mutamad. He was forced to face the invasion of Sahib-Al-Zanj, who raided Hejaz and Yemen and let loose the hounds of loot and arson thoroughout the Abbaside kingdom, subjecting the administration of Baghdad, the capital, to utter chaos. Al-Mutamad was, therefore, naturally too occupied by warfare to pay any attention towards Janab-e-Nargis, who was consequently released after six months and questioned no further about the birth of the twelfth Holy Imam.

CHILDHOOD·

The Holy Imam was brought up by his father Imam Hasan Askari, the eleventh Imam who resorted to the same underground and secret measures in rearing his child as Hazrat Abu Talib had adopted in connection with safe-guarding the Holy Prophet Muhammad. He used to take care of his child in one portion of the house for a few days and then shift him to another with a view not to let the exact whereabouts be known.

While Imam Hasan Askari kept the birth of the young Imam-to-be and the affairs of his infancy a well-guarded secret, he did put him within the access of some exclusive devotees and sincere friends in order to familiarise them with their would-be Imam to whom they would pledge their allegiance.

Below mentioned are the few names, quoted from the authentic books of both Sunni and Shia sects, of people who had the honour of having personally seen the Holy Imam Mehdi.

It is mentioned by Abi Ghanim that when Imam Hasan Askari's son was born he named him after Muhammad and on the third day after his birth, bringing forth the child to show him to some of his followers, declared thus:

"Here is my successor and your would-be Imam! He is that very Qaim to whose reverence your heads will bow down. He will re-appear to fill the earth with blessings and justice after it will have been abounding with sins and vices."

Muawiya Ibne Hakeem, Muah Muhammad Ibne Ayyub and Muhammad Ibne Usman mentioned that they called upon Imam Hasan Askari with a deputation of forty persons. The Holy Imam showed them his newly-born child and said,

"This is your Imam after me! All of you should unanimously submit your allegiance to him and should not allow any controversy on the subject which will lead you in peril! Mind that he will no more be visible to you".

IMAMAT:

Imam Hasan Askari died on the 8th Rabi-ul Awwal 260 A.H. and the day marked the inception of his son's Imamat and his elevation to the Apostolic office being the source of

139

spiritual guidance for the whole universe. As, according to God's Will, all the affairs pertaining to the Holy Imam were to remain strictly behind the curtain, he commissioned some of his deputies and ambassadors, who had been looking after the religious affairs from the time of his father to act as the associates between the people and the concealed Imam. They conveyed the problems and religious queries of the people to the Imam and brought back the verdicts and the answers of the Imam to the people.

It was by the Will of God that he disappeared and will again reappear by the Will of God. This will be a prelude to the Day of Judgment.

HAZRAT ABBAS ALAMDAR ALAIHIS SALAAM

Name : Abbas

Title : Qamar-e-Bani Hashim (the moon of Hashemites)

Kunyat : Abul Fazl

Born at Medina on 7th Rajab 26 A.H.

Father's name : Hazrat Ali Ibne Abi Talib

Mother's name : Fatema bint Huzam Ibne Khalid

Martyred at Kerbala, aged 34 years, on Monday, 10th Muharram 61 A.H.

Buried at Kerbala

Hazrat Abbas was the son of Hazrat Ali Ibne Abi Talib. His mother's name was Fatema, who was well-known as "Ummul Banin". She was the daughter of Huzam Ibne Khalid, an illustrious person of the tribe of Kalb—a tribe distinguished for its chivalry.

Hazrat Abbas was born at Medina on 7th Rajab 26 A.H. When the news of his birth reached Hazrat Ali, he prostrated himself on the ground as a token of his humble thanks to God.

140

Imam Husain took the baby in his arms and recited the Azan and Eqamat (calls for prayers) in his right and left ears respectively. Then the new-born baby opened his eyes to see the face of Imam Husain, before looking at anyone else. On the 7th day of his birth, the ceremony of Aqeeqa (which is one of the emphasised sunnats) was performed and Hazrat Ali named him Abbas.

Hazrat Abbas was a towering and a handsome personality. His dauntless courage, supreme confidence and unflinching loyalty earned him many titles. He was called "Qamar-e-Bani Hashim" (the moon of Hashemites), because of his imposing appearance. His remarkable horsemanship made him "Syed-ul-Forosan" (the chief of horseman). His ability to lead people resulted in his being called "Rais-ul-Shujan" (the leader of the valiant), and the manner in which he sacrificed his life earned him the title of "Afzal-ul-Shohada" (the choicest of the martyrs) and "Saqqa" (water carrier), because he sacrificed his life in an effort to procure water for Imam Husain's children in the tragic battle of Kerbala. He fully lived up to his name Abbas, which in Arabic stands for Lion.

Hazrat Ali, who himself was known as the 'Lion of God', brought up Hazrat Abbas and ably guided him till he was 14 years old. The next ten years of Hazrat Abbas' life were spent under the careful eye of Imam Hasan, and the last ten years with Imam Husain. Thus it was no small wonder that Hazrat Abbas acquired near perfection in so many aspects of life. His gallantry, boldness and courageous outlook were inherited from Hazrat Ali. Imam Hasan taught him patience and tolerance. His lion-hearted loyalty and the self-sacrificing nature were the results of his association with Imam Husain.

Imam Jafer Sadiq has said: "I bear witness, O Abbas, that you have reached the zenith of perfection in the matter of self-resignation, loyalty and obedience."

Imam Zain-ul-Abedin has said: "May God shower His blessings on my uncle Abbas. The manner in which he laid down his life for his brother, Imam Husain, showed supreme self-sacrifice. He fought valiantly to protect Imam Husain, and it was only after he lost both his arms that he fell. God recompensated him by conferring upon him in Heaven, two wings to fly with. Verily, the place of Hazrat Abbas before God is so high, that all the martyrs will envy him on dooms-day.".

Hazrat Ali's desire was to ensure that Hazrat Abbas preached the religion of Islam and served the prophet's family. Hazrat Abbas saw his first battle when only eleven. This was the battle of Siffen. One day he appeared fully disguised, masked and armoured, on the battle-field. When Ibn-e-Shasa, a brave and famous Syrian fighter saw this masked person, he asked one of his seven sons to slay him. Instead, the son was quickly put down. Similarly, the other six sons tried to fight this masked warrior, but they all met the same fate. Finally, Ibn-e-Shasa himself came forward and the manner in which he was also beaten, made all the other people stare in disbelief. They then thought this masked fighter to be Hazrat Ali, and no one dared to come forward to fight. But, when Hazrat Abbas removed the mask, people were surprised to note that he was not Hazrat Ali, but instead, the inheritor of Hazrat Ali's gallantry.

HIS DEVOTION FOR IMAM HUSAIN:

Hazrat Abbas' devotion, respect and affection for Imam Husain was so deep, that he used to worship the very ground that Imam Husain walked on. In fact, it is said that he used to apply to his eyes, the dust from Imam Husain's feet. He detested anyone taking precedence in serving Imam Husain. Even as a young child, he prevented others from serving Imam Husain. It is said that once Imam Husain, while present with his Holy father Hazrat Ali in the mosque of Kufa, felt thirsty and asked for water from Qamber (a well-known and obedient servant of Hazrat Ali). When Qamber rose to bring water, Hazrat Abbas, who was then a very young child, asked Qamber to stop, saying that he would himself bring the water for his master.

He stayed besides Imam Husain ever since they left Medina and he was loved by all the members of the Imam's family. He was so devoted to Imam Husain, that when Shimr Ibne Ziljoshan, the second-in-command of Yezid's army came towards Imam Husain's camp and called out: "Where are my nephews, Abbas, Abdullah, Jafar and Uthman?" Hazrat Abbas refused to even reply. It was only after Imam Husain told him: "Answer him, because, despite the fact that he is corrupt he is also one of your relations", that Hazrat Abbas asked Shimr what he wanted. Shimr replied: "O my nephews, I have specially asked Obaidullah Ibne Ziad for the safety of you all. So why do you wish to kill yourselves with Husain? Why do you not join the forces of the mighty Yezid?"

Hazrat Abbas looked at him with contempt and retorted, "May God's wrath fall upon you and upon your proposition, O enemy of God! How dare you counsel us to desert our master, Imam Husain and tie ourselves up with the corrupt and misguided Yezid?" Shimr turned around and went away angrily.

At length the battle started and the companions of Imam Husain, heavily outnumbered by the enemy, began to fall. The three brothers of Hazrat Abbas; Abdullah, Jafar and Uthman, as well as Hazrat Abbas' two sons, Fazl and Qasim, fought with rare gallantry before being killed.

The cries of water raised by the children in Imam Husain's camp on the day of Ashura, deeply grieved Hazrat Abbas. After taking permission from Imam Husain, he took the empty water-bag of Janab-e-Sukaina, the daughter of Imam Husain, and rode off towards the river Euphrates. Cutting through the rank and file of Yezid's army he rushed to the bank of the river, filled the bag with water, and started towards the camp. Yezid's army encircled the gallant Hazrat Abbas. He kept the water-bag in one hand and started fighting with the other. When both his hands were severed, he gripped the water-bag strap with his teeth. The severe blow from a mace on his head shook him badly and he fell off his horse, and called out to Imam Husain. Imam Husain reached him with great difficulty, and placed his head on his lap. Hazrat Abbas then opened his eyes to cast a last look on the Holy Imam's face and breathed his last.

JANAB-E-ZAINAB ALAIHAS SALAAM

Name : Zainab

Title : Siddiqa-E-Sughra

Kunyat : Umm-ul-Massaib

Born at : Medina on 1st Shaban 6 A.H.

Fathers Name : Hazrat Ali-Al-Murtaza

Mother's Name : Janab Fatema Zahra

Died : On 16th Zillhajj—

Janab-e-Zainab was born in Medina on the 1st of Shaban 6 A.H. Her father was Hazrat Ali-Al-Murtaza, the first Apostolical Imam, and her mother was Janab-e-Fatema Zahra, the beloved and only daughter of our Holy Prophet.

On the seventh day after her birth, the Holy Prophet solemnised her Aqeeqa and named her Zainab. Her epithets were Umm-ul-Hasan and Umm-ul-Masaib. Her popular titles were Sharikat-ul-Husain, Siddiqa-e-Sughra and Aqila-e-Bani Hashim.

The Holy Prophet, because of his deep affection, constantly took care of her and brought her up. Unfortunately, when she was only five years old, the Holy Prophet expired and just two months later, she lost her mother. Thus the sole responsibility of her upbringing fell on the shoulders of Hazrat Ali. The knowledge that was imparted to her by the Holy Prophet and Janab-e-Fatema Zahra, and later on by Hazrat Ali, quite naturally resulted in her being gifted with great virtues. Benevolence, sacrifice, truth, courage and devotion to God, became her way of life. She had a commanding knowledge of the Holy Quran and the Ahadees (traditions) of the Holy Prophet.

Even though she was married at the age of eleven to Hazrat Abdullah, son of Janab Jafer-e-Tayyar, the nephew of Hazrat Ali, she continued to remain by her father, and kept serving him, along with her husband. In fact, when Hazrat Ali decided to make Kufa his headquarters, both she and her husband also moved out to Kufa, enabling her to continue attending to her father.

144

Raziq-ul-Khairi, a Sunni scholar, writes in his book, "Sayyida Ki-beti": Her concern over the domestic economy was so deep, that only the necessities of life were kept at home. She did not believe in luxury, and avoided all unnecessary expenses. She was most thrifty and even the food was prepared in strict proportion to the consumption. She observed strict discipline and she would not eat until after all the male members and the children had been served. She had inherited the moral and ethical character of her grandfather, the Holy Prophet. She was tremendously courteous and hospitable to the women folk who visited her. Her simplicity in dress and her devotion to social service, made her a living example for others to follow. The young girls of the neighbourhood frequented her house for learning such discipline and she taught them without hesitation."

The extent of Janab-e-Zainab's devotion to God can be judged through the words of her brother, Imam Husain, who while departing from her on the day of Ashura, said, "O my dear sister! Forget me not in thy nocturnal prayers." Imam Zain-ul-Abedin said, "My aunt Zainab was subjected to un mentionable agonies in Kerbala, but even under these horrible conditions she never missed "Namaz-e-Shab" (the prayers offered after midnight and before true-dawn").

The sermons of Janab-e-Zainab bear ample evidence of her tremendous faith, and knowledge of the Holy Quran, Ahadees (traditions), Fiqh (religious laws), etc.

After the martyrdom of Imam Husain, Janab-e-Zainab and the other women folk in her camp were treated roughly and were almost shelterless. They remained as captives for a week or so in Kufa, and were then sent to Damascus. It was during this long journey to Damascus that Janab-e-Zainab successfully conveyed the principles and practices of Islam, and explained the purpose of Shahadat to the general public. She along with Imam Zain-ul-Abedin, explained to the public that they were the Aale Rasool who had the true principles and practices of Islam with them, and who were responsible for the spread and safeguard of the message delivered by the Holy Prophet. They also explained to the public that it was for this very reason that Yezid and his army mercilessly killed, not only the relations and followers of Imam Husain, but also the Imam himself.

Later on in Damascus, Janab-e-Zainab delivered many historic sermons in the courts of Yezid and Ibne Ziad. She elaborated upon the Islamic Ideals as taught by the Holy Prophet, and she immortalized the mission of Imam Husain. An example of her brilliant oratory is given as follows:

"Praise and glory be to God and blessings to my grandfather Muhammad Mustafa and on his pure kindred. Oh Kufis! Oh deceitful and treacherous ones! Do you weep! May your weeping never cease and may there be no pause in your cries of lamentation. You are to be compared to a woman who strengthens some thread, only to break it later. You have doomed yourselves by your wiles and deceit. The only things you know are envy, hatred, flattery and backbiting."

"You have harmed your souls with such terrible deeds that God is angry and you are doomed for eternal torment. You have forfeited your right to laugh and now there is nothing left for you but to mourn and weep. The stains of your vices are such that you can never wash them away. Do you realize that you have shed the blood of the Holy Prophet's successor, Imam Husain, the person who could have been your saviour? Imam Husain, the leader of the Youths of Paradise, was the one you needed for guidance and towards whom you could have turned in your time of need.

"The burden of your sins is terrible and will result in your destruction! Your efforts will be brought to nothing and you will suffer the eternal curse of disgrace and humiliation. Woe be to you, oh Kufis, have you ever considered how badly you have hurt and grieved the Holy Prophet? Have you assessed the nobility and purity of him, whose blood you have shed and have you realized how greatly respected were his kindred whom you have disrespected? You have, contrary to God's Pleasure, subjected us to misery upon misery. Are you surprised that blood poured from the sky? The torments of the Hereafter shall be more dreadful and there shall be none to help you." The narrator relates. "By God, I saw the multitude dumbfounded and all hid their faces in their hands and wept."

THE FOUNDATION OF AZADARI (MOURNING):

The Ahl-ul-Bait were released from prison, and Yezid in compliance with Janab-e-Zainab's wish, allocated a house in the vicinity of Darul-Hijara at Damascus to accommodate the bereaved family of Imam Husain. In this house Janab-e-Zainab laid the foundation of Azadari (mourning) of Imam Husain. In this house Janab-e-Zainab spread a mat and got Imam Zain-ul-Abedin to sit on it. All the Quraishite and Hasmite women came in their mourning dress to participate in this first "Majlis" in which the woeful and tragic accounts of the Holy Imam's martyrdom were narrated by Imam Zain-ul-Abedin and Janab-e-Zainab. This caused the audience to burst into tears. They lamented and bemoaned over the grandson of the Holy Prophet and his companions. After this the women offered their condolence to Janab-e-Zainab and Imam Zain-ul-Abedin.

Having returned from Syria to Medina, Janab-e-Zainab devoted the rest of her life to prayers and to mourning over her slain brother Imam Husain. Her two sons Aun and Muhammad were also martyred along with Imam Husain in Kerbala.

147

Supplications

Dua-e-Kumail

Imam Zain-ul-Abedin's Prayers for :−

Every day of the week

His Prayers for his parents

His Prayers for the removal of Anxieties

He Prayeth for safety and for grace.

"*O Thou who hast favoured Thy creatures with benevolence and kindness and lavished on them goodness and bounty, how manifest, amongst us, are Thy blessings; and how perfect, upon us, is Thy favour; and to what extent has Thou particularly favoured us with Thy goodness! Thou hast guided us to Thy religion which Thou hast chosen, and to Thy creed which Thou hast approved, and to Thy path which Thou hast made easy: And Thou hast shown us the way of approaching Thee, and the means of achieving Thy graçe.*"

An intelligent reading of the Dua-e-Kumail, the worded supplication granted by Hazrat Ali to one of his intimate devotees, Kumail Ibne Ziad, will disclose to the reader the unique nature of the touching appeal it has for invoking Divine Mercy, as well as the eloquence it presents.

Once Kumail requested the Holy Imam Ali Ibne Abi Talib for some prayer with which he could get his heart tranquilled. The Holy Imam granted this prayer, saying:

"Kumail! Take this prayer and recite it every night. If thou cannot do it every night, recite it once a week. If thou cannot do it, recite it once a month. If thou cannot do it, recite it once a year. And Kumail! if thou cannot do that even, recite thou it at least once in thy life."

This Dua has been split into twenty-four verses. It is advisable to recite at least one verse a day to realise the beauty and power of this supplication.

IN THE NAME OF ALLAH,
THE BENEFICENT, THE MERCIFUL

1

O My God! I beseech Thee through (the medium of) Thy Mercy which encompasses all things,

and through (the medium of) Thy Might which overpowers all things, to which all things submit and compared to which all things are humble,

and through (the medium of) Thy Power through which Thou hast conquered all things,

and through (the medium of) Thy Greatness against which nothing can stand up (or can rise), and through (the medium of) Thy Grandeur which prevails upon all things,

and through (the medium of) Thy Own self which will continue existing when all things will pass away (cease to exist),

and through (the medium of) Thy Names (attributes) which manifest Thy Power over all things,

and through (the medium of) Thy Knowledge which pervades all things,

2

O Thou (who are) the Light, O Thou (who are the most Holy.)

O Thou who existeth before the foremost things (from time without beginning), O Thou who shalt exist after the last things will cease to exist (Thou art Eternal—no beginning and no end.)

3

O my Lord! forgive my such sins as would disgrace virtue;
O my Lord! forgive my such sins as would bring down retribution (from the Heavens);

O my Lord! forgive my such sins as would change prosperity and happiness (into afflictions and sorrows);

O my Lord! forgive my such sins as would intercept my invocations and prayers;

O my Lord! forgive my such sins as would suppress hope;

O my Lord! forgive my such sins as would bring down afflictions;

O my Lord! forgive all the sins that I have committed and all the vices that I am guilty of.

O my Lord! I endeavour to achieve Thy favour through Thy praises and invocations to Thee; I pray to Thee to intercede Thyself on my behalf; I entreat of Thine benevolence to grant me Thy nearness, to bestow on me the quality of feeling (truly) grateful to Thee and to inspire me to keep on remembering and invoking Thee.

O my Lord! I entreat Thee begging submissively, humbly and meekly to treat me mercifully, to take pity on me, to make me contented, satisfied and pleased with what is allotted to me by Thee, and to keep me gentle and modest in all circumstances (in all phases of life).

5

Lord! I beg Thee as one who is passing through extreme privations and in his misery supplicates his needs to Thee, and (as one) whose cravings are great for the things which are Thine. ......

Lord! Great is Thy Kingdom, exalted is Thy Place, inscrutable are Thy Ways, evident is Thy Authority, overwhelmnig is Thy Might, ever-operating (acting) is Thy Power and no escape is possible from Thy Domain.

6

Lord! except Thee I do not find any one (so kind as) to pardon my sins, to conceal my degradations (despicable actions) and to divert me (my mind) from vices to virtues.

7

There is no God but Thou, Glory and praise be to Thee, I have harmed myself (by foul deeds), I have boldly taken to sins and vices as I was ignorant (of Thy Wrath and Power) and confident of my past prayers and invocations and Thy (constant) mercies and blessings on me (which I took for granted).

My God! O my Lord! How many of my vices hast Thou covered (from public gaze), how many calamities (descending upon me) hast Thou reduced the severity of; how many of my mistakes hast Thou corrected, how many misfortunes hast Thou averted (from me) how many elegant praises hast Thou alowed to be propagated about me which I did not merit!

8

O my Lord! my trials and misfortunes are great, and my sorrows and sufferings are intense,

and my good deeds are few, and my manacles (liabilities and responsibilities) lie heavily upon me.

And inordinate (remote) desires keep me away even from lawful gains.

The world has deceived me with its vanities and my mind has deceived me with dishonesty and procrastination.

Therefore, my Lord, I implore Thee in the name of Thy greatness not to let my sins and vices hinder my prayers from access to Thy realm, and not to disgrace me by exposing my (hidden) sins and vices of which Thou hast knowledge, and not to hasten Thy retribution for the vices I have committed secretly and which were due to evil-mindedness, sinfulness, ignorance, lustfulness and negligence.

So my Lord (I crave Thee) for the sake of Thy Greatness under all (those) circumstances before giving and under all conditions be merciful unto me.

9

O my God! have I any one besides Thee, O my Lord! to whom can I turn in my hour of afflictions to relieve me of my sorrows and to put my affairs in order!

10

My God! My Master! Thy commandments came into force for me (to obey) but I followed (evil) intentions of my (warped) mind, and I heeded not (those commandments) on account of allurements staged by my enemy who deceived me through my passions (evil desires), and my ill luck also favoured him (my enemy) in this.

Thus I transgressed some of the bonds set by Thee (for human freedom) and I disobeyed some of Thy commands.

Praise be to Thee, my Lord! Thou hast proof against me in all these matters, and I have no argument (no reasoning) to protest against Thy Judgment and Thy Orders and Afflictions (sent down by Thee).

11

I return to Thee, my Lord, after having committed the sins of omission and commission againt myself apologetic, repentant, broken-hearted, imploring forgiveness, begging pardon (for my sins) confessing (my vices), submissive and admitting (my faults).

I see no escape from that which has been done by me, and I find no refuge to which I may turn except that Thou mayest (kindly) accept my excuse (plea).

And allow me to enter the realm of Thy Mercy.

12

O my Lord! accept my apology, and have pity on my intense sufferings, and set me free from the strong fetters (put on by my evil deeds).

Lord! have mercy on the weakness of my body, and on the tenderness of my skin and on the brittleness of my bones.

O Thou! Who originated my creation (and then) granted me fame and honour, (Who) arranged for my upbringing and ensured my welfare and made provisions for my food, as Thou hast been generous to me from the very beginning of my life, please continue Thy Favours and Blessings as before.

13

O my God! O my Master! wilt Thou see me punished in Thy hell after I have faithfully believed in Thy Unity?

And when my heart has been truly and loyally filled with knowledge about Thee?

And when my tongue has persistently praised Thee and repeated Thy name, and I have conscientiously, faithfully, and constantly loved Thee, and after sincere confessions (ot my sins and vices) and after the moving and humble entreaties made by me?

No, My Lord! such an action is far from Thee, Thou art far too kind and generous to lay waste one whom Thou hast nourished, maintained and supported, or drive away from Thyself one whom Thou hast kept under Thy protection.

Or to scare away one whom Thou hast given shelter, or to abandon one to afflictions and trials whom Thou hast protected and hast shown Kindness and Mercy.

14

O my Master! My God and my Lord! I can never believe that Thou wilt empower the fire (of hell) to burn the faces which have submissively bowed in prostration before Thy Greatness.

Or (Thou wilt burn in the fire of hell) the tongues which have sincerely declared Thy Unity and have been always thankful (for kindness and Mercy).

Or (Thou wilt permit the fires of hell to consume) the hearts which have acknowledged Thy Divinity with conviction.

Or (thou wilt allow to be cremated in hell) the minds which have gathered such knowledge about Thee as to feel humble and submissive before Thee.

Or (Thou wilt consent to consumption by fire in hell) of bodies whose endeavours, wherever they lived, were directed towards obedience and service to Thee and which have exerted themselves with deserving humility to seek Thy Forgiveness.

Such an attitude can never be expected of Thee (O my God) nor Thy Kindness and Grace will allow me to hold such a belief, O Generous One!

15

O Lord! Thou art aware of my weakness to bear even minor afflictions and calamities of this world or their consequences, and also of adversities which befall men inhabiting this world, though all those trials and afflictions are momentary, short lived and transient.

(Lord!) How can I bear the retributions and the punishments of the hereafter which are enormous and of intensive sufferings, of prolonged period or of peretual duration, and which shall never be reduced or alleviated for those who deserve these punishments; because those retributions will be the result of Thy Wrath, Thy Punishment and Thy Anger which neither the heavens nor the earth can withstand and bear.

O my Lord! how can I, a weak, insignificant, humble, poor and destitute creature of Thine bear them?

16

O my God! My Lord! My King! and my Master! about how many things (of hell) shall I complain to Thee and about how many shall I bewail and weep;

About the pain and pangs of punishment and its intensity or about the prolongation of sufferings and their duration.

Because, my Lord! if Thou wilt submit me to the penalties (of Hell!) together with Thy enemies and cast me with those who deserved those punishments, and if Thou wilt separate me from Thy friends and from those who love Thee, I realise that Thou hast the right to do so, but my God, my Lord and my Master! (please let me submit that) though I may patiently bear thy punishments, how can I calmly accept the separation from Thee (Thy Grace and Mercy?)

(And) please Lord, let me submit that though I may patiently endure the scorching fire of Thy hell ,yet how can I resign myself to the denial of Thy pity and clemency; how can I remain in the fire (of hell) while I have hopes of Thy forgiveness?

Truly do I swear by my honour, O my Lord and O my Master that, if Thou wilt allow my power of speech to be retained by me, I will, from amongst the inmates (of hell), cry out unto Thee with the cry of those who have faith in Thy Kindness and Compassion.

And I shall loudly beseech Thee for help and mercy with the voice of those who shriek for succour, and I shall lament like those who are desperately in need of Thy help, and I shall keep on calling unto Thee; "Where art Thou, O Friend of the believers! O (Thou who art) the last hope and resort of those who have faith in Thy Clemency and Kindness; O the Helper of those who seek Thy help! O (Thou who art) dear to the hearts of those who truly believe in Thee! and O (Thou who art) the Lord of the Universe."

Seest Thou my plight, O my Lord! Glory and Praise be unto Thee, Thou wilt be hearing from inside hell the voice of Thy humble creature (myself) who is thrown in there in punishment for his disobedience and who tastes the chastisements (of hell) for his sins, and who is confined within its layers because of his crimes and vices and who cries to Thee (my Lord) with the voice of one who has faith in Thy Mercy and calls out to Thee in the language of those who believe in Thy Unity, and who seeks Thy Grace and Help (with a firm belief) in Thy Authority and Lordship.

18

O My Lord!

How could he remain in the abode of chastisement who puts his confidence in Thy past Forbearance and Clemency?

How could the fire of hell hurt him who has hope in Thy Kindness and Compassion?

How could the flames of hell burn anybody while Thou hearest his voice and seest his plight?

How could the roaring (fires) of hell terrify anyone whose weaknesses Thou art aware of?

How can he, whose sincerity is known to Thee, be tossed into the layers of hell?

How can the flames of hell torture him who keeps on calling Thee as his Lord?

How is it possible that while a person has faith in Thy Kindness and Mercy to set him free from hell, Thou shouldst abandon him there?

No, my Lord! nobody can believe Thee to be thus, neither Thy Grace has such a reputation; nor hast Thou through Goodness and Clemency ever dealt in this way with those who have faith in Thy Unity.

19

I am positively certain (my Lord) that hadst Thou not ordained punishment for those who disbelieve in Thee, and hadst Thou not decreed Thy enemies to remain in hell, Thou wouldst have turned the fire of hell cold and pleasant, and it (the burning and blazing hell) would never have become an abode or a halting place for any one.

But sanctified be Thy names, Thou hast sworn to fill hell with all the disbelievers from amongst the Jinns and mankind and to throw in it (hell) all Thy enemies (and to keep them there) forever.

Thou, exalted be Thy praise, hath said in the beginninng and, out of Thy Generosity and Kindness hath come to the generous decision that faithful followers (of Thy Orders) can never be (treated) like those who are sinners.

20

My Lord! My Master!

I, therefore, implore Thee by that Power and Might which Thou possesseth and by that faith of Thine (not to treat alike the good and bad) which Thou hast finalised and ordained and thereby hath overpowered those upon whom Thou hast imposed it, to forgive tonight and during this very hour all the transgressions that I am guilty of.

All the sins that I have committed, all the vices that I have kept secret and all the evil deeds that I have done, which I may have done secretly or openly, and which I may have tried to keep hidden or may have committed publicly, and all my evil actions that Thou hast ordered the two immaculate (and accurate) Scribes to note down, they are appointed by Thee to keep a correct record of all of my actions and to act along with the limbs of my body as witnesses to all of my doings and beside them all Thou (my Lord) doeth, keep a watch over me.

And Thou knowest the things which have been hidden from them, but hast through Thy Mercy kept my vices secret (from everybody) and through Thy Kindness drawn a curtain over them.

And I pray to Thee (my Lord) to increase my share in all the good that Thou dost bestow; and all the favours that Thou dost grant; all the virtues that Thou dost allow to be known everywhere; all the sustenance and livelihood that Thou dost distribute (in greater and greater quantities);

All the sins that Thou dost forgive and all the vices that Thou dost cover up.

21

O Lord! O Lord! O Lord!

O my God! my Lord! my King!

O master of my freedom! O Thou! who holdeth my destiny and art aware of my suffering and my poverty, O Thou! who knoweth my destitution and starvation, O Lord! O Lord! O Lord!

I beseech Thee by Thy Glory and Thy Honour, by Thy Supremely high attributes and Thy Names to make me busy day and night with Thy Remembrance, engaged in serving

Thee (Thy Cause) and to let my deeds be such as to be acceptable to Thee, so much so that all my actions and offerings (prayers) may be transformed into one continuous and sustained effort and my life may take the form of constant and perpetual service to Thee (Thy Cause).

22

O My Master! O Thou! on whom I rely, O Thou! unto whom I supplicate about (the miseries and sufferings of) my life.

O my Lord! my Lord! my Lord!

Strengthen my limbs for Thy service and sustain my strength and perseverance to continue it.

(Lord) Grant me that I may continuously endeavour to keep Thy fear (in my mind) and to be occupied constantly in Thy service.

Till I can successfully compete (with those striving) to reach Thee (Thy Grace) faster and quicker than the ones who are in the first rank; and I may hasten with those who eagerly surge to be near Thee, so that I may be as close to Thee as those sincere ones who have attained Thy Nearness, and I may keep on fearing Thee like those sincere believers who constantly keep Thy fear in their minds and thus I may join the assemblage of the faithful (gathered) near Thee.

23

O Allah, (please) let ill befall on him who, wishes me ill, (please) bring distress to him who plots against me.

And assign unto me a place in Thy Presence with the best of Thy servants whose place is nearest to Thee, for verily that position cannot be attained except through Thy Favour.

Lord! please treat me benevolently and through Thy Greatness extend Thy Favour towards me, and through Thy Mercy protect me and let my tongue be constantly busy in Thy Remembrance and let my heart be filled with Thy Love and be kind to me with Gracious acceptance (of my service and prayers), and weaken the force and intensity of my vices and forgive my evil doings.

For verily, Thou hast ordained that Thy creatures should obey Thee and hast bidden them to pray unto Thee and hast assured their acceptance.

24

So, my Lord! I have fixed my gaze upon thee and my Lord! I have extended my hands (in supplications) towards Thee.

Therefore, for the sake of Thy Honour accept my prayers and allow me to attain my objective; and by Thy Favour (I implore Thee) do not frustrate my hopes, and thoroughly protect me from the enmity and malice of my foes, from among the Jinns and mankind.

O Thou! Who art readily pleased, forgive one who owes nothing but prayers, verily Thou doest what Thou wilt.

O Thou! Whose name is the remedy (for all ills) and whose Remembrance is a sure cure for all ailments, and whose obedience will make one independent of all, have Mercy on one whose only asset is his hope (in Thy Kindness and Mercy) and whose only armament is supplication to Thee.

O Thou! Who bestoweth cure and happiness, who granteth remedy and blessings and who wardeth off misfortunes, O Light Who illuminateth those who are in darkness (of sins and sorrows), O Omniscient! Who knoweth without (acquisition of) learning, bless Muhammad and the descendants of Muhammad and do that unto me which befitteth Thee (Thy Mercy, Kindness and Grace).

And my Lord! bless Muhammad and the blessed leaders amongst his descendants and bestow upon them peace and tranquillity to the utmost extent that Thou can.

Prayers of Imam Zain-ul-Abedin

EVERY DAY OF THE WEEK

SUNDAY

With the name of Allah, besides whose mercy, I hope for nothing; I fear nothing save His justice, and trust nothing but His word, and do not cling but to His string.

To Thee do I beg for shelter, O Lord of forgiveness and approbation, from tyranny and oppression, from the changes of time and succession of grief, and from a life ended without preparation.

And to Thee do I beg for guidance in which there be reformation and improvement.

And to Thee alone do I pray for help in granting me success and satisfaction.

And Thee do I request for the garment of safety and the granting of peace and its permanence.

And I seek Thy protection O Lord, from the suggestions of Satan, and with Thy power guard myself from the tyranny of kings.

Therefore accept whatever be of my prayers and fasts and let my morrow and thereafter be better than my present hour and day; and make me respected amongst my kindred and community; and guard me in my waking and my sleep; for Thou art God the best Preserver, and Thou art the most Merciful.

O Lord, in this my day and on Sundays to follow, I clear myself in Thy presence of ascribing partners to Thee and of infidelity, and pray unto Thee sincerely to obtain Thy answer and render obedience to Thee hoping for Thy reward.

Therefore, bless Muhammad, the best of Thy servants, the preacher of Thy truth; and honour me with Thy diginty which cannot be diminished, and watch me with Thy eye which does not sleep; and finish my affair so as to make me independant of others and rely on Thee alone, and terminate my life in forgiveness. Verily, Thou art the Forgiving, Merciful.

MONDAY

Praise be to God who called none to witness when He created the heavens and the earth, and took no assistant when He created the spirits.

Never had He any partner in His Godhead, nor was He ever helped in His Oneness.

Tongues are unable to praise Him to the fullest extent, reason incapable of knowing His essence, the mighty humble themselves before His Majesty their faces bent downward on account of His dread, and all the great submit to His Glory.

Therefore, unto Thee be all praise in increasing succession and unbroken continuance.

And may His favour be on His apostle eternally, and peace perpetually, forever.

O Lord, let the first part of this my day consist in amendment, the middle of it in prosperity, and the last of it in success.

And through Thee I seek refuge from a day which begins in fear, the middle of which causes distress, and which ends in pain.

O Lord, verily I ask Thy pardon for every vow I vowed every promise I promised and every covenant I made with Thee, and then failed to discharge them.

And I pray to Thee concerning wrongs done to Thy creatures; therefore whichever servant of Thine or handmaid of Thine has suffered from me any wrong which I may have done to his person or reputation or property or kith or offspring, or any slander whereby I may have spoken ill of him, or anything I may have imposed on him on account of inclination, or passion, or force, jealousy, or hypocrisy, or prejudice; he being absent or present, alive or dead; and, thereafter my hand become too short and my means too narrow to make amends to him or obtain his forgiveness; in that case, I beg Thee..... O Thou who art the Lord of requests (and they are obedient to Thy will and ready to conform to Thy wish), to confer favour on Muhammad and his Aal and reconcile him to me by whatever means Thou choosest, and let me have mercy from Thee:

Verily, pardon causes Thee no loss, nor does bounty injure Thee, O most merciful!

O Lord, grant me on every Monday two gifts from Thee, viz. good luck to obey Thee at the begining of the day, and the blessing of Thy pardon at the end of it.

O Thou who art the only object of worship, and except whom none can forgive sins.

TUESDAY

Praise be to God—and praise is His due, as He deserves it —abundant praise.

I betake me to Him for refuge from mischief of Satan who adds sin to my sin; and I guard myself through Him from every wicked tyrant, oppressive king and over-powering enemy.

O Lord let me be of Thy force; for verily Thy forces—they are victorious and let me be of Thy band, for verily Thy band they are happy: and make me one of Thy friends, for surely Thy friends have no fear, nor shall they be sorry.

O Lord reform my faith for me, for verily it is the safe-guard of my affairs and make easy for me my hereafter, for certainly it will be my place of rest, and to it will I retire from the company of the wicked.

And let my life be an enhancement of every good to me, and my death a comfort to me from every evil.

O Lord bless Muhammad, the Last of the Prophets, the one who concluded the number of the sent ones, and his Aal, the pure, the holy; and his chosen companions; and in this third day of the week, grant me three things, viz.: leave me no sin unforgiven and no sorrow unremoved and no enemy un-vanquished by Thee.

With the name of Allah, the best of the names; with the name of Allah, the Lord of the earth and the heaven, I drive away every evil, the first of which is His displeasure; and desire to achieve every good, the foremost of which is His approval. Therefore let my existence end in Thy pardon, O Lord of Benevolence!

WEDNESDAY

Praise be to God who ordained night (to be) a cover and sleep (to be a mode of) rest; and made the day (to be the time of) dispersion.

All praise be to Thee for raising me from my sleep, for hadst Thou wished so, Thou wouldst have made it everlasting; a praise perpetual, unceasing and which the whole of creation would be unable to count.

Praise be to Thee, O Lord, for, thou didst create, and didst so with symmetry, and Thou didst measure and dispose, and causest to die and to live, and makest sick and restorest to health, and givest safety and dost afflict, and Thou are exalted above the Arsh (Throne) and art in full possession of sovereignty.

I pray unto Thee like him whose cause is weak and whose resource is cut off, and whose death has approached and whose worldly hope has shrunk, and whose need for Thy mercy has become pressing, and whose regret for his default has grown intense, and whose guilt and error has been too frequent and whose repentance unto Thee is sincere.

Therefore bless Muhammad the Last of the Prophets and the members of his house, the pure, the holy, and let me have the intercession of Muhammad—may Thy favour be on him and his Aal (family) and do not deprive me of his company; verily, Thou art the most Merciful.

O Lord, in the fourth day of the week grant me four things: employ my strength in Thy service; let my delight consist in Thy worship; make me love Thy reward; and cause me to abstain from that which would make me deserving of painful chastisement from Thee. Verily, Thou art kind to whomsover Thou willest.

THURSDAY

All praise be to God who removed the dark night with His power and brought the bright day with His mercy; and clothed me with His light and gave me His blessing.

Therefore, O Lord, since Thou hast kept me alive for this day, be pleased to spare me for other days similar to it; and bless Muhammad and his Aal (family) and do not afflict me in it and in other nights and days for my having done things forbidden and for my having committed guilt; and confer on me its benefit, and the benefit of what be in it and the benefit of what follows: and turn away from me its mischief, and the mischief of what be in it and the mischief of what comes after it.

O Lord, verily I seek adherence unto Thee through the guarantee of Islam; and rely on Thee through the honour of the Quran; and seek intercession with Thee through Muhammad, the chosen, may God bless him and his Aal; therefore, O Lord, recognise my guarantee, whereby I hope for the satisfaction of my need, O most Merciful!

O Lord, in the fifth day of the week, grant me five things, which none has power to vouchsafe except Thy generosity, and which none can afford save Thy bounty: a soundness, whereby I may gain strength to serve Thee; and a devotion whereby I may deserve Thy magnificent reward; and an immediate prosperity by means of fair earnings; and guard me on occasions of danger with Thy protection and place me under Thy defence, against future sorrows and anxieties.

O Lord, bless Muhammad and his Aal (family), and let my adherence to him be an effectual intercession at the day of Judgment, verily Thou art the most Merciful.

FRIDAY

Praise be to God, who existed before creation and the giving of life, and who shall continue to exist after all things have perished.

The Knower, who forgets not him who remembers Him; Who does not diminish him who gives Him thanks; who does not disappoint him who prays to Him; and does not frustrate the hope of him who places hope in Him.

O Lord, I call Thee to witness—and thou art sufficient as a witness; and I call all Thy angels and inhabitants of Thy heavens and bearers of Thy Arsh (Throne) and Thy prophets and Thy apostles whom Thou didst entrust with Thy mission and the various creatures whom Thou hast created; to witness that I bear testimony that certainly Thou and Thou alone art God, there being no God but Thee; Thou art alone there being no associate with Thee nor peer, and there is no untruth in Thy word, nor change.

And that, verily, Muhammad—may Thy blessings be on him and his Aal—is Thy servant and Thy apostle; he delivered to Thy servants the message with which Thou didst entrust him, and exerted himself in the cause of God the Honourable, the Exalted, as it deserved; and he gave happy tidings of reward which was certain, and threatened with punishment which was true.

O Lord, keep me firm in Thy religion as long as Thou keepest me alive; and let not my heart deviate; after Thou hast guided me; and let me have mercy from Thee; verily, Thou and Thou alone art the Giver.

Bless Muhammad and his Aal and make us of the number of his followers and his adherents, and raise me (on the last day) amongst his band; and give me the grace to be regular in my performance of the Friday prayer and to win such of Thy bounty as Thou wilt allot to the deserving observers of Fridays, on the day of recompense. Verily, Thou and Thou alone art the Mighty, the Wise.

SATURDAY

"Bismillah," which is the creed of those who seek protection and the motto of those who want refuge.

I betake me to the Exalted Lord for shelter from the oppression of tyrants, from the devices of the envious and from the treachery of the wicked; and praise Him above the praise of all those who praise.

O Lord Thou art the One without associate and the king without being made a king:

Thy command is unopposed and Thy sovereignty undisputed.

I beg Thee to favour Muhammad Thy servant and Thy apostle, and to inspire me with such gratitude for Thy favours as would enable me to deserve the utmost extent of Thy approval; and with Thy loving-kindness help me to serve Thee and worship Thee regularly and deserve Thy reward.

And favour me by restraining me from acts of disobedience to Thee as long as thou keepest me alive; and give me the grace to do that which would benefit me as long as Thou sparest me; enlighten my mind with Thy Book and remove from me the burden of sin because of my reading it; and favour me by keeping safe my faith and my life; and let not those that love me be frightened from me; and continue Thy goodness to me during the rest of my life as Thou hadst done during the past, O most Merciful!

His Prayers for His Parents

O Lord bless Muhammad, Thy servant and Thy apostle, and the Holy Prophet of His house; and distinguish him with the best of Thy favour, mercy, blessings and peace.

And distinguish, O Lord, my parents with the excellence of Thy nearness and Thy grace, O most merciful.

O Lord bless Muhammad and his Aal and acquaint me by inspiration with the knowledge of what is due unto them from me; collect for me the complete knowledge of all this, and cause me to act according to what Thou reveal to me by such inspiration; give me the grace to absorb such of this knowledge as Thou teach me, so that I may omit to perform nothing Thou hast taught me; and do not let my limbs grow heavy (so as to prevent them) from the observance of what Thou hast revealed to me.

O Lord bless Muhammad and his Aal, as Thou hast exalted us with him; and favour Muhammad and his Aal, as Thou hast given us claim upon Thy creation because of him.

And make me fear my parents as I would fear a powerful monarch, and love them with the tenderness of an indulgent mother.

And let my obedience to my parents and my beneficence to them be sweeter to my eyes than sleep is to the drowsy, and cooler to my breast than drinking water is to the thirsty; till I ever give preference to their wishes over mine, and precedence to the satisfaction of their needs over mine.

And let me over-value their benevolence to me even in small things, and under-value my beneficence to them even in great things.

O Lord let me lower my voice for them and let my speech be agreeable to them, soften my conduct towards them and let my heart be kind to them, and make me tender and lenient unto them both.

O Lord reward them for bringing me up and recompense them for loving me and guard them as they guarded me in my infancy.

O Lord, and whatever pain they may have received from me or whatever displeasure may have been caused to them by me or whatever duty owed to them and left unperformed by me, let that be a pardon of their sins and an exaltation of their rank and an addition to their good deeds, O Thou who dost change evil deeds into multiplied good deeds!

O Lord, and that speech in which they were unjust to me or that action in which they were extravagant against me, or such of my claims as they failed to satisfy or such debts as they failed to discharge, verily, I forgive it to them, and favour them therewith; and I turn unto Thee with a view to removing the penalty thereof from them.

For, verily, I do not accuse them falsely of having done something to hurt me nor do I deem them negligent in doing good to me nor do I despise the care they took of me, O Lord.

Because, their claim upon me is so great and their benevolence to me so magnificent; and I am so highly obliged to them that I cannot fairly meet it, nor repay them as they deserve.

O my God, how can I repay them for their tedious employment in bringing me up? And for their hard labour in guarding me? And for their self-denial in lavishing comforts upon me? Alas! Alas! (I cannot).

Their claim can never be satisfied by me nor can I perceive what is due from me unto them, nor can I fully discharge the duty of serving them.

Therefore, bless Muhammad and his Aal and help me, O Best of all those whose assistance is solicited, and give me grace, O Greatest of Guides towards whom men turn, and do not let me be of those who wronged their fathers and mothers on the day wherein every soul shall be paid what it hath merited, and they shall not be treated with injustice (3:5).

O Lord bless Muhammad and his Aal and distinguish my parents with the best distinctions which Thou hast conferred upon the fathers and mothers of Thy true believing servants, O most merciful.

O Lord do not let me forget to remember them after my Namaz (the regular prayers) and at every time of my night, and at every hour of my day.

O God bless Muhammad and his Aal, and forgive me for the sake of my prayers for them, and grant a sure pardon to them because of their goodness to me.

And be perfectly satisfied with them through my intercession for them; and bring them by Thy mercy into places of safety.

O God, if Thy pardon for them has preceded (my prayers), then make them intercessors for me; and if Thy pardon for me has preceded (Thy forgiving them) then make me an intercessor for them; so that we may be gathered together by Thy mercy in the place of Thy Grace, and the place of Thy pardon and mercy.

For, verily, Thou art the one whose munificence is great, and whose kindness is eternal, and Thou art the most merciful.

His Prayer for Removal of Anxieties

O Remover of anxiety and Undoer of sadness, O Compassionate in this world and the next and Merciful in both; bless Muhammad and his Aal and dispel my anxiety and remove my sadness. O One—O Alone—O Eternal.

O Thou who begetteth not and who art not begotten, and there is none like unto Thee; preserve me and remove my distress.

(Here repeat the following verses:

Ayatul Kursi   —   2: 254, 255, 256 and 257
Sura Ikhlas   —   Purity (of faith)   112
Sura Falaq   —   The Dawn   113
Sura Nas   —   Mankind   114

O Lord I beg Thee as one whose want has become intense whose strength has diminished and whose sins are innumerable; I pray to Thee as one who finds none to attend to his want, none to strengthen his feebleness and none to forgive his sins except Thee, O possessor of Glory and Majesty.

170

I beg of Thee to make me do such work as would invoke Thy love for the worker; and I beg of Thee such a conviction as would invoke Thy benefits on him who is perfectly convinced thereby of Thy command being in force.

O Lord, bless Muhammad and his Aal and cause me to die in truthfulness, cut off my interest from this world, and cause me to love what is near to Thee in order to make me eager to meet Thee; and give me the grace to sincerely rely on Thee.

O Lord, let my earnestness in making my request be like the earnestness of Thy friends in making theirs, and let my fear be similar to the fear of Thy friends; and for earning Thy approval, employ me in a work whereby I may not omit any item of Thy religion through fear of any of Thy creatures.

O Lord this is my request, therefore increase my earnestness in it, and reveal therein my excuse; and teach me therewith my argument, and keep therewith my body in health.

O Lord there are those who rise in the morning having others than Thee for objects of trust and hope; but verily, I rose in the morning having Thee alone for my trust and hope in all my affairs. Therefore ordain for me their successful management, and save me from misleading temptation, by Thy grace, O Most Merciful.

And may God bless our Prophet Muhammad, and the Holy members of his house.

His Prayer for Safety and for Grace

O Lord bless Muhammad and his Aal and honour me with Thy safety, guard me and make me independent with it, bestow on me as alms and favour me with it, spread it out for me and make it suitable to me; and do not interpose distance between me and Thy safety either in this world or the next.

O Lord bless Muhammad and his Aal and grant me safety, sufficiency, health, exaltedness and growth; and a security that would create safety of my body and a safety of my life in this world and the next.

And favour me with health, security and peace in my faith and in my body, insight in my mind, success in my affairs, and fear of Thee and dread of Thee; and power to perform what

Thou hast commanded for Thy service; and the will to avoid what Thou hast forbidden.

O Lord, give me grace to perform in this and every future year, the Hajj and the Umrah and to visit the tomb of Thy Prophet—Thy blessings on him, and Thy mercy and favours on him and his Aal—and the tombs of the family of Thy Prophet (peace be on them) as long as Thou keepest me alive.

And let this be accepted, approved, remembered and stored up by Thee.

And let my tongue utter Thy praise, Thy thanks, Thy remembrance and a handsome eulogy upon Thee.

And enlarge my mind for receiving directions (for the acceptance) of Thy faith.

And protect me and my offspring from the devil, the one who was driven away with stones; and from the mischief of venomous and stinging creatures; and from the vulgar and the mean; and from the mischief of every obstinate devil; and from the mischief of every malicious king; and from the mischief of the envious and haughty amongst the rich; and from the mischief of the weak and the strong, the high and the low, the great and the small, the nigh and the distant, and from the mischief of every one of the genii or of mankind who insisted upon fighting against Thy Apostle or the people of his house; and from the evil of every creature that moveth on the earth and whose forelock is held by Thee; verily, Thou art the right path.

O Lord bless Muhammad and his Aal; and whoever intendeth to wrong me, turn him away from me and ward off from me his device and repel from me his evil, and put (the noose of) his fraud around his own 'neck, and place before him a barrier till Thou makest blind his eye from seeing me, and deafen his ear that he may not hear me, and lock up his mind when about to think of me and render his tongue dumb concerning me, and crush his head and disgrace his dignity, break his pride, humble his neck, demolish his greatness; and render me safe from all his mischief, evil, back-biting, tale-bearing, slander, envy, malice, toils, traps, and his foot soldiers and cavalry.

Verily, Thou art the possessor of glory and power.

Parents
and
Children

The Prayers of Hazrat Ibrahim Alaihis Salaam.

"O my Lord, make me one who establishes regular prayer, and also (raise such) among my offspring, O our Lord; and accept Thou my prayer."   14:40

"O our Lord, cover (us) with thy forgiveness—me, my parents, and (all) believers, on the day that the Reckoning will be established."   14:41

Duties of Parents and Children

The rights and duties of parents and children are inter-related. That which is the right of a child is the duty of a parent. Likewise, that which is the right of a parent is the duty of a child.

It is 'the parents who have to take the lead in this direction and see that their children are able to grasp the importance of their duties to them.

If parents fulfil their duties of proper training and the education of their children, the latter will be able to understand the Commands of Allah. But, to be able to impart this knowledge to their children, parents themselves should be well versed in religion.

This message was brought to us by the Holy Prophet, the last Messenger of God, and he laid great stress on the performance of the duties of parents towards children and vice versa.

There is an explicit Command of Allah in the Holy Quran which says: "O ye who believe! save yourselves and your families from the fire." (66:6)

Other Ayats of the Holy Quran say:

"O my Lord! increase me in knowledge." (20:114)

"For those who seek guidance, He increases the Light of Guidance; and bestows on them piety and restraint from evil." (47:17)

If children are not taught religion, they will plead ignorance on the day of Judgment and will say, "O Allah, our parents did not provide us with proper education and training." Here education and training mean the education of religious principles and acquaintance with religious practices.

BEFORE CONCEPTION:

When a man has intercourse with his wife, there is a chance of pregnancy, therefore they should recite Bism-illah-ir-Rahman-ir-Raheem. This will keep Satan away from them and the child born will be free from Satan's evil designs.

AFTER CONCEPTION:

Once pregnancy is confirmed, the parents should invoke Allah's blessings for a child that is pious, obedient and promising.

THE BIRTH OF A CHILD:

First and foremost, it is essential that the Azan and Eqamat be recited in the right and left ears respectively.

AQEEQA:

On the 7th day after the birth of a child, the parents should perform the "Aqeeqa" ceremony (the hair on the head of the infant being shaved and an animal or animals sacrificed), and name the child. One can also name the child on the day he is born, or even when the child is in the womb of the mother.

The performance of Aqeeqa is Sunnat (strongly recommended). In case it is not possible to perform this within seven days, then it is recommended that it be performed as soon as possible. If the parents fail to do this before the child attains puberty, then the child himself or herself should have it performed.

A Dua (invocation) is recited at the time the goat or some other animal is sacrificed. This Dua makes it clear that the flesh of the child, the skin, the hair and the bones, are all to be safe because of the meat, the skin, the bones of the animal being sacrificed. The Aqeeqa is a sort of charity and alms for the safety of the new-born baby. Therefore, it is not correct that people should entertain their friends and relatives on this occasion and neglect the poor, who are entitled to a portion of this meat.

Imam Jafar-as-Sadiq recited the following Dua at the time of Zibha of an animal: (Zibha means the slaughtering of an animal according to Islamic Law.) "In the name of Allah and with the help of Allah! O Allah, I slaughter this animal for Thine sake. This (animal) is the Aqeeqa (Special Sacrifice) for —————— (here mention the name of the child). Its meat for his meat, its blood for his blood and its bones for his bones. O Allah! make this child a shield for the Progeny of Muhammad. Allah's Blessings on Muhammad and his Aal.

CIRCUMCISION:

The circumcision of a male child on the 7th day is strongly recommended and is very hygienic from the health point of view. The performance of circumcision at an early age enables the child to recover quickly.

According to Imam Jafar-as-Sidiq, the following supplication at the time of the circumcision should be recited: "In the Name of God, the Merciful, the Compassionate. O Allah! the performance of circumcision is commanded by Thee, as such its performance is tantamount to Thy obedience, and this is so because Thou, under Thy will, intention and decree, hast declared it to be Wajib (obligatory); we submit to Thy order and abide by Thy judgment which is binding, and carry out that which is promulgated by Thee; and because of Thy Command the child has felt the sharpness of the knife, while being circumcised. O Allah, Thy Command leads to the bleeding of the child, the benefits of which Thou knoweth more than we do. Shower Thy blessings on the child."

Imparting religious knowledge is the first and foremost duty of parents. Therefore, when the child is capable of learning, the first thing to teach would be the Kalema and Salawat. Then the names of the 14 Masooms, Usool-e-Deen, Furoo-e-Deen and such other subjects as suit his age and understanding.

Once the parents have done their duty towards their children, it becomes incumbent upon the children to follow these teachings.

SAYINGS FROM THE HOLY QURAN, THE HOLY PROPHET AND HAZRAT ALI:

The Holy Prophet has said:

"Heaven lieth at the feet of mothers."

"God's pleasure is in a father's pleasure; and God's displeasure is in the father's displeasure."

"He who wishes to enter Paradise at the best door, must please his father and mother."

"A man is bound to do good to his parents, although they may have injured him."

"Any child who does good to his parents and looks upon them with kindness and affection, God will grant him a reward on every occasion, and this reward is equal to a Sunnat Pilgrimage."

Hazrat Ali has said:

"Disobedience of parents is one of the major sins."

"The right of a father is that he should be obeyed in all his commands, except where he asks to be done a thing which is forbidden by Allah and is a sin"

The Holy Quran says:

"My Lord hath decreed that ye worship none but Him, and that ye be kind to parents, whether one or both of them attain old age in thy life."

"Utter not to them a word of contempt but lower to them the wing of humility and say: "My Lord! bestow on them Thy Mercy even as they cherished me in childhood."

After this, children should ponder over the following questions:

God gave you life, but, who has reared you?

God has provided you with food, but who has fed you?

You were nothing, everything was bestowed by God, but whose blood is running through your veins?

God has given continuity to your life, but who has kept awake during the long nights for your care and welfare?

If these deeds are not favours and beneficence, then what else can be termed as such? After the Benefactor, who else than your parents are worthy of respect and veneration?

Prayers (Namaz)
and
Illustrations

The Five Wajib Daily Prayers
Tasbeeh (Rozary), Dua Hifzo Iman, Ziarat
Ziarat of 14 Masooms and of the
Martyrs of Kerbala
(Peace be on them)
Tasbeeh after every Namaz
Namaz-e-Ayat
Namaz-e-Shab
Namaz-e-Jamat

"Prayer is the heart of Religion and Faith, but how shall we pray? What words shall convey the yearnings of our miserable ignorant hearts to the Knower of all? The Inspired One taught us Prayer that sums up our faith, our hope, and our aspiration in things that matter. We think in devotion of God's name and His Nature; we praise Him for His creation and His cherishing care; we call to mind the Realities, seen and unseen; we offer Him worship and ask for His guidance; and we know the straight from the crooked path by the light of His Grace that illumines the righteous."

178

In Arabic, prayer is called "As-salaat", and in Urdu and Persian, "Namaz."

Prayers are the pillars of Faith, the means of attaining nearness to God, the expression of obedience to Him, the thanksgiving for His infinite Mercy, the emulation of the examples of the Holy Prophet and the Imams, the strong link with God, the constant means of seeking and receiving His Guidance and Assistance in avoiding errors and transgressions. Prayer is the only way in which faith that lives in the heart can be made manifest in our actions, and can ensure admission to the realm of everlasting happiness in life as well as after death.

Hence it is incumbent upon every man and woman of mature age and sane mind who believes in the One True God and His Messenger Muhammad, and obeys the twelve Immaculate Imams who are the divinely appointed guides for all mankind, to observe the Wajib (compulsory) prayers steadfastly and regularly, in health and sickness, at home and on journeys, until the summons of death comes and takes us towards the Seat of Judgment and on the Day of Resurrection.

THE WAJIB (OBLIGATORY) PRAYERS

1.	The five daily prayers.	7.	Namaz-e-Kasam.
2.	Namaz-e-Ayat.	8.	Namaz-e-Juma.
3.	Namaz-e-Mayyat.	9.	Namaz-e-Istejara.
4.	Namaz-e-Tawaf.	10.	Namaz-e-Qaza.
5.	Namaz-e-Ahad.	11.	Namaz-e-Ehtiyat.
6.	Namaz-e-Nazar.		

The occasions for saying the Namaz numbered 2 to 11, are:

2. Prayers which are to be said when acts of God, like earthquakes, eclipses and cyclones take place.
3. Prayer to be offered for the dead at the time of burial.
4. Prayer to be offered when going around the Kaaba during Hajj.
5. Prayer which one has vowed to perform.
6. Prayer undertaken to be offered on fulfilment of a certain desire.

7. Prayers said when one has taken an oath.

8. The Friday congregational prayer.

9. Prayers which one has undertaken to offer on behalf of a deceased person which he or she has omitted in his or her lifetime.

10. Prayers omitted by parents during their lifetime which are obligatory on the eldest son or daughter.

11. Prayers which are to be performed when certain doubts occur during everyday prayers.

The Five Wajib Daily Prayers

The Morning (Fajr) Prayer: (2 Rakats)
Fajr starts at Subhe Saadiq (i.e. about one hour and twenty minutes before sunrise) and ends at sunrise. At least one rakat should be over before sunrise otherwise the Namaz becomes Qaza .

The Midday (Zohar) Prayer: (4 Rakats)
Zohar starts at Zawaal (start of the sun's decline from the apparent noon) and ends before sunset, when just enough time is left for four rakats of Asr.

The Afternoon (Asr) Prayer: (4 Rakats)
Asr starts after Zohar is offered, and ends just before sunset.

The Sunset (Maghrib) Prayer: (3 Rakats)
Maghrib starts 8-15 minutes after sunset and ends before midnight when just enough time is left for four rakats for Isha.

The Evening (Isha) Prayers: (4 Rakats)
Isha commences as soon as Maghrib is offered and ends at midnight.

WAJIB means: The religious directives performance of which is rewarded and wilful neglect of which is a sin.

Sunnat means: Such recommendations, performance of which is rewardable and their omission not punishable.

All the above Wajib prayers add upto seventeen Rakats. This means that even the busiest man is expected to set aside about fifteen minutes of his precious time every twenty-four

180

hours, for no less an important duty than of communion with his Lord, Creator, Cherisher and Sustainer. Surely not an exacting demand by any standards.

NAWAAFIL PRAYERS

These prayers which are not obligatory—are highly recommended and are as follows:

Nawaafil Fajr : Prior to the Wajib Namaz of Fajr.2 Rakats.
Nawaafil Zohar : Prior to the Wajib Namaz of Zohar.

8 Rakats.

Nawaafil Asr : Prior to the Wajib Namaz of Asr. 8 Rakats.
Nawaafil Maghrib : After the Wajib Namaz of Maghrib.

4 Rakats.

Nawaafil Isha : After the Wajib Namaz of Isha. This is entirely performed in a sittng posture.

2 Rakats.

QASAR PRAYERS

While travelling, or staying away from home for less than ten days, the Wajib prayers are shortened. The traveller is required to offer:

2 Rakats for the Fajr prayer.
2 Rakats for the Zohar prayer.
2 Rakats for the Asr prayer.
3 Rakats for the Maghrib prayer.
2 Rakats for the Isha prayer.

This is a concession granted to travellers only when the return journey is over 44 Kilometers (27½ miles) and it is not permissible for them to exceed the limit of ten days.

It is preferable to say each of the prayers at the earliest time rather than to put them off until the last moment.

PURIFICATION FOR PRAYERS

Before addressing himself to prayer, the believer must make sure that his body and clothes and the place of prayer are all clean. Then he must make the necessary purification by one of the following three means, whichever form be applicable: Ghusl (bath), or Wazu (Ablution), or Tayammum (purification by means of sand if water be not available or if it be harmful).

GHUSL (BATH)

Ghusl becomes Wajib in the following circumstances:

1. Janabat, i.e. emission of semen or intercourse.
2. Haiz, i.e. the normal monthly period of menstruation—minimum 3 days, maximum 10 days. Any period beyond this would not be Haiz. During Haiz women are not permitted to observe the prayers (namaz).
3. Istehaza, i.e. discharge of menstrual blood for periods longer than ten days, or the normal period for the individual.

Istehaza may be:—

(a) Kaleela (in small quantities).
(b) Mutawassita (somewhat larger quantities).
(c) Katheera (in large quantities).

The discharge of Istehaza is usually not so dark in colour and not so dense as the blood of Haiz. In case of Istehaza Qaleela, it does not wet the cotton-wool through and through. In this case, therefore, all that is necessary is to change the sanitary pad and it is not necessary to take Ghusl. In the case of Mutawassita, the discharge of blood is sufficient in quantity to soak the cotton-wool. In this case, Ghusl should be taken in the morning and the sanitary pad be changed and only the Wazu should be performed before each prayer. In the case of Istehaza Katheera, the discharge of blood is in such quantities as to soak through the sanitary pad completely. In this case, Ghusl must be taken before each prayer, without, which the prayer would be invalid.

4. NIFAS: i.e. the discharge after childbirth. Ghusl is wajib after Nifas, in the same way as in the case of Haiz.

5. GHUSL-E-MAYYAT: i.e. the bathing of a dead body. It is Wajib-e-Kifaee for all Muslims. Men only may bathe male bodies, and women, female bodies; except in the case of husband and wife.

6. GHUSL-E-MASS-E-MAYYAT: This bath becomes Wajib on touching a corpse which has not been duly washed.

METHOD OF GHUSL

The method of performing Ghusl is, first to wash the whole body from head to foot so as to remove all oily substances and other extraneous matter from the entire surface of the skin. Then wash the hands, mouth and nostrils. Then perform the niyat. This is the intention you make in your mind, "that I perform Ghusl (naming the particular kind of Ghusl) to cleanse myself, Wajib Qurbatan Ilallah—("seeking the nearness to God.") Then thoroughly wash the neck and head. Then wash the body from the right shoulder down to the toes so as to wash the entire surface of the skin on the right side. Finally, wash the entire body from the left shoulder down to the toes on the left side.

For the Ghusl-e-Haiz, Nifas, etc., perform the Wazu after the Ghusl. But no Wazu need be performed after the Ghusl-e-Janabat.

Ghusl can also be performed by forming the Niyat and taking a complete dip in a pool of water so as to let the water reach all parts of the body.

WAZU
(Ablutions)

Before saying each of the prayers it is necessary for the devotee to make sure that he has performed the Wazu and the Wazu has not been broken.

The Wazu consists of two parts, namely

(a) Sunnat and (b) Wajib.

The Sunnat part of the Wazu consists of (1) Washing both the hands from the wrists (Fig. 1a, 1b); (2) Washing the mouth (gargle), (3) Rinsing the nostrils.

Washing of the Hands

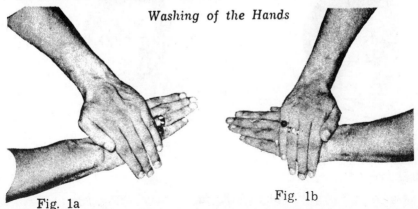

Fig. 1a

Fig. 1b

183

After these preliminaries, the Wajib Wazu begins :

1. The Niyat (intention) should be formed in ones mind as follows: "I perform the Wazu in order to cleanse myself from impurity and to make myself eligible for Namaz, Wajib Qurbatan Ilallah ("seeking the nearness to God.")

2. Washing the face once from the point where the hair of the head normally grows, down to the chin; and breadthwise as much of the face as comes between the outspread thumb and little finger of the hand. (Fig. 2a, b, c. & d.)

Fig. 2a

Fig. 2b

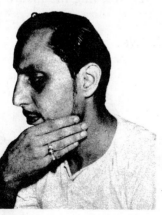

Fig. 2c   *Washing of the face*   Fig. 2d

3. Washing the right arm, from the elbow down to the finger tips once, spreading the water always from top to bottom. If the devotee is wearing a ring, etc., he must either move or remove it so as to enable the water to run over the entire surface of the skin. (Fig. 3a).

4. Washing the left arm from the elbow down to the finger tips, once, in the same way as below. Fig. 3b.

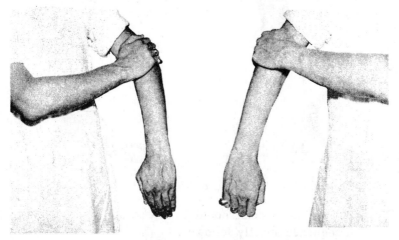

Fig. 3a　　　*Washing of the arms*　　　Fig. 3b

5. Masah : After washing the face and the hands, Masah of the head should be performed by drawing the wet fingers of the right hand from the middle of the head upto the edge of the hair. (Fig. 4a, b.)

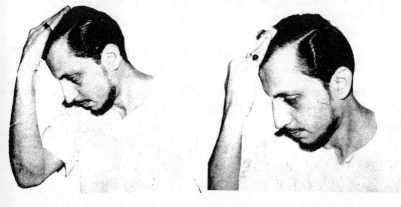

Fig. 4a　　　*Masah of the head*　　　Fig. 4b

6. Masah of the feet should be performed by drawing the wet fingers of the right hand over the upper part of the right foot from the tips of the toes to the ankle, and then similarly the left hand over the left foot. (Fig. 5 a, b.)

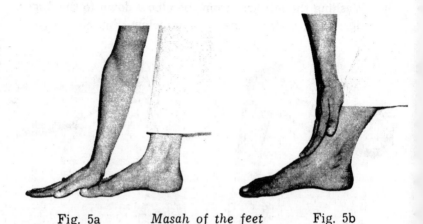

Fig. 5a   *Masah of the feet*   Fig. 5b

P.S.—All the above acts should be consecutive and the order of sequence strictly followed.

TAYAMMUM

When a worshipper is sick and cannot use water without injury to his health or when water is not available, he is allowed a simpler way of purifying himself called Tayammum. Thus instead of Ghusl or Wazu as the case may be, he may perform Tayammum, i.e. purification by means of clean pure sand or clean dry dust, as follows:

Form the niyat.. Strike with both palms a sufficient quantity of sand or clean dry dust (Fig. 6) and place both the hands on the forehead and pull them down, rubbing the forehead and the eyebrow (Figs. 7a, 7b.)

Rub your right hand with the left and the left with the right. (Fig. 8a, 8b)

Fig. 6
The Striking

Fig 7a The begining

Fig 7b The end

Masah of the face

Fig. 8a Right hand   *Masah of the Hands*   Fig. 8b Left hand

A fresh Wazu becomes necessary only if the previous one has lapsed, which may happen under any of the following conditions:

1. By defecation
2. By urination.
3. By emission of a flatus Ex ano.
4. By sleeping or dozing.
5. By fainting.
6. By Janabat (intercourse), Haiz, Nifas, etc.

Shakkiyaat-e-Namaz
(Occurrence of doubt during prayers)

Although the Namaz may be offered with full care and attention yet an error is committed sometimes. At other times doubts may arise about the performance of a particular part of the prayer. If these remain unresolved, certain rules should be observed.

Shakkiyaat (Doubts) to be ignored

A Namaz does not become invalid in the event of the following Shakkiyaats:

1. After having finished the Namaz, a doubt as to whether one has gone through all the rituals or not.
2. Doubt after passing of the event, for example, while in Sajdah, a doubt about having missed a rukoo.
3. Doubt after the time has passed, for example, doubt at the time of Maghrib whether the Asr Namaz was offered or not.
4. Doubt either by an Imam (one who leads the Namaz) or Mamoom (one who follows the Imam in Namaz). In this case, the Imam may be sure of his performance but the Mamoom is doubtful, or vice versa. In such a case whoever is in doubt will follow the one who is sure.
5. Doubt during a Sunnat (non-obligatory) Namaz.

Mubtil Shakkiyaat

The following doubts if arising render the Namaz invalid. In this case the Namaz has to be offered again.

1. Doubt about the number of the rakat being prayed in a two rakat Namaz, e.g. Fajr, or Qasr.
2. Doubt about the number of the rakat being prayed in a three rakat Namaz e.g. Maghrib.
.3 Doubt during a four rakat Namaz whether it was the first, second or third rakat.
4. Doubt during a four rakat Namaz before the second Sajdah whether it was the second or the third rakat.
5. Doubt during a four rakat Namaz .whether it was second, fifth or higher rakat.
6. Doubt during a four rakat Namaz whether it was third, sixth or higher rakat.
7. Doubt during a four rakat Namaz whether it was fourth, sixth or higher rakat.
8. Doubt during a four rakat Namaz as to the number of rakats offered and the balance to be offered.

Saheeh Shakkiyaat

Arising of the following doubts do not render Namaz invalid (batil), provided the remedial procedure as prescribed in each case is carried out:

1. Doubt during a four rakat Namaz after both the Sajdahs whether it was the second or the third rakat. In such a case it should be regarded as the third rakat and the Namaz be finished after offering the fourth rakat. Thereafter Namaz-e-Ehtiyat (precautionary prayer) of one rakat standing or two rakats sitting be offered.
2. Doubt after the two Sajdahs whether it was second, third or fourth rakat. In such a case, Namaz be finished by considering it as the fourth rakat and Namaz-e-Ehtiyat of two rakats standing, and then another two rakats sitting be offered.
3. Doubt after two Sajdahs, whether it was second or fourth rakat, in such a case the Namaz should be finished by considering it as the fourth and Namaz-e-Ehtiyat of two rakats standing be offered.
4. Doubt whether it was third or fourth rakat. In such a case, the Namaz should be finished considering it as the

189

fourth rakat, and Namaz-e-Ehtiyat one rakat standing. or two rakats sitting be offered.

.5 Doubt whether it was third, fourth or fifth rakat. In such a case, if standing one should at once sit down and after finishing the Namaz offer two rakats Namaz-e-Ehtiyat standing and two rakats sitting.

6. Doubt before rukoo whether it was third or fifth rakat. In such a case if standing, one should at once sit down and after finishing offer two rakats Namaz-e-Ehtiyat, standing.

7. Doubt whether it was fourth or fifth rakat. In such a case the Namaz should be completed then and there and two Sajdahs of Sahv should be offered immediately.

8. Doubt while in Qayam (standing posture) whether it is fourth or fifth rakat. In such a case one should sit down at once and finish the Namaz. Thereafter Namaz-e-Ehtiyat one rakat standing or two rakats sitting should be offered. If this doubt arises after the two Sajdahs, then the Namaz should be finished and thereafter two Sajdahs of Sahv as Wajib should be performed.

9. Doubt whether it was fifth or sixth rakat. In such a case, the Namaz should be finished at once and two Sajdahs of Sahv be done.

NAMAZ-E-EHTIYAT

Soon after finishing a Namaz that requires the remedial procedure for its validation without looking away from the Qibla, the worshipper should rise (or keep sitting if it has been offered sitting) and form the following Niyat (intent):

"I offer one two rakats Namaz-e-Ehtiyat Wajib Qurbatan IIallah, and recite Allaho Akbar."

Then after reciting only Sura-al-Hamd the worshipper goes into the Rukoo and Sajdah and then recites the Tashahhud and Salaam as is done in a usual Namaz.

SAJDAH OF SAHV

The Sajdah of Sahv is Wajib if any one has spoken by mistake during the Namaz, or has omitted one Sajdah or has forgotten to recite Tashahhud or has recited Salaam at the wrong place.

For the Sajdah of Sahv, immediately after finishing the Namaz, the following Niyat should be formed:

"I do Sajdah of Sahv in lieu of (Tashahhud, Salaam or Sajdah as the case may be) Wajib Qurbatan Ilallah."

After the Niyat, "Allaho Akbar" is said and the Sajdah is performed, when the following is recited once:

"Bismillaha wa billahe Allahumma salle'ala Muhammadin wa Aale Muhammad." Then the head is raised and after sitting, "Allaho-Akbar" is said. Thereafter "Astaghfirullaha rabbi wa atoobo ilaihi" is said and again the Sajdah is done and the above mentioned phrase repeated. Thereafter, while sitting, Tashahhud as under is recited:

Ashhado an la ilaha illahlah wa Ashhado anna Muhammadar Rasoolullah. Allahuma salle 'ala Muhammadin wa aale Muhammad: asallamu 'alaikum wa Rahmatullahi wa barakatuh.

SOME ESSENTIALS

While offering Namaz some of the actions and performances, though apparently of little significance, need special care. The Shariat has laid great emphasis on these, so much so that their irregularity or improper performance may render the Namaz batil (invalid). These are as follows.

1. If any of the Wajib rukn (below) are missed deliberately or even due to a lapse then the Namaz is batil.

The Wajib Rukn are five:

1. Niyat
2. Takbeeratul Ehram
3. Qayam Muttasil ba rukoo
4. Rukoo
5. Sajdatain

"Qayam muttasil ba rukoo" means that having finished the recitation of al-Hamd and Qul ho Wallah one must remain in a standing posture and say Allaho Akbar. And after a pause one should perform the rukoo. In case this pause is missed the Namaz is rendered batil.

During Namaz the performance of such acts, which if seen by some one else may lead him to conclude that the person was not offering Namaz, must be avoided.

191

Whatever is recited during Namaz, is to be recited very patiently, e.g. Allaho Akbar before rukoo. "Samey Allaho Layman Hamaydah" after rukoo, "Astaghfiroollaha Rabbee wa atoobo ilaih" and "Allaho Akbar" in between the two Sajdahs and "Allaho Akbar" after the 2nd Sajdah. All these must be recited while one is not moving.

Reciting during a movement is only permitted when one is getting up from a sitting posture after the second Sajdah (page 196 — 10), — and during this getting up process one has to recite : "Bay-haulillahay wa Qoowateyhee aqoomo Wa-aqood".

The Qibla

Qibla means Kaaba, which is a cubical in Masjidul Haraam at Mecca in Saudi Arabia. Around this cubical is the Qibla in every direction.

It is obligatory that every Salaat (Namaz) must be offered while facing Qibla. At places distant from the Kaaba we have different ways of finding out the direction of Qibla. The easiest way is by using the magnetic compass. The direction of Mecca will approximately give the direction of Qibla.

Sajdagah

In the Sajdah which is the position of prostration (fig. 12), the forehead must not rest on any mineral, cloth, jewel or the skin or fur of any animal. Sajdah is valid on grass, straw, clean dry rock, earth, or leaves which are not eaten by human beings. Highest preference is given to Kerbala earth readymade tablets which are available and called "Sajdagah."

Azan and Eqamat

These are the Calls to Prayer and the Declaration of Belief which are proclaimed aloud at the time of each Namaz calling the Faithful to prayer.

The Azan consists of :

1. "Allaho Akbar" — 4 times ("God is Great")
2. "Ash-hado-an la ilaha illallah" — twice ("I bear witness that there is no God except Allah.")
3. "Ash-hado anna Muhammadan Rasool-Allah" — twice ("I bear witness that Muhammad is the Messenger of Allah.")
4. "Ash-hado anna Aliyan Wali-Allah" — twice ("I bear witness that Ali is the friend of God.")
5. Hayya alas-salah" — twice ("Hasten towards prayer.")

6. "Hayya alal-falah" — twice ("Hasten towards prosperity.")
7. "Hayya ala Khairil-amal" — twice ("Hasten towards the best of actions.")
8. "Allaho Akbar" — twice ("God is great.")
9. "La ilaha illallah" — twice ("There is no God except Allah.")

The Eqamat or Declaration of Belief follows the Azan and consists of :

1. "Allaho Akbar" — twice.
2. Same as in Azan.
3. Same as in Azan.
4. Same as in Azan but recite only once.
5. Same as in Azan.
6. Same as in Azan.
7. Same as in Azan.
8. "Qad qamatis-salaat" — twice ("Lo, prayer has been established.")
9. "Allaho Akbar" — twice.
10. "La ilaha illallah" — once.

THE NAMAZ
The Namaz consists of the following parts :

The First Rakat

The Niyat : The devotee should stand erect facing the Kaaba, (the feet of a male person should be 4 to 8 inches apart. and those of a woman joined together) and form the following intention consciously in his mind : "I offer, the————— prayer (here name the particular prayer), of—————rakats, Wajib Qurbatan Illallah, (seeking nearness to God, in obedience to Him.")

2. THE TAKBIRAT-UL-EHRAM : Lift both hands up to the ears and say, "Allaho Akbar" (God is Great) (Fig. 9)
Then stand erect. (Fig. 10).

After the Takbirat-ul-Ehram all excessive movement, looking about. turning, speech, laughter, etc., are forbidden until the end of the Namaz.

Fig. 9

QAYAM :

Whilst reciting the Sura-al-Hamd, and any other Sura, one should stand erect and motionless with the eyes fixed on Sajdagah. (Fig. 10).

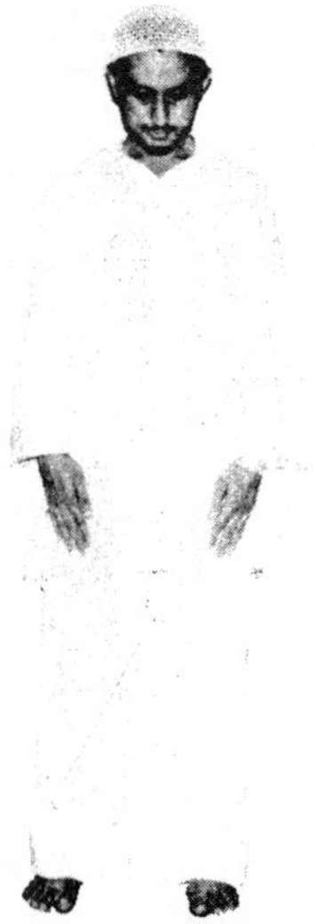

Fig. 10

3. RECITATION OF SURA-AL-FAATAYHA (The opening).

This is also known as Sura AL-HAMD :

Bism-illah-ir-Rahman-ir-Raheem

(In the Name of God, the most Compassionate, the Merciful)

Al-hamdo Lillahay Rabbil Aalemeen; Ar Rahma nir Raheem; Maalikay yau-middeen; Eeyaka na bodo wa Eeyaka nastaeen; Ehdaynas Siratal Mustaqeem, Siratal lazeena an amta alaihim ghairil maghzoobay alaihim walaz zaalleen.

All praise belongs to Allah, the Cherisher, Sustainer, Developer and Perfector of the worlds; the most Compassionate, the Merciful, Master of the Day of Judgment.

Thee only do we worship and Thee alone do we ask for help.

Guide us along the straight path—the path of those whom Thou has blessed, not of those with whom Thou art angry, nor of those who go astray.

194

4. After this recite any other appropriate Sura (e.g., SURA AL-KAUSAR. CVIII. (The abundance of good)

Bism-illah-ir-Rahman-ir-Raheem.

(In the name of God, the Most Compassionate, the Merciful.)

Innaa aatainaa kal Kausar. Fasallay lay Rabbayka wanhar. Inna shanay-aka howal abtar.

To thee have We granted the Fount (of abundance). Therefore pray to your Lord and make a sacrifice. Surely your enemy is the one cut off (from good).

5. RUKOO : Bend from the waist, resting both hands on the knees with eyes fixed at a point midway between the toes and say : "Subhana Rabbee-Al-Azeemay wa bay Hamdeh" ("Free from all defects is my Lord, and with His praise I bow") Or "Subhan Allah" 3 times ("Glory to God.")

(Women should rest their hands on their thighs and men on their kness as in Fig. 11.)

Note :— Immediately after Rukoo and Sajdah one must recite Salawat.

6. QAYAAM BAAD RUKOO : Resume erect posture, saying "Samey-Allaho Layman hamedah" (God listens to one who praises Him.")

7. FIRST SAJDAH : It is performed by prostrating on the ground (Fig. 12) with the forehead resting on Sajdagah, the palm of the hands, the knees and the toes touching the ground and saying :

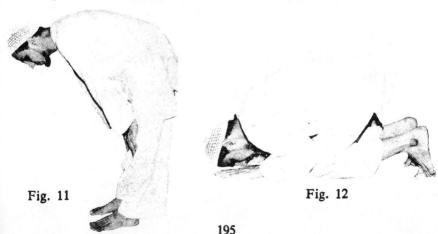

Fig. 11   Fig. 12

195

Subhana Rabbee-al-aa-laa Wa Bey Hamdeh." or 3 times Subhan Allah	Free from all defects is my All-Highest Lord, and with His praise I adore Hiim

NOTE : When going into Sajdah men should first rest their hands on the ground, but women need not. During Sajdah, women should rest their elbows on the ground but men should not.

8. SITTING BETWEEN THE TWO SAJDAHS : Sit up in a kneeling position with the ankle of the right foot in the sole of the left, hands resting on thighs, and say :

"Astaghfir-oollaha Rabbee wa Atoobo Ilaih"	I ask God, my Lord, to cover up my sins and unto Him I turn repentant.

9. SECOND SAJDAH : The adoration described in (7) above is repeated.

NOTE : Before and after the Rukoo and after each Sajdah it is preferable to say without moving, "Allaho Akbar."

10. Sit up for a moment and then rise (a man must support himself with his hands on the ground for rising and a woman should support herself with her hands on her legs and rise) to begin the second rakat and reciting in the process :

"Bay Hawlillahay wa Qoowateyhee Aqoomo wa Aqud."	Due to the vigour given by Allah and because of the vitality from Him I rise and stand.

The Second Rakat

1. Recite Sura-al-Hamd as in the first Rakat.
2. Recite Sura Tauheed (The Unity) CXII :
   Bism-illah-ir-Rahman-ir-Raheem.

(In the name of God, the Most Compassionate, the Merciful.)

"Qul-ho-Wallaho Ahad; Allah-hus-Samad; Lam yalid wa lam youlad, Wa lam yakunl lahoo kofowan ahad."	Say : He is God, the One, the Unique. God the Changeless the Independent. He begets not, nor is He begotten. And equal to Him there is no one.

QUNOOT :

3. Raise the hands in a posture of begging (see Fig. 13) this is know as "Qunoot" — and say either of the two Dua's given below or any other preferred :

Fig 13

"Rabbana Aatayna Fiddoonya Hasanatawn wa fil Aakheratey Hasanatawn wa Qena Azaban Nar."

O our Lord ! Bestow upon us good in this world and good in the Hereafter, and protect us from the torment of the fire.

or

"Rabbanaghfirli wa ley Walaydaiyya wa lil momeneena yauma yaqoomool hisab."

O Lord ! Forgive me and my parents and the faithful on the day of Judgment.

4. The Rukoo as described in para 5 of the first Rakat.
5. The Qayaam as described in para 6 of the first Rakat.
6. First Sajdah, as described in para 7 of the first Rakat.
7. Sitting, as described in para 8 of the First Rakat.
8. Second Sajdah as described in para 9 of the First Rakat.

9. The kneeling posture as described in para 8 of the first Rakat is resumed (see Fig. 14) — this is known as the "Tashahhud" — and say :

Fig. 14

197

"Ash-hado-an la ilaha illallha wahdahu la sharika lah, wa ash-hado anna Muhammadan Abdu-hoo wa Rasooluh"

I bear witness that there is no God except Allah, He is the One, without any partner; and I bear witness that Muhammad is His slave and Messenger.

10.   After this, whilst remaining in the same position, say ALLAHOOMMA SALLAY ALA MUHAMMADIN WA AALEY MUHAMMAD.

(O our God, bless Muhammad and the Progeny of Muhammad).—This is known as the "Salawat".

10A.   Now, in the case of the morning prayer which consists of only two rakats, recite the salaam as below, while still kneeling and terminate the Namaz by reciting "Allaho Akbar" three times whilst touching the ears as in para 2 of the first Rakat, each time:

"As-salaamo alaika aiyuhan-nabiyo wa rahmat-ullahey wa barakaatoh."

Peace be unto thee, O Apostle and the mercy of God and His bounties;

"As-salaamo alaina wa ala ibad-Illah-his-Saleyheen."

Peace be unto us and unto the virtuous servants of God.

"As-salaamu alaikum wa rahmat-ullahey wa barakaatoh."

Peace be unto ye all, and the mercy of God and His bounties.

11.   Then if the prayer is of more than two rakats, stand to begin the third rakat.

The Third Rakat

1.   Recite the Sura-al-Hamd; or "Tesbeehaate Arbaa" which is:

Subhaan Allahey Wal-Hamdo lillahey wala Ilaha Illallaho Wallaho Akbar

Glory to God, all praise belongs to God, and there is no God but Allah and God is Great.

2.   Rukoo as described in para 5 of the first Rakat.

3.   Qayam as described in para 6 of the first Rakat.

4.   First Sajdah as described in para 7 of the first Rakat.

5.   Sitting up as described in para 8 of the first Rakat.

6.   Second Sajdah as described in para 9 of the first Rakat.

7. Sitting up as in para 10 of the first Rakat.

Now, in case of the Maghrib prayer which consists of only three rakats; recite the Salaam as in 10A of 2nd Rakat and end the prayer. But in case of the Zohr, Asr and Isha prayers, stand up for the Fourth Rakat.

The Fourth Rakat

1. Recite the Sura-al-Hamd or Tasbeehaate Arbaa as in 3rd Rakat.
2. Rukoo as in para 5 of the first Rakat.
3. Qayam as in para 6 of the first Rakat.
4. First Sajdah, siting up and second Sajdah as in paras 7, 8 and 9 respectively of the first Rakat.
5. Tashahhud and Salawat as in paras 9 and 10 of the second Rakat.
6. Salaam as in para 10A of the second Rakat.

The Namaz may be followed by the Tasbeeh (rosary) and two Dua's given below, or any supplication the devotee may wish to make, then the Sajdah-i Shukr (the adoration of thanksgiving) and finally the Ziarat.

Tasbeeh

A Tasbeeh is a rosary having 100 beads.

The following Tasbeeh is to be recited after every Namaz and is known as Tasbeeh-e-Zahra.

> 34 times Allaho Akbar (God is Great)
> 33 times Alhamdo Lillah (All praise be for God)
> 33 times Subhan-Allah (Glory to God)

After the above Tasbeeh one should recite the following Dua: 3 times. Bism-illah-ir-Rahman-ir-Raheem. ("In the name of God. The Merciful, The most Compassionate.")

"Astaghferullah Hul Lezee, La Ilaha Illah Howal Haiyul Qayum Ar-Raman Nir-Rahim, Zul Jalaley Wul Ikrame, Wa Atoo Bo Ilai." which means:

I seek pardon from God. There is no God but Allah,
The merciful, The compassionate. Lord of bounty,
majesty and power, and unto Him I turn repentant.

After this the following Dua, known as Dua Hifzo Iman is recommended.

Dua Hifzo Iman

Bism-illah ir-Rahman-ir-Raheem

(in the Name of Allah, The Merciful, The Most Compassionate)

Razeeto billahey rabbun, wa bey Muhammadın sallallaho 'alaihey wa aalehi wa sallam nabian, wa bil Islamey deenan, wa bil Quraney kitabun, wabbil Kaabatey Qiblatun, wa bey Ali-yin waliyan wa imama, wabil Hasan wal Husain, wa Ali-ibnil Husain, wa Muhammad ibne Ali, wa Jafar ibne Muhammad, wa Moosa ibne Jafar, wa Ali ibne Moosa, wa Muhammad ibne Ali, wa Ali ibne Muhammad, wa Hasan ibne Ali, wal Hujjat ibnil Hasan, salawatullahey 'alaihim a-immatan. Allahoomma innee razeeto beyhim a immatun fa-arzeni lahoom innaka' ala kulley shai-in Qadeer.

"I willingly believe in the light of reason that Allah is my Rab (Lord), Muhammad (blessing of Allah upon him and his Progeny) is my Nabee (Prophet), Islam is my Deen (Religion), Quran is my Kitab (Book), Kaaba is my Qibla. Ali is my Walee (Master) and Imam (Guide); and I further willingly submit in the light of reason that Hasan and Husain, Ali Ibne* Husain, Muhammad Ibne Ali, Jafar Ibne Muhammad, Moosa Ibne Jafar, Ali Ibne Moosa, Muhammad Ibne Ali, Ali Ibne Muhammad, Hasan Ibne Ali and Hujjat Ibne Hassan, blessing of Allah be upon them all, are my Imams O Allah! I have willingly submitted in the light of reason to the belief that they are my Imams so Thou make them pleased with me. Verily! Thou has power over all things."

*Ibne means son of.

SAJDAH-I-SHUKR

The worshipper prostrates himself in a Sajdah and utters any words of thanksgiving and repentance which need not be in Arabic.

Finally, the following Ziarat ought to be recited:

Ziarat

1. *Facing slightly right of the Qibla.*
   "As Salaamo Alaika Yaa Aabaa Abdilla.
   As Salaamo Alaika Yub-ne Rasoolullah

As Salaamo Alaika Yub-ne Amir-il-Momeneen
As Salaamo Alaika Yub-ne Fatemetuz-Zahra Syedetay
Neesaa-il-Aalemeen.
As Salaamọ alaika wa rahmat-ullahey wa barakaatoh."

2. *Facing a little further towards the right than above.*

"As Salaamo Alaika yaa Garib-ul-Gurba,
As Salaamo Alaika yaa Sultan ya Ali Yibne Moosur-Reza
Wa Rahmatullahi wa Barakaatuh."

3. *Facing straight towards Qibla.*

"As Salaamo Alaika Yaa Saheb-uz-Zaman
As Salaamo Alaika Yaa Khaleefetar Rahman
As Salaamo Alaika Yaa Imamul Inse Wul Jaan
As Salaamo Alaika Yaa Muzharal Imam
As Salaamo Alaika Yaa Shareekul Quran
As Salaamo alaika wa rahmat-ullahey wa barakaatoh."

Meanings of Ziarat

1

"Peace be upon thee, O Aabaa Abdilla (pet name for
Imam Husain).
Peace be upon thee, O son of the Holy Prophet, (The
Holy Prophet always called his grandson Imam Husain
his son).
Peace be upon thee, O son of Hazrat Ali, the Commander
of the faithful.
Peace be upon thee, O son of Janab-e-Fatima Zahra, Chief
of the women of the world
Peace be upon thee and the mercy of God and his
bounties."

2

"Peace be upon thee, O one who lies far away from his
domain.
Peace be upon thee, O Ruler, O Ali son of Moosur-Reza.
And the mercy of God and His bounties."

3

"Peace be upon thee, O king of the times.
Peace be upon thee, O merciful leader.

Peace be upon thee, O Imam of the jinns and men.

Peace be upon thee, O companion of the Quran.

Peace be upon thee and the mercy of God and His bounties."

Ziarat of 14 Masooms and of the Martyrs of Kerbala

The following is a Ziarat which may be recited and is highly reccommended.

Bismilla Hir Rahman Nir Rahim. (In the name of Allah, the Merciful, the Compassionate.)

As Salaamo Alaika Ayyo han Nabiyo wa Rahmatullahi wa Barakaatuh

As Salaamo Ala Aliyin Amiril Momeneen

As Salaamo Ala Fatemetuz–Zahra Syedetay Neesaail Aalemeen

As Salaamo Alal Hasan wul Husain Syeday Shababey Ahlil Jannat

As Salaamo ala Ali Ibnil Husain Zain-ul-Abedin

As Salaamo ala Muhammad-Ibne Ali Baqir-Ilmin Nabiyeen

As Salaamo Ala Jafar-ibne Muhammadus Saadeeq.

As Salaamo Ala Musa-ibne Jafar-ill Kazeem

As Salaamo Ala Ali Ibne Moossur-Reza

As Salaamo Ala Muhammad-Ibne Ali-yil Jawad

As Salaamo Ala Ali Ibne Muhammad Haadi

As Salaamo Ala Hasan-Ibne Ali-iz-Zaki Askeri

As Salaamo Alul Hujjut-tib-nil Hasan-il-Faa-e-mil Mahdi

As Salaamo Alaikoom Shohedaa-e-Kerbala Jameeaun wa rahmat-ullahey wa barakaatoh."

Meaning:

Peace be upon thee, O Apostle and the mercy of God and His bounties.

Peace be upon thee, O Hazrat Ali, Commander of the faithful.

Peace be upon thee, O Janab-e-Fatima, Chief of the women of the world.

Peace be upon thee, O Imam Hasan and Imam Husain, Chiefs of the youths of paradise.

Peace be upon thee, O Imam Ali, son of Imam Husain, the Ornament of worshippers.

Peace be upon thee, O Imam Muhammad, son of Imam Ali, the Exponent of sciences.

Peace be upon thee, O Imam Jafar, son of Imam Muhammad, The True.

Peace be upon thee, O Imam Moosa, son of Imam Jafar, The Patient.

Peace be upon thee O Imam Ali, son of Imam Moosa, The Agreeable.

Peace be upon thee, O Imam Muhammad, son of Imam Ali, The Munificent.

Peace be upon thee, O Imam Hasan, son of Imam Ali, The Guide.

Peace be upon thee, O Imam Muhammad, son of Imam Hasan, The One whom we await.

Peace be upon all the Martyrs of Kerbala and the Mercy of God and His bounties.

This Ziarat may be followed by two rakats Sunnat Namaz.

Tasbeeh after every Namaz

It is highly recommended to recite the following Tasbeehs after each namaz along with the Tasbeeh-e-Zahra.

After Morning Prayers: La Ilaaha Illallah al Malekul Haqqul Mubeen. (There is no God except Allah, Who is the Sovereign Lord and Truth Manifest.)

After Zohar Prayers: Allahoomma Sallay Ala Muhammadin wa Aaley Muhammad (O God, send Thy blessings on Muhammad and his Progeny.)

After Asr Prayers: Astaghferullaha wa atoobo ilaih. (I seek pardon from God and unto Him I turn repentant.)

After Maghrib Prayers: La Ilaaha Illallah Muhammudun Rasoolallah. (There is no God but Allah, and our Prophet Muhammad Mustafa is the Messenger of God.)

After Isha Prayers: Subhaan Allahey Wal-Hamdo lillahey wa-la ilaha illallah wallaho Akbar, Wa la havla wa la qoovata illa billa hill Ali-yil Azeem. (Glory to God and all praise for Him, there is no God but Allah, Allah is Great, and there is neither might nor power but in Him.)

Namaz-e-Ayat

This prayer is Wajib at the time of the manifestation of any of the "signs of God", which show his Power and Glory, such as earthquakes, total (or nearly total) eclipses of the sun and the moon, severe tornadoes, hurricanes, and similar Acts of God.

The prayer consists of ten rukoos, five qunoots and four Sajdahs, as follows :

(1) Perform Niyyat, and recite Takbirat-ul-Ehram.

(2) Recite Sura al-Hamd, followed by any other Sura, e.g., the Sura-az-Zalzala :

Bism-Illah-ir-Rahman-ir-Raheem

(In the name of God, the Most compassionate the Merciful)
SURA AZ-ZALZALA (The Convulsion) XCIX.

Izaa zulzay-latil arzo zilzaalaha; Wa akhrajatil arzo asqaalaha; wa qaalal insaano maalaha; Yaumaayzin tohadday so akhbaraha; Bay anna rabbaka awhaa laha; Yaumaay zeen yesdoroon-naaso ashtaa-ta; Lay yorau aamaalahoom; Fa main yaamal misqala zarratin khairain-yarah; Wa mainyaamal misqala zarratin sharrain yarrah.	When the Earth shall tremble with a mighty shaking, Her burdens from within outbreaking, And man will ask, "Wherefore is she aching?" She, on that Day, her statements making, Inspired thereto by thy Heavenly King. On that Day shall men issue forth (from their graves) separately, to witness their doings. Then whoever hath done an iota of good shall see it; And whoever hath done an iota of wrong shall see it.

(3) First rukoo.

(4) Straighten up and again recite Sura-al-Hamd and Sura Tawhid, followed by

(5) Qunoot.

(6) Second Rukoo.

204

(7) Straighten up again and recite Sura-al-Hamd and any other Sura.

(8) Third rukoo.

(9) Straighten up again and recite Sura-al-Hamd and Sura Tawhid.

(10) Second Qunoot.

(11) Fourth rukoo.

(12) Straighten up again and recite Sura-al-Hamd and any other Sura.

(13) Fifth rukoo.

(14) Straighten up and say "Same-Allaho Liman Hamidah" and go into first Sajdah.

(15) Sit up and ask for the Lord's pardon. (As in No. 8 of First Rakat, page 196).

(16) Second Sajdah.

(17) Stand up and recite Sura-al-Hamd and Sura Tawhid

(18) Third Qunoot.

(19) Sixth rukoo.

(20) Straighten up and recite Sura-al-Hamd and any other Sura.

(21) Seventh rukoo.

(22) Straighten up and recite Sura-al-Hamd and Sura Tawhid.

(23) Fourth Qunoot.

(24) Eighth rukoo.

(25) Straighten up and recite Sura-al-Hamd and any other Sura.

(26) Ninth rukoo.

(27) Straighten up and recite Sura-al-Hamd and Sura Tawhid.

(28) Fifth Qunoot.

(29) Tenth rukoo.

(30) Straighten up as in 14 above and go into Sajdah (Third Sajdah).

(31) Sit up and ask for the Lord's pardon.

(32) Fourth Sajdah.

(33) Tashahhud, Salawat and Salam.

It will be noticed that the Namaz-e-Ayat consists of two rakats; each rakat having five rukoos and the qunoot being recited before each alternate rukoo; i.e. before the 2nd and 4th rukoo in the first rakat and before the 6th, 8th and 10th rukoo in the second rakat.

With a little concentration, it will not be found too difficult to remember the method of this prayer.

This prayer helps to keep the mind alert and active in spite of distress and anxiety.

Namaz–e–Shab

This Namaz is not Wajib, but it is highly recommended. It can be prayed after midnight till true dawn which is known as Subhe Saadiq (i.e. one hour and twenty minutes before sunrise).

The Ayats of the Holy Quran referring to the Namaz-e-Shab say:

Truly the rising by night is most potent for governing (the soul) and most suitable for (forming) the word (of prayer and praise). (73 : 6)

Their limbs do forsake their beds of sleep while they call on their Lord in fear and hope. And they spend (in charity) out of the sustenance which we have bestowed on them.

(32 : 16)

And pray in the small hours of the morning an additional prayer (of spiritual profit) for thee. Soon will thy Lord raise thee to a station of praise and glory. (17 : 79)

The Namaz consists of 3 parts and a total of 11 Rakats to be prayed as follows:

  a) *Niyat*: Namaz-e-Shab—8 Rakats. (4 Namazs' of 2 Rakats each, to be prayed like the morning Namaz.
  b) *Niyat*: Namaz-e-Shafa-2 Rakats. (like the morning Namaz).
  c) *Niyat*: Namaz-e-Witr—One Rakat. (as follows)
     1. Recite Sura-Al Hamd—Once
     2. Recite Sura Tauhid—Thrice
     3. Recite Sura Falak—Once
     4. Recite Sura Nas—Once
     5. Qunoot—as in any 2nd Rakat. Keep hands in same position for Dua (supplication), and after Dua repeat whilst in the position of Qunoot.

1) 100 times:
   Astaghfir-Ullaha Rabbi wa Atoobo Ilaih (if necessary one can keep a Rosary (Tasbeeh) in hand, to help keep count.
2) Recite 40 names of male momeens, each to be preceded by Allah-hoom mughfirlil. If it is difficult to recall the names of 40 momeens, then recite "Allah-hoom mughfirlil momeeneen wul momeenat."
3) Then repeat 300 times "Al-afv (please forgive), and complete the namaz by Rukoo, Sajdah and Salaam.

Namaz–e–Jamat

(Congregational Prayer)

There is much more reward attached to prayers offered in a congregation than when offered alone. Reward increases in proportion to the number of persons offering prayers in a congregation.

For the five daily prayers, there must be at least two persons to form a congregation. One an Imam, and the other a Mamoom. An Imam is one who leads the prayers, and a Mamoom is one who follows the Imam. In the case of Friday prayers however, there must be at least five persons—one leader and four followers.

In congregational prayers, Mamooms have to follow the Imam in all actions. The Niyat should be performed by Mamooms immediately after the Imam has done so. It must be borne in mind, that the Mamooms directly behind the Imam should perform the Niyat very quickly, as then the people next to them and behind them can pick up without delay. Rukoo, sajdah, etc., should all be performed after the Imam. In fact, a Mamoom has to follow the Imam in all respects.

The most important things to be remembered are:

1. The Takbirat-ul-Ehram should under no circumstances be said before the Imam has done so. (The phrase Allaho Akbar is called Takbeer. And Allaho Akbar recited just after determining the Niyat is called Takbirat-ul-Ehram.)

2. Whilst in the position of Qayam, no sura is to be recited in the first two rakats by the Mamoom who has merely to stand to attention behind the Imam.

In the Fajr, Maghrib and Isha prayers, the Imam recites the Suras during Qayam for the first two rakats with his voice raised. Here if the Mamoom is unable to hear the recition he may if he so wishes utter "Zikr", which consists of repeating "Subhan-Allah" or "Alhamdo—Lillah" or other appropriate words. In the first two rakats when the Imam completes reciting Sura Al-Hamd, the word "Ameen" should never be said by the Mamoom, but he may say "Alhamdo-Lillah" if he so wishes.

3. In the third and the fourth rakats the Mamoom should recite Tasbeehaate Arbaa thrice or Sura-al-Hamd once.

4. Salaam should never be recited by the Mamoom before the Imam.

A Mamoom, in case he is late, can join the congregation only in the state of Qayam, or in the Rukoo before the Imam has raised his head from the Rukoo.

A Mamoom can offer any of his prayers, Ada or Qaza in any prayer of the congregation. For example, a Mamoom can offer his Zohar or any other prayer whilst the Asr or any other prayer is being said by the congregation. Great care must be taken to perform "Niyat" for the prayer he may be offering.

Congregational prayers can be held in one's home or anywhere else. But the greatest reward is attached to the congregational prayers in the mosque.

In a congregation each row of devotees should be formed after the one in front is completed.

Qaza Namaz.

It is obligatory for every Muslim to offer his prayers during the times fixed. If however for some reason this has not been possible and the time has passed, there is a compensation. The Namaz may be offered as Qaza. A Qaza Namaz is simalar in all respects to the regular Namaz, except that in the Niyat, the word Qaza is to be used before "Wajib Qurbatan Ilallah"

FOR THOSE UNABLE TO PERFORM THE REGULAR NAMAZ

1. If a man cannot stand without support, he should (or may) stand with support.

2. If he cannot stand, even with support, he should sit without support.

3. If he cannot sit without support, he must sit with support. He may even sit on a chair, using a table for Sajdah.

4. If this is not possible, then he must lie on his right side, facing Qibla.

5. If this is not possible, then he must lie on his left side, facing Qibla.

6. If this is not possible, then he should lie on his back, his feet towards Qibla.

In the last three alternatives, he should bow down for Rukoo and Sajdah; the bowing down for Sajdah should be more than that for the Rukoo. If he cannot bow down, he should perform Rukoo and Sajdah with his eyelids.

Ziarats
at
Different
Places

"Think not of those slain in God's ways as dead. Nay, they live, finding their sustenance in the Presence of their Lord." 3:169 The Holy Quran.

O God always give me grace to perform the Hajj and the Omrah, and to visit the tomb of Thy prophet — They blessings on him, and Thy mercy and favours on him and his Al (family) and the tombs of his Al, peace be on them, as long as Thou keepest me alive, in my present year and every future year.

Ziarats at Different Places

MESHED

1. Roza of Hazrat Imam Ali Reza
2. Masjid-i-Goharshad
3. Museum
4. Roza of Imamzada Sultan Ahmed

TEHRAN

1. Roza of Shah Abdul Azim
2. Roza of Hazrat Hamza Ibne-Imam Moosa-e-Kazim
3. Roza of Imamzada Shah Tahir
4. Roza of Imamzada Moosa
5. Koh-e-Bibi Shehrbanu
6. Roza of Imamzada Saleh-bin-Imam Moosa-e-Kazim at Shemiran

QUM

1. Roza of Bibi Massoma-e-Qum
2. Masjid-e-Hazrat Imam Hasan Askari near Roza.

IRAQ

KERBALA

1. Roza of Hazrat Imam Husain
2. Roza of Hazrat Ali Akbar
3. Roza of Hazrat Ali Asghar
4. Roza of Hazrat Abbas
5. Roza of Hazrat Ebrahim, descendent of Hazrat Imam Moosa Kazim
6. Roza of Hazrat Habib-ibne-Mazahir
7. Ganj-i-Shahidan
8. Katal Ghah
9. Garden of Hazrat Imam Jafar Sadiq
10. Garden of Saheb-ul-Asr
11. Khaimagah
12. Tal-e-Zainabia
13. Roza of Hazrat Hur (3 miles from Kerbala)
14. Roza of Janab Aun (6 miles from Kerbala)

MOOSAYAB (between Kerbala and Kazmain)

1. Roza of Hazrat Muhammad and Hazrat Ebrahim Ibne Hazrat Muslim (Tifflan-i-Muslim)
2. Roza of Hazrat Hamza Ibne-Hasan-Ibne Abdullah-Ibne Hazrat Abbas
3. Makam of Saheb-uz-Zaman

KAZMAIN

1. Roza of Hazrat Imam Moosa-e-Kazim
2. Roza of Hazrat Imam Muhammad Taqi
3. Mazar of Sheikh Moofid
4. Mazar of Sheikh Kooleyani
5. Mazar of Khwaja Nasiruddin Toosi

BAGHDAD

1. Masjid-e-Boorasa (between Kazmain and Baghdad)
2. Mazar of Janab Usman Ibne Saeed
3. Mazar of Janab Muhammad Ibne Usman
4. Mazar of Janab Ali Ibne Muhammad Foor
5. Mazar of Janab Husain Ibne Rooh
6. Mazar of Janab Qambar A.R. Ghulam-i-Hazrat Ali
7. Mazar of Janab Hafiz Muhammad-bin-Yaqoobi-Koolaini

} These persons were the Naibs of Sahebul-Asr during Ghaibat-e-Sughra

MADAYAN (SALMAN PAK) (30 miles from Baghdad)

1. Roza of Hazrat Salman Farsi
2. Roza of Hazrat Hoozaifa-i-Yamani
3. Roza of Hazrat Jabir-bin Abdullah Ansari
4. Masjid-i-Jooma (near Roza of Janab Salman Farsi
5. Taq-i-Kisra

BALAD (between Kazmain and Samarrah)

1. ROZA of Hazrat Muhammad-bin-Imam Ali Naqi

SAMARRAH

1. Roza of Hazrat Imam Ali Naqi

2. Roza of Hazrat Imam Hasan-Askari
3. Roza of Hazrat Bibi Hakima Khatoon-binte-Harzat Ali-Naqi
4. Roza of Hazrat Bibi Narjis mother of Saheb-uz-zaman
5. Cave of Saheb-uz-zaman (Maqam-e-Ghaibat)

HILA (between Kazmain and Najaf)
1. Roza of Janab Hamza
2. Roza of Janab Qasim-bin-Imam Moosa-e-Kazim
3. Roza of Janab Hazrat Ayub
4. Roza of Janab Danyal
5. Makam-i-Sahib-uz-zaman

NAJAF
1. Roza of Hazrat Ali
2. Roza of Hazrat Adam
3. Roza of Hazrat Koomail
4. Makam of Saheb-uz-zaman
5. Moosalla of Hazrat Imam Zain-ul-Abedin
6. Masjid-e-Hannana (between Koofa and Najaf)

MASJID-E-SAHLA
1. Kooba of Janab Ebrahim-ibne-Hassan-i-Mooana ibne-Hazrat Imam Hasan
2. Moosalla of Hazrat Imam Jafar Sadiq
3. Moosalla of Hazrat Ebrahim
4. Moosalla of Hazrat Idris
5. Moosalla of Hazrat Khizer
6. Makam-i-Saleheen
7. Makam-i-Hazrat Imam Jafar Sadiq
8. Makam of Janab Koomail Ibne Ziad
9. Mazar of Maysum-i-Tammar
10. Mazar of Zaid A.R., near Masjid-e-Sahela

KOOFA
1. Masjid-i-Koofa
2. Roza of Hazrat Muslim Ibne Aqil (cousin of Hazrat Imam Husain)
3. Roza of Hazrat Mokkhtar
4. Roza of Hani-ibne Urwa
5. Court-room of Hazrat Ali

6. Moosallas of several Prophets in Masjid-i-Koofa
7. Place where Hazrat Nooh made his boat
8. Roza of Janab-e-Khadijatul-Sogra-Binte - Hazrat Ali (outside Koofa Masjid)

SYRIA

DAMASCUS

1. Roza of Hazrat Bibi Zainab (at Zainabia)
2. Roza of Hazrat Janab Sakina Binte Imam Husain
3. Roza of Hazrat Ume Kulsum Binte Hazrat Ali
4. Roza of Hazrat Janab Salma and Janab Ome Habiba wives of the Holy Prophet
5. Roza of Hazrat Bibi Fizza (Kaniz of Bibi Fatema
6. Roza of Hazrat Hajar bin-Odey (Ashab of Hazrat Ali)
7. Roza of Hazrat Mikad-bin-Asvadul Kindi (Ashab of Hazrat Ali)
8. Roza of Hazrat Obay-i-Ibne-Kaab husband of Janab Halima Bibi (wet nurse of Hazrat Muhammad)
9. Place where the Head of Hazrat Imam Husain is asserted to be buried
10. Place where the Head of Hazrat Imam Husain was kept in Yazid's treasury
11. Roza of Hazrat Yahya-bin-Zakaria
12. Mimber of Hazrat Imam Zain-ul-Abedin
13. Roza of Janab Rukkaya Binte Hazrat Imam Husain
14. Prison for Ahl-ul-Bait
15. 1300 years old door in bazar of Sham
16. Ancient Masjid (building bult 3000 years ago)
17. Roza of Janab Abdullah-bin-Jafar-i-Tayyar
18. Roza of Janab Bilal (Moazzin)
19. Roza of Abdullah-bin-Omme-Maktoom (Moazzin)
20. Roza of Hazrat Abdullah-ibne-Hazrat Imam Zain-ul Abedin
21. Roza of Hazrat Abdullah-ibne-Hazrat Imam Jafar Sadiq
22. Roza of Fatima Soghra-binte-Hazrat Imam Husain
23. Gunj-i-Sar-i-Shohada

24. Mehrab where Hazrat Imam Zain-ul-Abedin used to pray Namaz
25. Place where Imam Zain-ul-Abedin prayed when he went to take the Head of Hazrat Imam Husain
26. Well of Nabi Hood and stone pot for Wazoo
27. Museum

SALEVA

1. Masjid-i-Sulaiman
2. Koh-i-Raqim
3. Small Masjid
4. Footmark of Hazrat Ali
5. Cave of Ashab-e-Kahf and their dog
6. Khotba written through figures by Hazrat Ali

ON OTHER HILL

1. Place where Kabeel killed Hazrat Habeel
2. Two eyes of the hill from which water drops like tears
3. Hazrat Jibrail's fingerprints
4. 40 Moosallas of Prophets in the Mosque

JORDAN

JERUSALAM (Baitul Mukkadas)

1. Masjid-i-Aqsa
2. Mehrab of Hazrat Ali
3. Room of Bibi Maryam
4. Room in which there are Moosallas of 40 Prophets
5. Stable of Hazrat Sulaiman (now closed)
6. Masjid-i-Sakhra (first Qibla)
7. Court room of Hazrat Sulaiman
8. Moosallas of 9 Prophets
9. Sakhratullah
10. Tongue of stone which replied to the Holy Prophet
11. Moosallas of Hazrat Sulaiman, Hazrat Dawood, Hazrat Ebrahim, Hazrat Muhammad and Hazrat Jibrail
12. Well of Rooh (now closed)
13. Roza of Hazrat Maryam
14. Ghar-i-Ambia (between Damascus and Jerusalam)
15. Roza of Nabi Ozair
16. Roza of Hazrat Moosa (10 miles from Jerusalam)

215

BAITULHEM: and CHURCH NO. 2
1. Christian monuments and birthplace of Hazrat Isa (Jesus)

HEBRON (KHAILILUR RAHMAN) (In the Mosque)
1. Roza of Hazrat Ebrahim Khalillullah
2. Roza of Bibi Sarah, w|o Hazrat Ebrahim
3. Roza of Hazrat Ishaq
4. Roza of Bibi Rafka, w|o Hazrat Ishaq
5. Roza of Hazrat Yaqoob
6. Roza of Bibi Lanika, w|o Hazrat Yaqoob
7. Roza of Hazrat Yousuf

SAUDI ARABIA

MECCA

Khana-e-Kaaba:
1. House of God and the birthplace of Hazrat Ali
2. Maqam-e-Ibrahim
3. Multazim (between Rukne-e-Yamani and Hajar-e-Aswad)
4. Mustajar (between Hajar-e-Aswad and door of Kaaba)
5. Hateem (Hazrat Ismail and Hazrat Hajra are said to be buried there)
5. Well of Zum Zum

Jannat-ul-Moa'lla
1. Grave of Ummul Mommeen Hazrat Khadijatul Kubra
2. Grave of Hazrat Amena (mother of the Holy Prophet)
3. Grave of Hazrat Abu Talib (uncle of the Holy Prophet and father of Hazrat Al)
4. Grave of Janab Abde Manaf (great grandfather of the Holy Prophet)
5. Grave of Janab Hashim (great grandfather of the Holy Prophet)
6. Grave of Hazrat Abdul Muttalib (grandfather of the Holy Prophet and other graves of Holy Personages)
   (Tombs on all these graves were destroyed by the late King Abdul Aziz Ibne Saud in 1926)

216

7. Ghar-e-Hira
8. Ghar-e-Saur

In Mecca City
1. Holy Prophet's birthplace
2. Hazrat Ibrahim's house
3. Hazrat Abu Talib's house
4. Hazrat Fatima's birthplace (daughter of the Holy Prophet)
5. Masjid-e-Jin
6. Masjid-e-Bilal

ARAFAT
1. Jabal-e-Rahmah
2. Masjid-e-Numrah

MINA
1. Masjid-e-Kheef
2. Masjid-e-Kausar

JEDDAH
1. Grave of Bibi Hawwa

MEDINA
1. Roza of the Holy Prophet
2. Hujra-e-Hazrat Fatima Zahra
3. Maqam-e-Hazrat Jibrail

JANNATUL BAQIE
1. Grave of Hazrat Fatima Zahra (Khatoon-e-Jannat, the daughter of the Holy Prophet)
2. Grave of Hazrat Imam Hasan
3. Grave of Hazrat Imam Ali Zain-ul-Abedin
4. Grave of Hazrat Imam Muhammad Baqir
5. Grave of Hazrat Imam Jafar Sadiq
6. Grave of Hazrat Abbas (Holy Prophet's uncle)
7. Grave of Hazrat Ibrahim (son of the Holy Prophet)
8. Grave of Hazrat Ummul Baneen (wife of Hazrat Ali A.S. and mother of Hazrat Abbas')
9. Grave of Hazrat Fatema-binte-Asad (wife of Hazrat Abu Talib and mother of Hazrat Ali

10. Grave of Hazrat Jafar Tayyar
    (Tombs on all these graves were destroyed by the late King Ibne-Saud in 1926).

MASJIDS IN MEDINA

1. Masjid-e-Ghammah (in the city)
2. Masjid-e-Quba (outskirts of Medina)
   (The first mosque on earth built by the Holy Prophet and Hazrat Ali
3. House of Hazrat Ali near Masjid-e-Quba
4. Masjid-e-Zuqiblatain (where Qibla was changed)
5. Masjid-e-Fatah
6. Masjid-e-Salman
7. Masjid-e-Fatima
8. Masjid-e-Mariyah Qibtiah
   (mother of Hazrat Ibrahim)
9. Masjid-e-Rajatus Shams
10. Bir-e-Ali (Well)
11. Masjid-e-Ali (also known as Masjid-e-Shajarah)-Miqat for Ehram

OHAD (On the outskirts of Medina)

1. Grave of Hazrat Hamza (uncle of the Holy Prophet S.A.)
2. Graves of other Shohada

Islamic Calendar

and

Important Dates

"Believe in God, for He is Perfect in Knowledge and Power, forgives sin and accepts repentance, and justly enforces His Law. Those who reject Him are but in deceit; His Glory is sung by the highest and the purest."

Islamic Calendar and Important Dates

There are twelve months in a Muslim year. Each month commences with the visibility of the New Moon.

These are:
1. Muharram
2. Safar
3. Rabi-ul-Awwal
4. Rabi-ul-Akhar
5. Jamadi-ul-Awwal
6. Jamadi-ul-Akhar
7. Rajab
8. Shaban
9. Ramazan
10. Shawwal
11. Zilkad
12. Zilhajj

MUHARRAM

Date   EVENT

1. Prophet Zakaria kept fast and invoked God for the birth of a son. (The prayer was accepted and Prophet Yahya was born.)
2. Imam Husain arrived in Kerbala 61 A.H.
3. Prophet Yousuf (Joseph) was rescued from the well.
5. Prophet Moosa (Moses) passed safely through the river Nile, while Fir'aun and his army were drowned.
7. Prophet Moosa talked with God on the mount of Toor. River Euphrates made out of bounds for Imam Husain and his entourage before Battle of Kerbala.
8. The camps of Ahl-ul-Bait surrounded by the enemy.
9. Prophet Younus (Jonah) extricated from the belly of a fish.
10. Martyrdom of Imam Husain and his companions 61 A.H.
11. Allama Hilli, a great scholar of Islamics, died in 726 A.H.
12. Ziarat of Imam Husain.

Date	EVENT

17. King Abraha's attack on the Khana-e-Kaaba. (The event is remembered in the annals of history and the year is named 'Ammul Feel' or The year of the Elephant).

22. Shaikh Toosi, a great authority on Islamic Sciences, died in 460 A.H.

25. Martyrdom of the 4th Imam, Hazrat Ali Zain-ul-Abedin, 95 A.H.

SAFAR

1. Battle of Siffin commenced, 37 A.H.
   Heads of the Martyrs of Kerbala brought to Damascus, 61 A.H.
   Zaid Bin Ali martyred, 122 A.H.

2. Martydrom of Hazrat Ammare Yasir, 25 A.H.

4. Death of Syed Murtaza, 436 A.H.

7. Birth of Imam Moosa Kazim at Abwa (a place between Mecca and Medina), 128 A.H.

9. Battle of Naherwan won by Hazrat Ali, 40 A.H.

10. Lailatul Hareer, 37 A.H.

12. Battle of Siffin won by Hazrat Ali, 38 A.H.

17. Martydrom of Imam Ali Reza, 203 A.H.

20. Chehlum (40th day) of the Martyrs of Kerbala.
    Jabir Ibn-e-Abdullah Ansari, a pious companion and devoted friend of the Holy Prophet, first visited the graves of the Martyrs of Kerbala, in 61 A.H.

28. Death of the Holy Prophet, 11 A.H.
    Martyrdom of the second Imam, Hazrat Imam Hasan, 50 A.H.
    Death of Hujjatul Islam Maulana Shaikh Abdul Qasim Najafi Kashani, 1350 A.H.
    Death of Ayatullah Shaikh Muhammad Hassan Najafi, 1387 A.H.

RABI-UL-AWWAL

1. The day of Hijrat. The Prophet left Mecca leaving Hazrat Ali sleeping in his (the Prophets's) bed.

4. The Prophet emerged from the cave and set out for Medina.

221

Date	EVENT

5. Death of Janab Masooma-e-Qum (sister of Imam Ali Reza).
8. Martyrdom of Hazrat Imam Hasan Askari, 260 A.H.
9. Ahl-ul-Bait changed their mourning dress.
10. Death of Abdul Muttalib 44 years before Hijrat.
12. The Holy Prophet arrived at Kuba, a place on the outskirts of Medina, and waited for Hazrat Ali and the other members to join him.
17. The Holy Prophet's departure from Kuba for Medina. The birth of the Holy Prophet, 52 B.H. (570 A.D.). The birth of Hazrat Imam Jafar-e-Sadiq, 83 A.H. (702 A.D.)
18. The birth of Janab Kulsum (sister of Imam Husain).

RABI-UL-AKHIR

8. The birth of Hazrat Imam Hasan Askari, 232 A.H. (847 A.D.)

JAMADI-UL-AWWAL

10. Muhammad bin Makki, an adherent of Ahl-ul-Bait, martyred, 782 A.H.
14. Death of Janab-e-Fatema Zahara [(the beloved and only daughter of the Holy Prophet)] 11 A.H. 632 A.D.
15. Birth of Hazrat Imam Zain-ul-Aabedin, 37 A.H. (658 A.D.)

JAMADI-UL-AKHAR

20. The birth of Janab-e-Fatema Zahara [(the beloved daughter of the Holy Prophet)] 8 years before Hijrat (615 A.D.)
26. Martyrdom of Hazrat Imam Ali Naqi, 254 A.H. (868 A.D.)

RAJAB

1. Birth of Hazrat Imam Muhammad Baqir, 57 A.H. (676 A.D.)
7. Birth of Hazrat Abbas Alamdar-e-Husain, 26 A.H. (654 A.D.)
10. Birth of Hazrat Imam Muhammad Taqi, 195 A.H. (811 A.D.)

Date	EVENT

13. Birth of Hazrat Ali Amir-ul-Momineen, (599 A.D.) 22 B.H.
15. Martyrdom of Hazrat Imam Jafar Sadiq, 148 A.H. (765 A.D.)
16. Imamat Day of Hazrat Moosa Kazim.
20. Birth of Janab-e-Sakina (daughter of Imam Husain),
24. Birth of Janab Ali Asgar (son of Imam Husain). Hazrat Ali's conquest of Khyber, the invincible fort of the Jews, 7 A.H.
25. Martyrdom of Hazrat Imam Moosa Kazim, 183 A.H. (793 A.D.)
26. Death of Hazrat Abu Talib.
27. Meraj, 621 A.D.

SHABAN

1. Birth of Janab-e-Zainab (sister of Imam Husain), 6 A.H. (627 A.D.)
3. Birth of Hazrat Imam Husain, 4 A.H. 626 A.D.
5. Birth of Janab Ali Akbar (son of Imam Husain).
7. Birth of Janab Kasim (son of Imam Hasan).
15. Birth of Hazrat Imam Mahdi Saheb-uz-Zaman, 255 A.H. (869 A.D.)

RAMAZAN

10. Death of Ummul Momeneen Bibi Khadeeja, the first wife of the Holy Prophet and the first lady in Islam.
15. Birth of Hazrat Imam Hasan, 3 A.H. (625 A.D.)
19. The first Imam, Hazrat Ali wounded in the Mosque at Kufa whilst praying, 40 A.H.
21. Martyrdom of Imam Hazrat Ali, 40 A.H. (652 A.D.)

SHAWWAL

1. I'd-ul-Fitr (Ramazan I'd).
8. Holy shrines in Jannat-ul-Baqi destroyed by Ibne Saud in 1343 A.H. (1925 A.D.)
10. Ghaibat (occultation) of Imam Saheb-uz-Zaman began, 328 A.H. (939 A.D.)

Date   EVENT

.ZILKAD

11. Birth of Hazrat Imam Ali Reza 148 A.H. (765 A.D.)
25. Birth of Hazrat Ibrahim (Prophet Abraham).
    Birth of Hazrat Esa (Prophet Jesus Christ).
29. Martyrdom of Hazrat Imam Muhammad Taqi 220 A.H. (865 A.D.)

ZILHAJJ

7. Martyrdom of Hazrat Imam Muhammad Baqir, 116 A.H. (733 A.D.)
9. Martyrdom of Hazrat Muslim bin Aquil.
10. I'd-uz-Zoha (Bakri I'd).
15. Birth of Hazrat Imam Ali-un-Naqi, 212 A.H. (828 A.D.)
16. Death of Janab-e-Zainab.
18. I'd-e-Ghadir.
23. Martyrdom of the sons of Hazrat Muslim ibne Aquil.
24. I'd-e-Mubahala.

224

Glossary
of
Important
Terms

"O my Lord: increase me in knowledge." The Holy Quran
2:114

"Those who reject the light of Truth are obstinate. Why should they persist in evil ways when the Clear Evidence has come before them? The straight Religion is simple; to adore with a pure heart the God of Truth, to draw nigh to Him in prayer sincere, and to serve our fellow-creatures in charity and love."

"To do aught else is to fall from Grace. But Faith and Good Life lead straight to the Goal, the beauteous Gardens of Bliss Eternal, and the mutual good pleasure of the Soul in her Lord. They are the Khairul-Bareeya (The best creatures)."

Glossary of Important Terms

Allaho Akbar	..	God is Great.
A.S.	..	(Short for "Alaihis Salaam") May peace be upon him.
A.H.	..	Short for "After Hijrat"—the day the Holy Prophet left Mecca for Medina.)
Azan	..	Call to Prayer.
Aqeeqa	..	A custom observed by Muslims on the birth of a child. The hair on the head of the infant is shaved on the 7th day and an animal is sacrificed.
Arsh	..	Throne.
Akhirat	..	Hereafter.
Aman	..	Peace or Tranquillity.
Ambia	..	Plural of Nabi or Prophet.
Bismillah	..	In the name of Allah.
Balig	..	Of age. For the purpose of fulfilling religious obligations, a boy becomes Baligh on completion of his fifteenth year and a girl in her ninth year.
Gharib-ul-Watan	..	Foreigner.
Ghibat	..	Backbite.
Ghuroob-i-Aftab	..	Setting of the sun.
Haram	..	Acts prohibited by Islam.
Halal	..	Religiously allowed.
Hafiz	..	Preserver.
Hajat	..	Need.
Haq	..	Right.
Hazir-o-Nazir	..	Omnipresent.
Hijrat	..	The day the Holy Prophet left Mecca for Medina.

Ibaadat	..	Devotion, worship.
Iman	..	Faith.
Insha-Allah	..	God willing.
Injil	..	The New Testament.
Inteqaal	..	Death.
Istigfaar	..	Seeking forgiveness of God.
Iqamat	..	A call for prayer after Azan.
Jehad	..	To strive or fight in the way of God. Strive and striving can be of various kinds, not necessarily violent.
Jaahil	..	Illiterate.
Jism	..	Body.
Jannat	..	Paradise.
Kalema	..	Creed.
Khuda	..	Persian word for God.
Khuda Hafiz	..	May God preserve you, or May God keep you safe.
Kafan	..	The shroud for the dead.
Kafir	..	One who does not believe in God.
Kaaba	..	The cube-like structure in the centre of the Mosque at Mecca which contains the Hajarul-Aswad or the Black-Stone.
Khairaat	..	Almsgiving.
Laash	..	A dead body.
Marhoom	..	Deceased.
Masjid	..	Mosque.
Maatam	..	Mourning. A term used specially for the mourning of Imam Husain and the martyrs of Kerbala which is accompanied with the beating of chest and head.
Mohtaj	..	Needy.

227

Maut	..	Death.
Mazhab	..	Religion.
Mushkil-Kusha	..	Solver of difficulties.
Makruh	..	Things better avoided by Muslims though not prohibited outright.
Muslim	..	One who believes in Allah, His prophet Muhammad and the day of Resurrection, recites the Kalema, and accepts the commands of God and His Prophet as true.
Momin	..	The Muslim who believes in Tawheed, Adl, Naboovat, Imamat and Qiyamat.
Mushrik	..	One who believes that God has a colleague or a partner.
Munafiq	..	One who proclaims his belief in God and His Prophet, recites Kalema, but does not have faith in them at heart.
Mujtahid	..	A person who dedicates his life to the study of the Quran and Hadith and specialises in the knowledge of Islam.
Muqallid	..	One who follows a Mujtahid.
Mizan	..	A balance, the scales in which the actions of all men shall be weighed.
Mutah	..	A marriage contracted for a limited term.
Mimber	..	The pulpit in a Mosque from which the Khutba or Sermon is recited.
Munajat	..	Supplications.
Musalla	..	The prayer rug of a Muslim.
Muezzin	..	The caller of Azan.
Masoom	..	Sinless, infallible.
Mahsher	..	The eventual place of the gathering of souls.

Nabi	..	Prophet.
Nubuwat	..	The work of Prophethood.
Na-Baligh	..	A minor for the purpose of assuming Islamic duties.
Namaz	..	Prayer.
Nesha	..	Intoxication.
Niyat	..	Intention.
Nar	..	Hell fire.
Qiyamat	..	Day of Resurrection.
Qudrat	..	Nature.
Qurbani	..	Sacrifice.
Qibla	..	The direction of the Kaaba, in which all Muslims must pray.
Qamar	..	Moon.
Quraish	..	The Arabian tribe from which the Holy Prophet descended.
Qari	..	A term used for one who reads the Quran correctly and is acquainted with the science of reading it.
Roza	..	A fast..
Ruh	..	Soul.
Sunnat	..	Things recommended for a Muslim though not obligatory.
Salaam	..	Peace—Salutation.
Salaam Alai Koom	..	Peace be upon you. (A form of greeting.)
Shams	..	The sun.
Salaat	..	Prayers.
Swalawat	..	The reciting of 'Allahooma Swalle Ala Muhammad Wa Ale Muhammad. Meaning: O God, bless Muhammad and the progeny of Muhammad.

Sura	..	A chapter of the Holy Quran.
Sadaqah	..	Almsgiving.
Subah Saadiq	..	Early dawn. i.e. 80 minutes before sunrise.
Tauba	..	Repentance.
Taqleed	..	Performing deeds as prescribed by a Mujtahid.
Tafsir	..	A term used for a commentary of any book, specially of the Holy Quran.
Tasbeeh	..	A Rosary.
Takbir	..	The recitation of Allaho-Akbar.
Tarjuma	..	Translation.
Usool	..	Principles.
Wajib	..	Things which are obligatory for a Muslim to do.
Waaleed	..	Father.
Waaleda	..	Mother.
Wafat	..	Death.
Wiladut	.	Birth.
Wazu	..	Ablution for prayer or for any other purpose required for.
Zubur	..	The Psalms of David.
Zikr	..	Mention.
Zibah	..	To slaughter.

TRIBUTES TO HAZRAT ALI

"Had Ali been allowed to reign in peace" says Oelsner, "his vir-tues, his firmness, and his ascendancy of character would have perpetuated the old republic and its simple manners." The dagger of an assassin destroyed the hope of Islam. "With him," says Major Osborn, "Perished the truest-hearted and best Moslem of whom Mohammedan history has preserved the remebrance." Seven centuries before, this wonderful man would have been apotheosised; thirteen centuries later his genius and talents, his valour, would have extorted the admiration of the civilised world. As a ruler, he came before his time. He was almost un-fitted by his uncompromising love of truth, his gentleness, and his merciful nature, to cope with the Ommeyyades' treachery and falsehood.

(From The Spirit of Islam by Ameer Ali Page 283.)

"Had," says Sedillot, "the principle of hereditary succession (in favour of Ali) been recognised at the outset, it would have prevented the rise of those disastrous pretentions which engulf-ed Islam in the blood of Muslims.... The husband of Fatima united in his person the right of succession as the lawful heir of the Prophet, as well as the right by election. It might have been thought that all would submit themselves before his glory; so pure and so grand. But it was not to be."

In summing up Hazrat Ali's worth, Maswoodi says, "If the glo-rious name of being the first Muslim, a comrade of the Prophet in exile, his faithful companion in the struggle for the Faith, his intimate associate in life and his kinsman! if a true knowledge of the spirit of his teachings and of the Book; if self-abnegation and practice of justice; if honesty, purity and love of truth; if a knowledge of law and science, constitute a claim to pre-emin-ence, then all must regard Hazrat Ali as the foremost Muslim. We shall search in vain to find, either among his predecessors or among his successors, those virtues with which God had en-dued him."

Sermons of Hazrat Ali from Nahj-ul-Balagha
Have you fully realised what Islam is? It is a religion founded on truth. It is such a fountainhead of learning that from it flow out several streams of wisdom and knowledge. It is such a

231

lamp that from it several lamps will be lighted. It is a tall beacon lighting the path of God. It is a set of principles and beliefs which will satisfy every seeker of truth and reality.

Know you all that God has made Islam the most sublime path towards His Supreme Pleasure and the highest standard of His worship and obedience. He has favoured it with noble precepts, exalted principles, undoubtable arguments, unchallengeable supremacy and undeniable wisdom.

It is upto you to maintain the eminence and dignity granted to it by the Lord, to follow it sincerely, to do justice to its articles of faith and belief. to implicitly obey its tenets and orders, and to give it the proper place in your lives.

Salutations and Duas on Visiting A Graveyard.

When one visits a graveyard, it is always better to offer salutations to the 'Dwellers of the Graves'. One such salutation is given below:

"Us salaamo ala ahlidh-diyaray minal Momineena wal Mooslaymeena untoom lana faratoon wa nahno Insha-Allaho baykoom la hayqoon."

"Peace be upon you, O ye of the Believers and Muslims dwelling in these graves, ye have gone ahead of us. When God so willeth, we shall join you."

As one proceeds further towards the graves of one's near and dear ones, one should recite Sura Al-Hamd followed by Sura Tauheed three times. This should be followed by the Duas given below:

"Allah-hoom maghfirlil Momineena wal Mominaat, wal Mooslaymeena wal Mooslaymaat al ahya-ay minhoom wal amwaat. Taabay bainana wa bainahoom bil khairaat. Innaka moojibood dawaat. Innaka ala koolay shai-in-qadir."

"O our Lord! Forgive the faults of the believing men and women, and Muslim men and women, the dead and the living, and keep us in the company of the righteous. Indeed Thou art the Answerer of all prayers and Thou hast power over all things."

The above Dua should be immediately followed by the one given below:

"Innallaha wa malaa-ay katahoo you saloona allan Nabi, yaa aiyo hal lazeena aamanoo salloo alaihay wa sallaymoo tasleema. Allahoomma sallay ala Muhammadin wa Aalay Muhammad. Subhaana rabbayka rabbil izzatay amma yasayfoon. wa salaamoon alull moorsaleen wal hamdolillaahay rabbil aalameen."

"God and His angels send blessing on the Prophet. O ye who believe, send blessings on him and salute him with all respect. (O Lord! Bless Muhammad and the Progeny of Muhammad). Glory be to Thee Lord. The Lord of Honour and Power. He is free from what they ascribe to Him.

And peace be on the Apostles. and praise be to God the Lord and Cherisher of the worlds."

When leaving the graveyard, it is better if one prays to God for all those who are buried there. The same procedure should be followed but the intention (Niyat) should be for all those that are buried there.

DUA—E—MASHLOOL
(The Prayer of the Paralytic)

The effective prayer is undoubtedly an inspired work. Any one who is acquainted with the soul stirring experience of great religious thoughts cannot help seeing in these immortal words of Hazrat Ali the dazzling light of Universal Truth.

Imam Husain relates that once on a cold, wintry night he accompanied his father Hazrat Ali to the Sacred Mosque of the Kaaba and performed the circumambulations. The night was pitch dark and there was no one there except my father and myself. Everybody was asleep. Not a soul was stirring as it was the dead of night. Presently we heard a mournful voice of some one reciting the following poem:

"O Thou that answereth the prayers of the disconsolate in the depth of darkness;

O Thou that wardeth off the baneful influences of calamities and diseases.

233

Lo, those who surround the Kaaba sleep and wake up:

But Thou, Exalted be Thy Name, never sleepest.

Forgive me by the Grace of Thy Bounty and Thy Mercy.

O Thou towards whom all creation bows down in this
    Sanctuary !

If Thy Mercy be not such as giveth hope to the transgressors,
    Then who is there to take pity on the sinners except
    by Thy Bounty?"

The Story of Manzil Ibn Lahiq, the Paralytic

Imam Husain continues to relate :—

My father sent me towards the man who was reciting these
lines of poetry and I brought him with me into his presence.
Hazrat Ali asked his name and he said, "My name is Manzil Ibn
Lahiq. In my youth I was persisting in sin, while my father used
to guide me towards repentance. But I heeded him not. Instead
of listening to him I used to beat him. Now it came to pass that
my father had kept some money hidden away from me. One
day I found it and was going out with the money, to spend it
on my follies, when he stopped me and tried to take it away
from me, but I twisted his wrist and ran away with the money.
Thereupon my father kept a fast and went and performed the
rites of the Sacred Mosque. Then he lifted up his hands and
prayed that God may inflict upon me the disease of paralysis.
Hardly had he done so when I was struck with paralysis and my
father went back to his home. I then besought my father to pray
for my recovery in the same place where he had prayed for my
affliction. My father, in his infinite love and kindness, granted
my request and we both set out towards Mecca, but as my ill-
luck would have it, on the way thither my father's camel
suddenly took fright, and he was thrown from its back and killed
in a moment. Now I am left to spend the rest of my days in
this condition, helpless and forlorn, and people taunt me, saying
that I am being punished for courting my father's displeasure."

On hearing the sad tale, Hazrat Ali was moved by pity and
compassion and taught him the following prayer and said:

"Perform the ablutions and recite this prayer tonight". He did so, and the effect was miraculous ! Next morning when he came to my father, he was perfectly cured and carried the text of the prayer in his right hand and exclaimed, "Really this prayer is the 'Isme Azam' because when I lifted up my hands and read this dua several times, a deep sleep fell upon me and I dreamt that the Holy Prophet Muhammad came and massaged by body with his own hands. When I woke up, I found that the illness had completely departed from me. May God reward thee, O Amir-ul·Momineen for this miraculous prayer". In view of the above-mentioned incident, this dua is called **"The prayer of the paralytic"**.

Imam Husain continues to state that this dua contains the Isme-Azam. Whoever recites it will be relieved of sorrow; cured of illness; his debts will be paid up; his poverty will be changed to prosperity, his sins forgiven; his defects hidden; and he shall be granted Safety and Security from all evil, whether from satan or from any worldly potentate, and if any of God's obedient servants recite this prayer, the mountains can be moved from their place; the dead can be restored to life and water can be turned into ice thereby. Hence this prayer has come to us as a source of rejoicing and I have learnt it from my father. Imam Husain further directs that this prayer should never be recited in a state of impurity or pollution. This prayer is also referred to as "Dua-e-Khizr".

The Prayer

1

O Allah. I beseech Thee with (the help of) Thy Name : —
(with the help of) the Name of Allah. the Most Merciful, the Benign.

2

O Lord of Majesty and Generosity;
O Living; O Self-Subsisting.
O Ever-living, there is no God but Thou.

3

O Thou that art "He" of whom no one knoweth what "He" is, nor how "He" is, nor where "He" is, except "He".

4

O Lord of the Great Kingdom and Supremacy.
O Lord of Honour and Omnipotence:
O Sovereign Lord, O Holy One!
O Peace;
O Keeper of Faith; O Guardian
O Revered One; O Compeller;
O Superb.*

5

O Creator; O Maker of all things from nothing;†
O Artist; O Beneficient; O Administrator;
O Severe (in wrath); O Inventor; O Restorer;
O Originator; O Most Loving;
O Praised; O Adored.

6

O Thou that art distant yet near;
O Answerer of prayer; O Observer (of all deeds);
O Reckoner.

7

O Innovator; O Exalted;
O Unassailable; O Hearer.

8

O Knower; O Wise; O Bountiful;
O Forbearing; O Eternal; O Lofty; O Great.

9

O most Compassionate; O Giver of all good;
O most perfect Requiter of good and evil;
O Thou whose help is sought for.

---

* Surah 59, verse 24.
† Surah 59, verse 23.

10

O Majestic; O Glorious; O Trusted; O Guardian;
O Alleviator of suffering; O Fulfiller of hopes;
O Guide; O Magnanimous.

11

O Giver of guidance; O Commencer;
O First; O Last; O Evident; O Hidden.

12

O Established; O Everlasting;
O Knowing; O Ruler; O Dispenser of justice;
O Equitable; O Thou that disjoineth and uniteth;
O Pure; O Purifier; O Powerful;
O Almighty; O Great; O Magnificent.

13

O One; O Matchless; O Eternal; O Absolute;

O Thou that bareth none and is born of none; nor is there
equal unto Thee anyone; ‡ nor hath Thee any spouse; nor any
bearer of Thy burden; nor any consultant to give Thee advice;
nor does Thou need any supporter; nor is there with Thou any
other deity; There is no God but Thou, and Thou art far exalted
with great excellence above all that which the unjust folk do
say concerning Thee.

14

O High and Lofty; O most Glorious;

15

O Opener; O Diffuser of fragrance;
O Tolerant;

16

O Helper; O Victorious; O Overtaker;
O Destroyer; O Avenger; O Resurrector;
O Inheritor; O Seeker; O Conqueror;
O Thou from Whom no fugitive can escape.

---

‡ Vide Surah 112.

17

O Acceptor of repentance; O Ever-forgiving;
O Great Bestower; O Causer of all causes;
O Opener of doors (of relief and salvation):
O Thou that answerest howsoever Thou art invoked.

18

O Purifier; O Giver of manifold rewards; O Excuser;
O Pardoner; O Light of all lights;
O Director of all affairs.

19

O Ever Blissful;
O All-Aware;
O Protector; O Lumnious; O Seer;
O Supporter; O Great.

20

O Lone; O Unique; O Everlasting;
O Upholder; O Eternal and Absolute.

21

O Sufficer; O Healer; O Fulfiller of promises;
O Deliverer.

22

O Benefactor; O Beautifier; O Bestower of grace;
O Grantor of favours; O Gracious; O Peerless.

23

O Thou that being Exalted overwhelmest;
O Thou, that being Master of all, hast absolute power;
O Thou, who being hidden art well informed;
O Thou that being disobeyed forgiveth;
O Thou Whom no thought can fully comprehend; nor sight perceive nor from whom any impression is hidden, O Nourisher of Mankind: O Ordainer of every ones's destiny.

24

O Thou of Exalted position;
O Thou Formidable in Thy foundations;

O Changer of times; O Acceptor of sacrifice;
O Thou full of favours and benefactions;

O Lord of Honour and Supremacy; O All Merciful; O most Compassionate; O Thou that has each day a distinctive Glory while no aspect of Thy Glory is erased by the prominence of another aspect. O Thou that art present in every place.

25

O Hearer of all voices; O Answerer of prayers; O Giver of success in all requirements; O Fulfiller of all needs; O Bestower of blessings; O Thou that taketh pity on our tears.

O Thou that raiseth from the pitfalls; O Thou that relieveth agonies; O Thou that art the Cherisher of good deeds.

O Thou that raiseth men in rank and degree; O Thou that accedeth to requests; O Thou that bringeth the dead to life; O Thou that gathereth together that which is scattered.

O Thou that art informed of all intentions; O Thou that restoreth that which has been lost: O Thou that art not confused by a multiplicity of voices; O Thou that art not harassed by a multitude of petitions; and Whom no darkness can hide or cover; O Light of heaven and earth.

26

O Perfector of blessings; O Averter of calamities;
O Producer of zephyrs;
O Gatherer of nations; O Healer of disease;
O Creator of light and darkness;
O Lord of generosity and munificence;
O Thou whose throne no one can set foot !*

27

O Thou more generous than the most generous;
O Thou more munificent than the most munificent;
O Thou more keen of hearing than the most keen of hearing;
O Thou more keen of vision than the most perceiving; O Protecting neighbour of those that seek Thy neighbourhood.

---

* Surah AL ARAF — Verse 45.

O Refuge of the fearful; O Giver of shelter to those who flee unto Thee; O Patron of the faithful; O Helper of those that seek Thy help;

O ultimate Goal of those that aspire.

28

O Companion of all strangers; O Friend of all the lonely ones;

O Refuge of all outcasts;

O Retreat of all persecuted ones;

O Guardian of all those who stray.

29

O Thou that takest pity on the aged and decrepit; O Thou that nourisheth the little baby; O Thou that joineth together broken bones; O Liberator of all prisoners;

O Enricher of the miserable poor;

O Protector of the frightened refugees;

O Thou for Whom alone, are both destiny and disposal; O Thou for Whom all difficult things are simple and easy : O Thou that doth not need any explanation.

O Thou Mighty over all things; O Thou Knower of all things.

O Thou Seer of all things.

30

O Thou that maketh breezes blow;

O Thou that cleaveth the day-break;

O Reviver of the spirits; O Lord of Generosity and Clemency; O Thou in Whose hands are all keys.

31

O Hearer of all voices; O Thou earlier in time than all that have passed away; O Giver of life to every soul after death.

32

O my Means of defence in confronting hardships; O my Guardian in strange lands; O my Friend in my loneliness; O my Master in my bliss; O my Refuge at the time when: the journey doth tire me out and my kinsfolk hand me over to my foes.

And all my comrades forsake me.

33

O Supporter of those who have no support;
O Guarantor of those who have no guarantee;
O Wealth of those who have no wealth;
O Means of those who have no strength;
O Refuge of those who have no refuge;
O Treasure of those who have no treasure;
O Helper of those who have no helper;
O Neighbour of those who have no neighbour.

34

O my Neighbour that art adjacent; O my Support that art firm; O my God that art worshipped by virtue of positive knowledge (1); O Lord of the Ancient House (the Ka'ba); O Thou full of loving kindness; O nearest Friend.

35

Liberate me from the choking fetters, Remove from me all sorrow, suffering and grief, Protect me from the evil that I am unable to bear, and help me in that which I am unable to do.

O Thou that didst restore Joseph unto Jacob: (2)
O Thou that didst cure Job of his malady; (3) O Thou that didst forgive the fault of David; (4) O Thou that didst lift up Jesus and saved him from the clutches of the Jews; (5) O Thou that didst answer the prayer of Jonah from the darkness; (6) O Thou that didst choose Moses by means of Thine inspired words; (7) O Thou that didst forgive the omission of Adam (8) and lifted up Idris to an exalted station by Thy mercy; (9) O Thou that didst save Noah from drowning; (10) O Thou that didst destroy the former tribe of Ad and then Thamud, so that no trace of them remained, and destroyed the people of Noah aforetime, for verily they were the most unjust and most rebellious;

---

1. Belief in God must be by conviction, not by blind following.

See Quran

2 XII 99	5 IV 157, 158	8 II 37
3 XXI 84	6 XXI 87 88	9 XIX 56,57
4 XXXVIII 26	7 XIX 51,52	10 XXI 76

and overturned the ruined and deserted towns; (11) O Thou that destroyed the people of Lot; (12) and annihilated the people of Sho'aib; (13) O Thou that chose Abraham as a friend; (14) O Thou that chose Moses as one spoken unto; (15) and chose Muhammad (Thy blessings be upon him and his Progeny) as Thy Beloved; O Thou that gavest unto Luqman wisdom; (16) and bestowed upon Solomon a kingdom the like of which shall not be merited by anyone after him; (3) O Thou that didst afford succour unto the two-horned one against the mighty tyrants; (4) O Thou that didst grant unto Khizr immortality (5) and brought back for Joshua, the son of Nun, the sun after it had set; (6) O Thou that gave solace unto the heart of Moses' mother; (7) and protected the chastity of Mary, the daughter of Imran; (8) O Thou that didst fortify John, the son of Zacharias against sin (9) and abated the wrath for Moses; (10) O Thou that gave glad tidings of (the Birth of) John unto Zacharias; (11) O Thou that saved Ishmael from slaughter by substituting for him the Great Sacrifice; (12) O Thou that didst accept the offering of Abel and placed the curse upon Cain, (13) O Subduer of the alien hordes for Muhammad — the blessings of Allah be upon him and his Progeny — bestow Thy blessings upon Muhammad and his Progeny and upon all Thy Messengers and upon the Angels that are near Thee and upon all Thine obedient servants.

37

And I beg of Thee all the requests which anyone has begged of Thee with whom Thou has been pleased and unto whom Thou hast assured the granting thereof, O Allah O Allah, O Allah, O Most Merciful, O Most Merciful, O Most Merciful, O Most Beneficent, O Most Beneficent, O Most Beneficent, O Lord

---

See Quran

11 LIII 50-53	13 XXVI 189	15 IV 164
12 XXVI 172	14 IV 125	16 XXXI 12
3 XXXVIII 37	7 XX 40	11 XIX 7
4 XVIII 84-98	8 XIX 16-34	12 XXXVII 102-7
5 XVIII 66-83	9 XIX 12-15	13 V 27-30
6 XVIII 59-65	10 VIII 150-151	

of Majesty and Grace, O Lord of Majesty and Grace, O Lord of Majesty aand Grace. Here repeat seven times **"Through Thee"**

I beseech Thee with the help of all the Names whereby Thou hast named Thyself, or which Thou hast sent down in any of Thy inspired Scriptures, or which Thou hast inscribed in thy knowledge of the unknown; and (I beseech Thee) in the name of the honoured and exalted positions of Thy Throne, and in the name of the utmost extent of Thy Mercy as expressed in Thy Book (the Quran) and in the name of that which "If all the trees on the earth were to become pens and all the seven seas ink, the Words of Allah could not be fully written down. (14) "VERILY Allah is the Honoured. the Wise"; And I beseech Thee with the help of Thy Beautiful Names which Thou hast praised in Thy Book, saying, "Unto Allah belong the beautiful names — so call ye Him by Them"; (15) And Thou hast said "Call unto Me and I shall answer you"; (16) and Thou hast said, "And when My servants ask something of Me, lo, I am near, and I grant the prayer of the supplicant when he asks anything of Me. so pray ye unto Me and believe in Me, that ye may be made perfect"; (17) And Thou hast said, "O My servants who have wronged yourselves, despair not of the Mercy of Allah; verily Allah forgiveth all the sins; verily He is the Forgiving, the Merciful" (18).

38

Therefore I pray unto Thee, My God, and I ask Thee, My Cherisher and Sustainer, and I hope from Thee, my Chief, and I crave Thy acceptance of my prayer, O my Protector, even as Thou hast promised me, and I call upon Thee even as Thou hast commanded me — So, do unto me what pleases Thee O Generous One! **Here the Devotee should pray for the fulfilment of his valid desires.**

39

And all Praise be to Allah, the Cherisher and Sustainer of

See Quran

14 **XXXI** 27	16 **XL** 60	18 **XXXIX** 53
15 VII 180	17 II 186	

243

the worlds, and the blessings of Allah be upon Muhammad and all His Holy Descendents.

Translated by Mohammed Amir Hyder Khan.

HADEES-E-KISA

(The Event of The Blanket)

(How and for whom the Verse of Purity was revealed)

The fame and popularity of this Hadees is too well known, and none can deny its importance and authenticity. The verse of the Holy Quran **"Innama youreedoollaho lay-youz-hayba ankomoor-rijsa Ahlulbait wa you-tahay-rakoom tatheera".** meaning "Verily, verily Allah intendeth but to keep off from you (every kind of) uncleanliness, O ye people of the House, and purify you with a thorough purification". (Chp. 33, verse 33.) It was revealed to show the grandeur and the purity of the Ahl-ul-Bait. This Quranic verse is famous as the Ayat-e-Tathir, and is the basis of the Hadees-e-Kisa which points to the Ahl-ul-Bait.

At the revelation of this Ayat, the Holy Prophet (S. A.) assembled his daughter Fatima, her sons Hasan and Husain, and her husband Ali (who was also the cousin of the Prophet.) He covered them including himself under a blanket and addressed Allah as such :— **"Allahooma haa'oolaa-ay ahlo-baiti haa'oolaa-ay itrati"** "O Allah! these constitute my progeny. Keep them away from every kind of impurity, purified with a perfect purification".

Umme Salma, the wife of the Holy Prophet in whose house the Prophet was at that time, witnessing this marvellous occasion, humbly submitted to the Prophet, "O Messenger of Allah! may I also join this group?" To which the Prophet replied, "No, please remain where thou art".

The Holy Prophet has said:—"The likeness of my Ahl-ul-Bait is that of the Ark of Noah. Whoever got into it was saved, and whoever turned away from it got drowned and lost".

That the Ahl-ul-Bait enjoyed an exalted position by the order of Allah can be seen by the following Ayat of the Holy Quran:- "No reward do I ask of you except the love of those near of kin." Chp. 62, verse 23.

This verse is clear in its meaning that the Holy Prophet is being commanded by Allah to ask the believers to love his kith and kin, i.e. the Holy Ahl-ul Bait. This was the reward the Holy Prophet asked from his followers for having guided them all his life to the right path.

The Holy Prophet also said, "I leave behind among you, two Weighty Things, one of them is the Book of Allah and the other is My Itrat (progeny), who are My Ahl ul-Bait (People of My House). After me you shall not go astray if you adhere to both of them, and the two shall remain together till they meet me at the cistern of Kauser in the Heavens".

Authentic traditions clearly point out that none other than the Holy Prophet, Ali, Fatima, Hasan and Husain (may peace be upon them all) were included in the Ahl-ul-Bait.

One should recite this Hadees with purity, sincerity and devotion, and before and after the recitation, one should recite Salawaat 3 times on Muhammad and his descendants. One should recite this Hadees as often as one can, and especially on the night of Friday, or Friday itself. Insha-Allah with the blessings of the Ahl-ul-Bait your legimate desires will be fulfilled. The benefits of reciting this Hadees are numerous, and if recited regularly, all religious worldly wishes shall be fulfilled through its auspiciousness, Insha-Allah.

Below is given a list of scholars and commentators who have transmitted this Hadees through a great many traditions and narrations. These narrations have been related in different forms of which the following are some of the references :—

1—Saheeh Muslim, Kitab Fazaele Al-Sahabah Chapter Fazaele Ahlebaital Nabi. Part VII Page 130.

2—Imam Ahmad Hanbal, Musnad Part 1 page 331, Part III Pages 151-259 & 285, Part IV pages 5 & 107, Part VI pages 292, 296, 298, 304, and 322.

3—Saheeh Tirmizi, K-44 Surat H-7, K-56, B-31 and 60.

4—Jalaluddin Siyuti, Kitab Al-Dural Mansoor, Part V, Pages 198-199.

5—Shaikh Abdul Haq Muhaddis Dehlvi, Ash'tal Al-Lamaa't Volume IV, Pages 378-379.

6—Abu Daood Al-Tiyalsi, Musnad Part VIII, Page 474 Hadees No. 2055.

7—Sawaa'eqe Muhriqah, Allama Ibn-e-Hajar Makki, translation in Persian under Baraheene Qatiah.

8—The following Hadees has been taken from the manuscript of Awalim Al-Uloom Shaikh Abdullah Bin Nurullah Al-Bahraini, who relates it by precise narration from Hazrat Jabir Bin Abdullah Ansari who was one of the exalted companions of the Holy Prophet. (S.A.)

Bism-illah-ir-Rahman-ir-Raheem

(In the name of God, the Most Compassionate, the Merciful)

1

Hazrat Fatima, the Lady of Light, relates the circumstances of the revelation of the Verse of Purity, as follows: —

One day, my father, the Messenger of Allah, came to me and said, "Peace be unto thee, O Fatima", and I replied, "unto thee be Peace, O my Father".

Then he said, "My body is feeling weak today"[1] and I said, "May Allah protect you from weakness".

He said, "Bring me the Yamani blanket and cover me with it",

1-It may be observed that the things that strengthen the spirit, like continuous prayer, fasting and generosity, often tend to weaken the physical body. Weakness, shivering and other such symptoms usually attended our Holy Prophet before the approach of a divine revelation and marked the onset of inspiration.

So I brought, the Yamani blanket and covered him with it, and behold, his face began to shine like the full moon in all its glory.

2

After a while, there came my son, Hasan, and saluted me and I returned the salutation.

Presently, he said, "O Mother, I smell a sweet perfume like the fragrance of my grandfather, the Messenger".[2]

So I answered, "Yes, your grandfather is resting under the blanket."

At this, Hasan went and stood near the blanket and saluted the Messenger of Allah and he duly answered the salutation.

Then Hasan asked, "Have I your permission to come under the blanket?" and the Holy Prophet readily answered, "Yes", and so Hasan entered under the blanket with the Holy Prophet.

3

After a little while, there came Husain and having exchanged the Islamic greetings with me, he observed, "O Mother. I smell the same kind of odour as the fragrance of my grandfather, the Holy Prophet". And I answered, "Yes, my dear, your grandfather is resting under that blanket. along with your brother". So, Husain approached the blanket, respectfully saluted the Holy Prophet, and the Holy Prophet affectionately answered him. Then said Husain, "Do I have your permission to come under the blanket with you?" And the Holy Prophet answered. "of course, my dear". So Husain too entered under the blanket.

4

Ere long, there came the Commander of the True Believers, Ali ibn Abu Talib and said to me, "Peace be unto thee, O Fatima", and I answered, "Unto thee be peace. O Abul Hasan,

---

2-It goes to prove the spritual receptivity and sensitiveness of Imam Hasan and Imam Husain that even in their childhood they could perceive the presence of the Holy Prophet by the distinctive aura of a delightful aroma that surrounded him.

O Commander of the True Believers". Then Ali also observed, "How is it that I smell here the fragrance of the Holy Prophet's presence?" and I replied. "Yes, your cousin is resting along with your two sons underneath the blanket". So Ali stepped towards the blanket and said, "Peace be unto thee, O Holy Messenger of Allah" and the Holy Prophet answered, "Unto thee be Peace, O my cousin and successor, O standard bearer of Islam and Commander of the True Believers".[3] Then Ali said, "Have I your permission to join you under the blanket", and the Holy Prophet readily permitted him. Thereupon Ali also entered under the blanket.

5

After that I went near the blanket and saluted my father and he answered the salutation. Then I asked, "O messenger of Allah, do I have your permission to come under the blanket with you", and my father, the Holy Prophet answered, "Of course, O dearest one and O light of my eyes, you have my permission". So I also entered under the blanket.

6

Now when all of us were assembled together under the blanket, the Holy Prophet tucked in the corners of the blanket, lifted up his hands towards the heavens and prayed, "O Allah, these are the People of my House, they are my own near and dear ones; the flesh of my flesh and the blood of my blood—so, do Thou shower upon me and them blessings, favours, mercy and good pleasure and certify their purification to the utmost extent"

3-It was only Hazrat Ali and no one else who was known as Ameer-ul Momineen or the Ulul Amr in the time of the Holy Prophet. Other persons arrogated this title to themselves later on

4-This shows that the revelation of verse 33 of chapter 33 of the Holy Quran took place in answer to the Holy Prophet's prayer whereby he desired his Ahl-ul-Bait to be absolutely protected from the contamination of the ungodly and wicked environment of the world.

Then Allah, addressed his angels, saying, "O ye angels of Mine, and O ye denizens of My universe and of the heavens! Behold I would never have created either the high vaulted heavens or the wide-spread earth, or the radiant sun, or the shining moon, or the revolving sky or the billowing ocean, or the sailing ship, but for the love of these FIVE SOULS that are gathered together under the blanket".[5]

Then asked Gabriel, (on whom be peace) "O our Cherisher and Fosterer, who are the people under the blanket?"

And Allah answered saying, "They are the People of the House of Prophecy and the Treasurers of My Messengership, they are Fatima, her father, her husband and her sons.

At this the Archangel Gabriel prayed, "O Allah dost Thou permit me to go down to the earth and be the sixth person with them?"

And Allah said, "Yes, I permit thee". So Gabriel came down from heaven to earth and said. "Peace be unto thee, O Messenger of Allah. Lo, the All-Highest, Most Exalted Lord sends unto thee His Greetings and salutes thee with His Peace, and says:

"Verily I would never have created either the vaulted heavens or the wide-spread earth, or the radiant sun, or the shining moon, or the revolving sky, or the billowing ocean, or the sailing ship, but for your sake and for your love, and Lo, He hath permitted me to join your company, therefore, have I your permission O Prophet of Allah?"[6]

And the Holy Prophet answered saying, "Unto thee be peace, O Trustee of the Divine Inspiration, of course, I permit thee."

5-This is a Hadees-e-Qudsi, or sacred Hadees, emanating from the Almighty, though it is not a revelation of the Quran.

6-As Allah had already permitted the angel Gabriel, it might seem that it was quite unnecessary for the angel to ask the Holy Prophet's permission, yet such was the Holy Prophet's position that even Gabriel had to seek his permission before entering the Prophet's presence, as laid down in the Holy Quran.

Thereupon the Archangel Gabriel entered under the blanket and said to my father, "Lo, the Great Allah hath inspired thee saying: —

"IT HAS ALWAYS BEEN THE WILL OF ALLAH TO KEEP OFF FROM YOU ALL STIGMA (of sin, ignorance and disbelief) O PEOPLE OF THE HOUSE, AND TO PURIFY YOU WITH A PERFECT PURIFICATION."" (Holy Quran,

Chapter: 33, Verse: 33)

7

Then Ali asked the Holy Prophet, "O Messenger of Allah, relate unto us the advantages of this assemblage of ours under the blanket and the benefits that Allah shall bestow thereby". And the Holy Prophet said,

"O Ali, by Allah who has chosen me to be His Messenger and favoured me by making me His Prophet, whenever this event is narrated in any assemblage of the people of the earth, which shall be attended by our followers and devotees, Allah shall bestow His mercy upon them and the angels shall descend and pray for their forgiveness until the assembly dissolves."
So Ali remarked,

"By Allah herein is assured our success and the success of our followers."

8

Again the Holy Prophet said,

"Whenever this event is narrated in any assemblage of the people of the earth, which shall be attended by our followers and devotees, if there be therein any unhappy person, Allah shall make him happy and if there be therein anyone making a wish, Allah shall grant his wish, and there shall remain none distressed but Allah will dispel his distress'.[8]

7-This verse is meant as a guarantee and a reassurance regarding the perfect purity of the Ahl-ul-Bait so that all the Muslims should recognise their excellence.

8-This part of the Hadees gives the effects and advantages of its recitation.

At this Ali remarked,

"Hereby is assured our success and good fortune and likewise the success and good fortune of our followers forever, by the Lord of the Kabba."

ZIARAT-E-WARIS

SALUTATIONS TO IMAM HUSAIN
AS THE HEIR OF THE PROPHETS.

"Peace be unto thee,
O Abaa Abdillah
(KUNYA OF IMAM HUSAIN)

Peace be unto thee,
O son of the Holy Prophet
(THE HOLY PROPHET ALWAYS CALLED)
Imam Husain his son);

Peace be unto thee,
O son of Hazrat Ali, the Commander of the faithful.

Peace be unto thee,
O son of Janab-e-Fatima Zahra.
(CHIEF OF THE WOMEN OF THE WORLD)

Peace be unto thee,
and the mercy of God and his bounties;

Peace be unto thee,
O heir of Adam, (the chosen one of God);

Peace be unto thee,
O heir of Noah, (the prophet of God);

Peace be unto thee,
O heir of Abraham, (the friend of God);

Peace be unto thee,
O heir of Moses, (interlocutor of God);

Peace be unto thee,
O heir of Jesus, (the spirit of God);

Peace be unto thee,
O heir of Muhammad, (the beloved of God);

251

Peace be unto thee,
  O heir of Ali, (Prince of true believers and friend of God)
Peace be unto thee,
  O son of Muhammad, (the Chosen);
Peace be unto thee,
  O son of Ali, (the repository of God's pleasure);
Peace be unto thee,
  O son of Fatima, (the Lady of Light);
Peace be unto thee,
  O son of Khadija, (the Great);
Peace be unto thee,
  O thou that shalt be avenged by God. and O son of one
  who is avenged by Him, and O unique martyr unavenged
  and cut into pieces.

I bear witness that thou didst establish the worship of God,
      and the poor-due
      and bade (men) to do good,
      and forbade (them) from evil-doing;
      and obeyed God and His messenger
      until the inevitable (death) came to thee.

Wherefore, the curse of God be upon the people who slew
thee,
  and the curse of God be upon the people who wronged thee,
  and the curse of God be upon the people who felt happy on
hearing about it.

Lord, O Aba Abdilla,
I bear witness that thou were a light
from the time of Thy revered (ancestors).

The stains of ignorance never tainted thee with their uncleans-
ing touch,
  and the ignominious garment (of disbelief) never cast its
shadow upon thee.

I bear witness that verily, thou art a pillar of faith and a
source of inspiration to the true believers,

252

and I bear witness that verily, thou art the righteous Imam, virtuous,

pious, repository of divine pleasure, pure and holy guide, and divinely guided.

And I bear witness that the Imams who are descended from thee are the word of piety, the banners of guidance, the strong rope of God and the conclusive proof of God unto the whole world.

And I call as my witness God and His angels, prophets and messengers.

that I have faith in thee and I believe in thy resurrection, and I am (convinced) of the laws of my religion and of the results of my actions:

and that my heart is surrendered unto thee, and my affairs are in obedience to your command.

The blessings of God be upon you and on your spirits and on your bodies, quick or dead, and on those of you who are witnesses and on those of you who are absent, and on matters manifest or secret.

And unto you be peace, and the mercy and grace of God."

TRANSLITERATION.

As-Salaamo alaika yaa Aba Abdilla, As-Salaamo alaika yab-na Rasoolillah. As-Salaamo alaika wa rahmatoollahay wa barakaatoh. As-Salaamo alaika yaa waraysa Aadama safwatillah, As-Salaamo alaika ya waraysa Noohin Nabee-illah, As-Salaamo alaika yaa waraysa Ibraheema Khaleellillah, As-Salaamo alaika yaa waraysa Moosa Kaleemillah,, As-Salaamo alaika yaa waraysa Eesa Roohilla, As-Salaamo alaika yaa waraysa Muhammadin Habeebillah, As-Salaamo alaika yaa warasa Amir-Ail Momeneen Walee-Allah, As-Salaamo alaika yab-na Muhammadeenil Mustafa, As-Salaamo alaika yab-na Ali-yenil Murtaza, As-Salaamo alaika yab-na Fateymataz-Zahraa. As-Salaamo alaika yab-na Khadeejatal Koobra, As-Salaamo alaika yaa sarallaahay wab-na sareh, Wa witral mautooray ash hadau annaka qad aqamtas salaata, Wa aataitaz zakaata wa amartabil-

maroofay wa nahaita annil moonkaray. Wa atatallaha wa
Rasoolahoo hatta atakal yaqeen. Fala anallaho ummatan qatal-
atka, Wa la anallaho ummatan zalamatka, Wa la anallaho
ummatan samay-at bay zaaleyak farzeeyat bayh, Yaa Maulaa
yaa Aba Abdilla, Ash hadau annaka koonta noorun fil aslabish
sha may khatay. Wal arhamil mootah haratay lum tonajjiskal
jaahaylee ya tau, Bay anja sayha wa lam toolbiska min mood
lahimaatay see-yabayha. Wa ashadau annaka min de-aa-ay
middeennay wa arkaanil momineen. Wa ash hadau annakal-
eemaamool barroot-taqee yur-razee-yuz zakee-yul haadee-yul
mahdee. Wa ash hadau annal-a-immata mew-ooldayka kaley-
matat taqwa, Wa aalamool hodaa wal oorwatool ooska wal-
hoojjatoo aala ahliddoonya, Wa ooshhaydool laaha wa
malaaykatahoo wa ambeeya-a-hoo wa Roosoolahoo annee baykoom momeroon wa bay yeeya baykoom moqaynoon, Bay
sharaa-ay deenee wa khawaa-teemay a-malee wa qalbee lay
qalbay koom, silmoon wa amree lay amraykoom moottabay-oon,
Salawaatoollahay alaikoom wa ala arwaa-haykoom wa alaa
ajsaadaykoom, Wa alaa ajsamaykoom wa ala sha-hay-day-koom,
Wa alaa gha-ay-bay-koom wa alaa zaa-hay-ray-koom, Wa alaa
ba-tay-nay-koom.

SALUTATION TO THE IMAMS (ZIARAT-I-JAMI'A)

A shorter form of prayer for the use of pilgrims to the shrines
of any of the Imams is attributed by Majlisi to Imam Ali Reza.
Majlisi quotes "By this prayer, which is appropriate for each
and every Imam, their help sought, needs may be made known
to them, and blessings may be solicited."

"Peace be to the friends of the Chosen Ones of Allah;
Peace be to the Trusted and Favoured of Allah;
Peace be to the Helpers and Representatives of Allah;
Peace be to the places where Allah has been made known;
Peace be to the places where Allah is remembered.
Peace be to those who have revealed Allah's commands;
Peace be to those who call upon Allah;
Peace be to those who obey what Allah has approved;
Peace be to the tested followers of Allah's will.

Peace be to those who are Proofs for Allah (the Imams);
Peace be upon their friends, for they are the friends of Allah;
As likewise their enemies are the enemies of Allah.

Those who have known them have surely known Allah; and those ignorant of them are ignorant of Allah.

Those who take them by the hand, and commit themselves to them, have given their hands to Allah;

But those who abandon them have truly abandoned Allah.
I bear witness before Allah that I am loyal to whoever is loyal to thee, and I am ready to fight those who are not loyal to thee."

PILGRIMAGE BY PROXY

Definite instructions for the pilgrimage by proxy are given by Shaikh Tusi as follows: —

"Anyone who goes on a pilgrimage as a proxy for a believing brother should say (after he has performed his ablutions and attended to the necessary requirements of the pilgrimage), 'O Allah, keep me from weariness or illness or disorder or weakness, and reward*.........the son of*.........for this pilgrimage, and reward me for completing it.' And after he has made the pilgrimage, at the end he should say, 'Peace be on thee, O my master, from*...............the son of...............I have come to thee as a pilgrim on his account, so intercede for him with Allah."

Then he may offer Salutations on his account, from any of the set Salutations that are written to meet the situation.

* Here name the person.
* Here name the father of the person.

255

QUR'AN AND ISLAMIC LITERATURES AVAILABLE PLEASE WRITE FOR CATALOGUE.

BRAILLE EDITION OF THE HOLY QUR'AN

HOLY QUR'AN Translated by Muhammad Sarwar A†E (Arabic†English)

HOLY QUR'AN Translated by M. H. Shakir A†E Casebound

HOLY QUR'AN Translated by M. H. Shakir A†E Paperback

GLORIUS QUR'AN Translated by Pickthall

GLORIUS QUR'AN Translated by Pickthall with Transliteration by Elisi A†E Caseboung

GLORIUS QUR'AN Translated by Yusufali with Commentary A†E Casebound

THE QUR'AN Translated by N. J. Dawood

THE MESSAGE OF THE QUR'AN Translated by Hashim Amir Ali A†E Casebound

THE QUR'AN Seleccion from the Noble Reading by Dr. T. B. Irving

THE KOR'AN Translated by A. J. Arberry

THE HOLY QUR'AN Translated by S. V. Mir Ahmed Ali with Commentary Casebound

THE MEANING OF THE QUR'AN Translated by A'la Maududi Vol. I-X each vol.

THE MESSAGE OF THE QUR'AN Translated by Muhammad Asad with Commentary Casebound

HOLY QURAN - Spanish translation

HOLY QURAN - French translation

HOLY QURAN - Persian translation - Arabic † Persian

HOLY QURAN - Persian translation

HOLY QURAN - Gujarati

Published by
Tahrike Tarsile Qur'an, Inc.
Publishers and Distributors of Holy Qur'an
P.O. Box 1115
Corona Elmhurst Sta.
Elmhurst, New York 11373-1115

Name: --

Address: ---

City --- Zip ----------------------------